BRIEF PSYCHOTHERAPY

BRIEF PSYCHOTHERAPY
TIME-LIMITED AND EFFECTIVE TREATMENTS

Richard D. Parsons, Ph.D.

West Chester University

Bassim Hamadeh, CEO and Publisher
Amy Smith, Senior Project Editor
Abbey Hastings, Production Editor
Emely Villavicencio, Senior Graphic Designer
Kylie Bartolome, Licensing Associate
Natalie Piccotti, Director of Marketing
Kassie Graves, Senior Vice President, Editorial
Jamie Giganti, Director of Academic Publishing

Copyright © 2023 by Cognella, Inc. All rights reserved. No part of this publication may be reprinted, reproduced, transmitted, or utilized in any form or by any electronic, mechanical, or other means, now known or hereafter invented, including photocopying, microfilming, and recording, or in any information retrieval system without the written permission of Cognella, Inc. For inquiries regarding permissions, translations, foreign rights, audio rights, and any other forms of reproduction, please contact the Cognella Licensing Department at rights@cognella.com.

Trademark Notice: Product or corporate names may be trademarks or registered trademarks and are used only for identification and explanation without intent to infringe.

Cover image copyright © 2017 iStockphoto LP/erhui1979.

Printed in the United States of America.

Brief Contents

Preface xiii
Acknowledgments xv

PART I
An Overview of Brief Therapy — 1

CHAPTER 1
The Emergence of Brief, Time-Limited Therapy — 3

CHAPTER 2
Brief Therapy: More Than "Limited Sessions" — 17

PART II
Theories and Their Applications — 31

CHAPTER 3
Solution-Focused Brief Therapy — 33

CHAPTER 4
Time-Limited Dynamic Psychotherapy — 52

CHAPTER 5
Brief Cognitive Behavior Therapy — 69

CHAPTER 6
Acceptance and Commitment Therapy — 89

CHAPTER 7
Dialectical Behavioral Therapy — 105

CHAPTER 8
Emotion-Focused Therapy — 121

CHAPTER 9
Interpersonal Psychotherapy — 137

CHAPTER 10
Single-Session Therapys — 154

Index 171
About the Author 179

Contents

Preface   xiii
Acknowledgments   xv

PART I   An Overview of Brief Therapy   1

Chapter 1   The Emergence of Brief, Time-Limited Therapy   3

A Unique Perspective: Challenging the Mainstream   4
Individuals Key to the Evolution of Brief Therapy   6
   Sigmund Freud   6
   Sandor Ferenczi   6
   Milton Erickson   7
   Gregory Bateson   7
   Jay Haley   8
   The Mental Research Institute   9
Additional Forces Contributing to the Emergence of Brief Therapy   11
   Popularity of Behavior Therapy   11
   Outcome Studies   11
   Social/Economic Pressures   13
A Rich History and an Inviting Future   13
Keystones   13
Additional Resources   14
References   14

Chapter 2   Brief Therapy: More Than "Limited Sessions"   17

A Common Core: Multiple Presentations   17
Guiding Values and Principles   18
Shared Technical Characteristics   18
   Nonpathologizing   18
   Here-and-Now Focus   20
   Time Limited   21
Valuing Client Strengths   21
   A Collaborative Working Alliance   23
   Therapist: Proactive Agent of Change   23
   Outcome Focused   23
   Flexibility of Techniques   25

Engaging Client Systems: Therapy Outside of the Office   25
A Question of Suitability   27
   Severity and Complexity   27
   Impediments to Therapeutic Alliance   27
   Client's Stage of Change   28
Keystones   28
Additional Resources   28
References   29

PART II   Theories and Their Applications   31

Chapter 3   Solution-Focused Brief Therapy   33

History and Contributors   33
A Nontraditional Perspective   34
   More Than a Technique   35
Assumptions and Principles Guiding Practice   35
Principles in Action   37
   Problem Deconstruction Discourse   37
   Problem-Free Talk   38
   Collaboration   40
   Starting With an End in Mind: Goal Setting   42
   Value Small Steps: Scaling   44
   Finding Solutions   45
   Task Development   48
Supportive Research   48
Suitability   48
Keystones   49
Additional Resources   49
References   50

Chapter 4   Time-Limited Dynamic Psychotherapy   52

History and Contributors   53
   Sandor Ferenczi   53
   Otto Rank   53
   Alexander and French   53
   Brief Dynamic Therapy   54
A Shift in Perspective   55
   From Intrapsychic to Interpersonal   55
   Here-and-Now Attachment   55
   Experiential–Affective Theory   56
Assumptions and Principles Guiding Practice   56
   Emphasis on Attachment and Relationships   56
   Maladaptive Patterns Schematized   56
   Circular Causality   56
   Clients as Stuck, not Sick   57
   Goals   58
   TLDP Is Process Oriented   58

      TLDP Is Focused 58
      Therapist as Active 58
      Change Outside of Therapy 59
    Principles in Action 59
      Case Conceptualization 59
      Experiential Learning 62
      From Experience to Understanding 63
      Experience, Understanding, Change 64
      Strategies 65
    Supportive Research 65
    Suitability 65
    Keystones 66
    Additional Resources 66
    References 67

Chapter 5   Brief Cognitive Behavior Therapy   69
    History and Contributors 69
      Behavioral Therapy 70
      Cognitive Therapy 71
      The Blending of Cognition and Behavior 71
      Brief CBT 72
    Perspective 72
    Assumptions and Principles Guiding Practice 72
      Humans Are Meaning Makers 73
      Cognitions as Mediator 73
      Cognitions Operating at Varying Levels of Awareness 73
      Cognitions Can Be Functional and Dysfunctional 76
      Schemata Are Resistant to Change 76
      Cognitions Can Be Modified 76
      Cognitive Change Requires Work! 77
    Principles in Action 77
      Connecting Thoughts and Feelings 77
      Recognizing and Monitoring Cognitive Distortions 79
      Testing and Reformulating 81
      Time Limited 83
    Supportive Research 84
    Suitability 85
    Keystones 85
    Additional Resources 86
    References 86

Chapter 6   Acceptance and Commitment Therapy   89
    History and Contributors 90
      A New Look at "Distancing" 90
      Comprehensive Distancing 90
      Renaming ACT 91
    Perspective 91
    Assumptions and Principles Guiding Practice 92

Suffering as Normal   92
Language: Roots of Psychological Suffering   92
Experiential Avoidance   92
Functional Contextualism and Workability   93
Principles in Action   93
The Therapeutic Relationship   93
Acceptance   94
Diffusion   96
Self as Context   96
Contact With Present Moment: Mindfulness   98
Values   98
Committed Action   98
Supportive Research   101
Suitability   101
Keystones   101
Additional Resources   102
References   102

Chapter 7   Dialectical Behavioral Therapy   105

History and Contributors   106
Perspective: Acceptance and Change   106
Assumptions and Principles Guiding Practice   107
Biosocial Theory   107
Validation and Acceptance   108
Dialectics   108
Principles in Action   112
Targets of Therapy and Functions Served   112
Stages in a Comprehensive Program   114
Engaging Acceptance and Change Skills   115
Supportive Research   117
Suitability   117
Keystones   117
Additional Resources   118
References   118

Chapter 8   Emotion-Focused Therapy   121

History and Contributors   122
Perspective: I Feel, Therefore, I Am   122
Assumptions and Principles Guiding Practice   123
Dialectical-Constructivist View   123
Emotions Central to Thought and Action   124
Client Experiences: Guiding Practice Decisions   124
Process Versus Content   124
Therapeutic Relationship as Vital to Outcomes   124
Principles in Action   125
The Therapeutic Relationship   125
The Therapeutic Work   126
Therapeutic Tasks Responding to Markers   126
Phases of Treatment   130

Supportive Research   132
Suitability   132
Keystones   133
Additional Resources   133
References   134

Chapter 9   Interpersonal Psychotherapy   137

History and Contributors   137
Perspective   138
Assumptions and Principles Guiding Practice   139
  A Medical Model   139
  Goals   139
  Here and Now   139
  Time Limited With Phases   140
  Collaborative   140
  Therapist Active   140
Principles in Action   141
  Beginning (One to Three Sessions)   141
  Middle Phase (10–14 Sessions)   143
  Final Phase: Termination   147
Supportive Research   149
Suitability   150
Keystones   150
Additional Resources   151
References   151

Chapter 10   Single-Session Therapys   154

History and Contributors   155
Perspective: Mind-Set Not Mode   156
Assumptions and Principles Guiding Practice   156
  The Power of the One   156
  Not a Quick Fix, Nor Truncated Conventional Therapy   157
  Providing Help at Point of Need   157
  Constructive and Strength-Based   158
  Collaborative   158
  Mind-Set   159
Principles in Action   159
  Working Alliance: A Collaboration   159
  Maintaining Focus   161
  Finding a Path to Follow   161
  Phases of SST   161
  Clinical Guidelines   164
Supportive Research   166
Suitability   166
Keystones   167
Additional Resources   167
References   167

Index   171
About the Author   179

Preface

At some point in their careers, all clinicians will provide therapy that is limited in time and number of sessions. This may be in response to the nature of the client's presenting concerns, the operational mandates of one's place of employment, or even the constraints of a third-party payer. Such "brief" therapy is by default. This type of time-limited therapy is not that presented within this text. Brief therapy, as presented here, is not simply a shorter or truncated version of traditional forms of psychotherapy. The theories presented within this book reflect unique approaches to service delivery.

The development of innovative, time-limited models of brief therapy has been in response to several factors. There has been increasing demand for cost-effective types of treatment, especially in this era of health care inflation and cost containment policies in the private and public sectors. Clients have demonstrated by their actions that they prefer and seek models of shorter term treatment. However, the most substantial support for the ongoing development of brief therapy is the increasing amount of research evidence highlighting its effectiveness.

The theories discussed in the upcoming chapters differ in terms of their assumptions about the human condition and the promotion of mental health and wellness, the breadth of their goals, and even the emphasis placed on here-and-now issues versus there-and-then experiences. Although each theoretical model may emphasize different techniques or strategies, they share characteristics that extend beyond the obvious commitment to providing effective brief, time-limited therapy. The theories presented within this book are similar in that they value the power of the working alliance and therapeutic relationship, seek to engage the client and client's strengths and resources, and create conditions for rapid change.

About This Text

Brief Psychotherapy: Time-Limited and Effective Treatments is a text that offers the reader insight into the historical development of brief therapy models and describes and provides clinical illustrations of the assumptions and operating principles guiding the application of each theory. Throughout the text, case illustrations and directed practice activities are employed as teaching tools. Each chapter describes that theory's

- unique perspective on the human condition, wellness, and therapy;
- assumptions and principles guiding the practice;
- principles in action; and
- research supporting its suitability and effectiveness.

The Hope

I hope that *Brief Psychotherapy: Time-Limited and Effective Treatments* significantly contributes to your professional development. While the text provides a snapshot of the current state of brief psychotherapy, it is vital that you continue your reading and research as new models and expanding evidence supporting these models will continue to emerge. It is also essential that you move beyond simply reading about and comprehending what is presented in this or any other text to engaging in applying that knowledge under corrective supervision. Through application and supervision, you will transition from student knowing about brief therapy to effectively applying brief therapy professionally.

Acknowledgments

My appreciation of, and gratitude for, the support and guidance provided by Amy Smith, senior project editor and Abbey Hastings, production editor, cannot be overstated. If it were not for the keen eyes and copyediting prowess of Michele Mitchell, this book could have been a grammarian's nightmare.

Finally, to Kassie Graves, vice president, of editorial, I say thank you—thank you for your stimulating ideas and ever-present support, but mostly for simply being the person you are.

PART I

An Overview of Brief Therapy

CHAPTER 1

The Emergence of Brief, Time-Limited Therapy

There are people who have benefited from therapy without being confronted with the past at all.

—Alice Miller (psychologist, psychoanalyst, philosopher)

As noted in the preface, all clinicians will provide therapy that is short-lived at some point in their careers. In a national survey of almost 4,000 mental health professionals, Levenson and Davidovitz (2000) found that close to 90% of the respondents reported that they had engaged in some form of time-limited and focused therapy. Often these brief encounters are the unplanned results of the operational mandates and restrictions of the place of employment, due to restrictions imposed by insurance companies and their unwillingness to pay for more extended treatment, or simply in response to a client's desire to terminate (see Muran et al., 2009). These types of time-limited engagement are not the subject of this text. These are unplanned or at least not formally designed to be brief and time limited.

Brief therapy (which will be discussed in Chapter 2) is a unique approach to service delivery, one where the focus is on the application of therapeutic techniques specifically targeted to a symptom or behavior and oriented toward a limited length of treatment. Brief therapy is an approach with a rich history, expanding empirical support, and widening acceptance among the professional community. The current chapter looks at the history of brief therapy and the individuals and forces that contributed to the emergence of this unique perspective and approach to engaging in psychotherapy.

Upon completion of this chapter, the reader will be able to do the following:

1. Explain how brief therapy reflects a unique perspective and focus for mental health service.
2. Describe the contributions of Milton Erickson, Gregory Bateson, and the associates at the Mental Research Institute in Palo Alto, California, to the evolution of brief, time-limited therapy.

3. Identify social/cultural forces contributing to brief therapy's growth and increased interest and demand.

A Unique Perspective: Challenging the Mainstream

Perhaps as a reflection of its historic roots in medicine, psychiatry has approached the issue of mental health as physical ailments. Symptoms are grouped, diagnostic categories assigned, and syndromes established. The process, while perhaps assisting in research and communication, has also resulted in the focusing of therapists' attentions and energies in search of the etiology, the cause(s), the "why" underlying the client's presenting issues, and the emergence of these "syndromes." For perhaps too long, this application of the "medical model," that is, viewing symptoms as mere indicators of the actual underlying problem, has resulted in psychotherapists viewing all psychological issues as disease, with diagnosis as being fundamental to treatment.

Such a perspective assumes that should the cause of a syndrome be identified, and treatment and perhaps prevention measures could be developed and employed. This is a noble pursuit. It is a perspective that found support in the discovery of the cause (e.g., syphilis) and treatment (e.g., antibiotics) for *general paresis*, a severe neuropsychiatric disorder presenting with progressive cognitive and behavioral deterioration accompanied with psychotic and/or affective behavioral disorders. However, it is not the only perspective on the treatment of mental health issues and concerns.

As mental health practitioners, we understand biologically based mental disorders, including schizophrenia, schizoaffective disorder, major depressive disorder, bipolar disorder, paranoia, and other psychotic disorders. We also know that all psychological distress reflects some contribution of both biology and experience (i.e., nature-nurture). Theories have and continue to attempt to identify and articulate these biological and experiential contributors to a client's distress. However, while the pursuit of root causes continues, many theorists and psychotherapists challenge the notion that identifying the root cause or etiology for an individual's distress or conflict is a necessary precondition to finding a pathway toward resolution of that distress. For those engaged in time-limited, brief therapy, the focus and emphasis of engagement has shifted from seeking the cause to engaging in treatment.

There is an old joke about a person who goes to a doctor, and says "Doc, every time I do this I get a sharp pain." The doctor responds, "Stop doing that." While certainly an overly simplistic approach to treatment there is value in targeting energy to problem resolution, if and when understanding the cause is either not possible or necessarily required (see Case Illustration 1.1)

Brief therapy, as an approach to psychological service, is deliberate and planned in its brevity. It is not "brief" by default. It is "brief" by intention and planning. Brief therapy, as presented within this text, reflects an approach that, while brief, is planned as short term. The established therapeutic objectives and the resulting strategies employed to achieve those objects are well thought out and considered within the context of a limited time frame (Bloom, 1992).

CASE ILLUSTRATION 1.1

Do This ... Not That

Rob is a 15-year-old, high school student who has been referred to the school counselor because of three recent occurrences of fighting with classmates. Rob is academically gifted and a star athlete on both the school's football and hockey teams.

When invited to share his perspective on these incidences, Rob was quick to point out that in each case the other person made a negative comment that really "pissed [him] off." Rob understood that he shouldn't lose his temper and gave the counselor clear evidence that he did want to be getting into trouble, since that may threaten his ability to play on the teams.

Counselor: I can tell you are not happy with what has been happening.

Rob: I'm not, but they pissed me off.

Counselor: I know you said that each incidence was triggered by the other person making a crude comment.

Rob: Yeah ... I would be embarrassed to tell you.

Counselor: Okay, I get it. I'm wondering when you are playing hockey or in a football game, do any of the players on the other teams try to get you angry by making comments?

Rob: Are you kidding? All of the time. They would love it if I threw a punch and got ejected from the game.

Counselor: So they make comments like the ones your classmates made?

Rob: Sometimes worse.

Counselor: So do you throw a punch? Have you been ejected?

Rob (smiling): Never!

Counselor: Wow. That is pretty cool. How do you restrain yourself?

Rob: I know what they are doing, and I just stop listening, tell myself it isn't worth it.

Counselor: So when you are in game, you just stop listening. It's like you don't care about the comment, or you care more about staying in the game, avoiding a penalty?

Rob: Absolutely.

Counselor: It seems to me if you did more of that, you know, stop listening and not caring about the comments in school, things would be better for you?

Rob: I guess I should do more of that, rather than getting myself worked up and sent to this "penalty box" (smiling).

This perspective is sharply contrasted to the traditional long-term and often protracted course of psychotherapy. It is a perspective that challenges the status quo and continues to be challenged but that is continuing to evolve and take up strong roots as an alternative approach for mental health services.

Individuals Key to the Evolution of Brief Therapy

Few people would associate the name of Sigmund Freud or psychoanalysis with brief therapy. However, like much in psychotherapy, the roots for brief therapy can be traced to his name, that theory, and that time in history.

Sigmund Freud

In his early writings, Freud highlighted time-limited interventions. For example, in his "Studies on Hysteria" (1895), he described his work with a woman presenting with olfactory hallucinations, depression, fatigue, and chronic rhinitis. He reports successfully "curing" her of her olfactory hallucinations after working with her once a week for 9 weeks.

This was not the only case where clients were seen for brief periods and limited sessions. In the early days of psychoanalysis, the process was viewed as one of brief duration (Marmor, 1979). In fact, Freud was reported to have been "apologetic about the length of analyses even when they lasted only a few months (Strupp & Binder, 1984, p. 8).

As his theory of psychoanalysis grew in complexity, the goals became increasingly complex and ambitious. As such, treatment often extended into years of analysis, and psychoanalysis morphed from that which was brief to an elongated mode of treatment. As will be discussed in Chapter 4, a number of those initially associated with Freud, individuals such as Alfred Adler and Otto Rank, expressed concerns about this change in approach, changes that resulted in the extension of therapy into years.

Sandor Ferenczi

Sandor Ferenczi began in earnest to reverse the trend of extended therapy and passivity on the therapist's part. Ferenczi has been regarded as the first analyst to engage in modified analytic techniques to shorten treatment length (Marmor, 1979).

As a psychoanalyst, Ferenczi initially maintained an interest and focused on reliving of the Oedipus situation in the relation of the patient to the analyst (Ferenczi & Rank, 1924/1986). However, he began to challenge the need to assist clients in working through infantile neurosis. His perspective was that there was value in focusing on the client's current emotional experience (Strupp & Binder, 1984). Of significance to the development of brief therapy was his view that the goals of analysis could be achieved through more direct, active intervention on the part of the analyst (Ferenczi & Rank, 1924/1986). Ferenczi promoted the idea that therapists needed to take a more active role in making interpretations and manipulating transference. This was in direct contrast and challenge to Freud's position of therapist passivity and the idea of letting transference evolve freely.

Ferenczi's ideas and innovations to psychoanalytic methodology stimulated additional revision to the original Freudian model. Her insights provided a foundation for the development of contemporary brief therapy models (Bauer & Kobos, 1987), especially that of time-limited dynamic therapy (see Chapter 4).

Milton Erickson

"Milton H. Erickson, M.D., was the first strategic therapist. He might even be called the first therapist since he was the first major clinician to concentrate on how to change people" (Haley, 1985, p. vii). Erickson (1901–1980) introduced an experiential, phenomenologically based approach to problem solving, one that utilized clients' existing strengths while evoking natural processes of learning and adaptation (Short, 2019). While not a fully developed explicit model of therapy, his approach was goal oriented and focused on problem solving. Erickson believed insight was not always necessary. He emphasized the therapist's role was a strategic one, focusing on productive change, with or without promoting client understanding and insight.

Erickson is credited with introducing the term *brief therapy* to represent his pragmatic and directive approach to symptom reduction (Guedalia, 2015). Central to Erickson's position, and what is an essential tenet of brief therapy, was that individuals have the power, the resources, and the resiliency to solve their problems and that assisting them in tapping and configuring their strengths and resources to address their concern need not be a lengthy and involved process (Jones-Smith, 2012).

Erickson posited three basic principles to guide therapy, which we now consider theories of brief therapy: (a) meet clients where they are, (b) help clients gain control by changing their perspectives, and (c) allow for change that meets clients' needs (de Shazer, 1982).

The idea of meeting a client where they are was a significant change from more traditional theories. Rather than attempting to apply universal principles or theoretical constructs of pathology or, conversely, of health and wellness to all clients, Erickson emphasized understanding the client's unique world and phenomenal experience and the goals they sought. He would talk with the client, get to know them, and, based on their understanding of the client as an individual, would employ specific techniques to communicate with the client's subconscious mind about the issues. His approach was practical and solution based. He believed in addressing the issues and the symptoms directly, with little concern for their history or causation.

Gregory Bateson

An individual engaged in interdisciplinary work in anthropology, psychiatry, evolution, and epistemology, Gregory Bateson was profoundly influenced by the ideas outlined in systems theory, communication theory, information theory, and cybernetics. A complete discussion of Bateson and his interest in cybernetics is beyond the scope of this chapter. Readers interested in gathering additional information about cybernetics would do well reviewing the extensive essay prepared by Bale (n.d.).

The paradigm offered by Bateson challenged the current thinking in social/behavioral sciences (Bateson, 1977). Rather than emphasize the intrapsychic world of the client, Bateson pointed to the importance of systems, constructivism, and the power of communication and feedback both in terms of supporting psychological problems and structuring therapeutic resolutions of those problems.

In what has become known as the Bateson Project (1953–1963), Bateson and associates focused on investigating the holistic/nonsummative, self-stabilizing, self-organizing, systemic, and hierarchical traits formally identified in cybernetic systems as a lens through which to view human problems. The informational nature of cybernetic processes, including the concepts of feedback, mutual causality, and self-regulating systems (i.e., that cybernetic systems adapt to and alter their environments through sequences of self-stabilization around steady states), was being explored and adopted into therapeutic models (Bale, n.d.).

The Bateson group applied ideas from cybernetics and systems theory to the study of interpersonal communication, including communication in families of people labeled schizophrenic, and in so doing provided what many regard as the intellectual foundation of the family therapy movement (Hoffman, 1981). The Bateson group introduced a move from the tradition of individual psychopathology toward understanding and treating problems as facets of ongoing social interaction (Fisch & Schlanger, 1999).

Bateson emphasized the value of information processing as a means through which living systems generate and sustain order. Bateson believed that feedback was essential to self-organization and self-stabilization. He saw feedback as the process allowing for behavior and its results to be scanned so as to provide evidence of success or failure and allow for the modification of future behavior (Weiner, 1950). Bateson believed that feedback provided the base from which a system could assess the degree to which goals are attained and alter or regulate behavior in relation to such goal attainment (Bale, n.d.). With this as a perspective, it is not surprising that the focus shifted from the intrapsychic to that which was extra-personal and systemic. Social systems in which people functioned were viewed as significant to developing and resolving an individual's problem (Visser, 2013), and feedback was a primary vehicle for guiding such problem resolution.

The work of Bateson and his associates served as a primary influence on those at the Mental Research Institute (MRI) and their work on rapid problem resolution (Sluzki & Ransom, 1976).

Jay Haley

Haley was widely known for his pragmatic approach to psychotherapy. In 1959 he became the director of research at MRI, where he remained until the late 1960s.

Haley played a critical role in the founding and development of brief therapy. He emphasized treating a person's symptoms by advocating practical behavioral strategies and the development of coping skills. He posited that the therapist must identify specific, solvable problems and then set goals to resolve those problems. His perspective was that a therapist's goal is to foster measurable improvements in the client's life rather than understanding the etiology of a problem or fostering increased insight and client self-awareness (Haley, 1976). Haley's strategic therapy focused on short-term, targeted efforts to solve a specific problem.

As a member of the Bateson Project, Haley also emphasized the role of a client's environment—namely that of the family unit. He is credited as a pioneer in the field of family therapy. With his wife, Cloe Mandes, Haley helped establish the Family Therapy Institute in Washington, DC.

While more theoretical than the MRI model, their model remained invested in addressing the symptoms or presenting problems. As was true for those engaged in MRI brief family therapy, Haley and Madanes used strategic interventions to alter faulty interactions, with the intent of affecting concerning behaviors and interactions. They differed from the MRI model in that in addition to altering the sequence of interactions and ameliorating the presenting problem they also focused on changing the family structure.

The integration of structural and strategic approaches to family therapy led to the development of a problem-focused, planful, and practical treatment—focusing primarily on identifying and enacting the changes necessary to ameliorate the presenting problems. The model emphasized the therapist's active role, especially in assisting family members in goal setting: identifying the changes each member would like to see as the outcome of therapy. The emphasis was on delineating a solvable problem with achievable goals.

In his work with families, Haley provided homework or directives for continuing therapy outside of formal therapy sessions, a strategy employed by many brief therapists.

The Mental Research Institute

Founded in 1958 by Don D. Jackson and associates, MRI is recognized as a founding institute for brief and family therapy (Nichols & Schwartz, 2005). Following up on the work of Bateson, the MRI explored the use of interactional, systemic, and strategic concepts to effectively resolve human problems with individuals, couples, families, and all other levels of social organization. In the 1960s, a research associate at the MRI by the name of Richard Fisch proposed the idea of studying the effects of short-term interventions for treatment.

Fisch, along with his associates John Weakland and Paul Watzlawick, created the Brief Therapy Center at MRI. The work at MRI and the Brief Therapy Center produced the foundation of a comprehensive model of brief psychotherapy and an approach distinctive from more traditional therapies. The early research of the center developed a new set of assumptions about the formation and resolution of human problems. It resulted in developing many of the innovative procedures and techniques currently employed by those engaged in brief therapy (Nichols & Schwartz, 2005). The center embodied a paradigm shift in psychotherapy where the emphasis was placed on creating actionable change and results instead of the more traditional therapeutic pursuit of diagnosis and identification of the why for the problematic experience.

The brief therapeutic model developed at the center was designed to be a new goal-oriented and pragmatic approach to therapy. Those at the center embraced the somewhat controversial stance that intervening, rather than diagnosing and simply waiting for client insight, was the therapeutic process to follow. In opposition to the then generally held view that it was essential to understand the origin of a problem and the intrapsychic dynamics surrounding that problem, those at the center believed it was essential to intervene in the problem directly, regardless of where it came from or the nature of the pathology driving it (Anger, 2020).

> Regardless of their origins and etiology—if, indeed, these can ever be reliably determined—the problems people bring to psychotherapists persist only if they are maintained by ongoing current behavior of the client and others with whom he interacts. Correspondingly, if such problem-maintaining behavior is appropriately changed or eliminated, the problem will be resolved or vanish, regardless of its nature, or origin, or duration. (Weakland et al., 1974, p. 144)

The conceptual model and central tenets of the MRI brief therapy model are straightforward: Problems are part of life. Problems are mostly self-resolving and become significant difficulties when ineffective attempts to solve "inadvertently serve to maintain and perpetuate them" (Ray, 2007 p. 859). As such, efforts to stop such attempted solutions, solutions that were in fact problem maintaining, would allow for the problems to "resolve (correct) themselves and dissipate" (Ray, 2007, p. 859). It is almost like the old joke in which a man complains to his doctor, "Doctor, when I do this (moving his arm), it hurts." The doctor's reply? "Then stop doing that."

While perhaps somewhat silly, the directive is clear: Recognize that what you are doing is not only ineffective but that it is, in fact, exacerbating the problem. Stop, and the problem will most likely self-resolve.

This model of therapy made no assumptions about normality or pathology and instead focused on current, observable interaction around the presenting complaint (Rohrbaugh & Shoham, 2001). For example, therapists were directed to think in terms of description, not diagnosis. The focus was on defining the nature of the present concern and attempted solutions. The question of why a behavior occurs was not of concern. Seeking understanding and insight into the why was seen as a distraction to identifying what the person does in specific social contexts (Rohrbaugh & Shoham, 2001).

In 1974, two critical works were published by members of the MRI brief therapy project, *Change: Principles of Problem Formation and Problem Resolution* (Watzlawick et al., 1974) and *Brief Therapy: Focused Problem Resolution* (Weakland et al., 1974). These works impacted the field of family therapy and served as significant contributors to the development of brief/strategic approaches to psychotherapy. The approach taken was an apparent deviation from the more traditional methods of psychotherapy.

As presented in these manuscripts, the model focused on techniques of change rather than theoretical constructs. The approach was strategic, with therapists intervening deliberately based on a careful plan and assuming responsibility for the outcome (Haley, 1987). Therapists focused on assisting clients in understanding what they were doing in the present to enable their problems to persist. With this understanding, therapists would then assist the individual in engaging in more effective behaviors. These behaviors would lead to the achievement of their desired goals and preferred state of being.

Several principles established by this early work, principles that continue to influence contemporary models of brief therapy, include that therapy is symptom oriented, that change is effected most readily if the goals are relatively small and clearly stated, and that the presenting problem is both a representation of the problem and an index of progress. From these foundational principles, a straightforward formula for engaging in brief therapy emerged directing practitioners to (a) define the complaint in specific behavioral terms; (b) set minimum goals for change; (c) investigate solutions to the complaint; (d) formulate ironic problem-solution loops (how "more of the same" solution leads to more of the complaint, etc.); (e) specify what "less of the same" will look like; (f) understand clients' preferred views of themselves, the problem, and each other; (g) use client position to interdict problem-maintaining solutions; and (h) nurture and solidify incipient change (Rohrbaugh & Shoham, 2001).

Additional Forces Contributing to the Emergence of Brief Therapy

The emergence and continued development of brief therapy has also been facilitated by a number of somewhat ancillary forces, including the growing popularity of behavioral therapy, research data gathered from meta-analytic outcome studies pointing to the effectiveness of time-limited approaches, and social-cultural factors pushing toward more solution-focused interventions.

Popularity of Behavior Therapy

Behavioral therapists challenged the models that emphasized uncovering the etiology of a client's presenting concern. They also discarded the need for the therapist to promote client insight as fundamental to treatment. During the early years, behavioral therapists viewed client problems as developing with the exact mechanisms that contributed to the development of all behavior, both that which was functional and desirable and that which was dysfunctional or at least undesirable. The goal was to strengthen that which was desirable and reduce or eliminate that which was unwanted. The therapeutic principles employed were influenced by both Pavlovian classical conditioning and Skinnerian operant learning (Center for Substance Abuse Treatment, 1999). Behavioral therapy was, and remains, action based, with a specific focus on modifying problematic behavior in the here and now.

As behavioral therapy's effectiveness and brevity (relative to traditional psychodynamic approaches) became more widely established, its popularity and interest gained momentum among both professionals and the lay populations. This relative success and popularity of behavior therapy further set the stage for accepting active short-term therapeutic approaches.

Outcome Studies

The increasing interest in the engagement of brief approaches is at some level attributable to increased empirical support highlighting the efficacy of such treatments. Early research appeared to paint the picture that therapy was time and session limited regardless of theory or model. For example, Pardes and Pincus (1981) reported that most outpatient treatments, regardless of the therapist model or theory, last no longer than 20 sessions.

Given that most therapies appeared somewhat time limited, attention turned to assessing the relative effectiveness of such time-limited approaches. Outcome research, such as that of Toner et al. (2021) and meta-analytic studies (e.g., Corpas et al., 2021), support brief psychological therapies. Early research comparing the effectiveness of time-limited and time-unlimited individual therapy reported no reliable differences in effectiveness (e.g., Butcher & Koss, 1978; Orlinsky & Howard, 1986). In fact, following a review of the literature, Lambert (2013), concluded "Therapy is highly efficient for a large minority of clients, perhaps 30% of whom attain a lasting benefit after only three sessions," and when monitoring for "reliable improvement ... it appears 50% of patients respond by the 8th session, and 75% are predicted to need at least 14 sessions to experience this degree of relief" (p. 204). To further buffer the interest in brief therapies, some research has reported that while clients appear to experience relatively rapid improvement in early treatment stages, treatment effects seem to decrease in later stages (Stulz et al., 2013). Such a diminishment of return has called to question the value of elongated individual therapy models and has served as a force in the ongoing evolution and development of brief therapy models.

This research appears to challenge the intuitively appealing notion that more therapy, is better. Exercise 1.1 invites you to test the beliefs held by your colleagues and classmates regarding the association of length of therapy and outcome and contrast those to what the research has found.

EXERCISE 1.1

Is More Better?

Directions: Using the Lambert (2013) and Stulz et al. (2013) research as your reference, survey your classmates, colleagues, perhaps even your instructors, and ask them the following:

1. What is your opinion of the statement "When it comes to therapy, more is better"?
2. What percentage of clients would you predict experience lasting benefit after only three sessions? (Remember that Lambert [2013] reported 30%.)
3. If you plotted client improvement across treatment, how might that graph look? (Remember that Stulz et al. (2013) reported relatively rapid improvement in early treatment stages, effects that seem to decrease in later stages.)

Share the results of the Lambert (2013) and Stulz et al. (2013) studies with the individual you interview. Were they surprised?

Social/Economic Pressures

Data supporting the relative effectiveness of time-limited therapy and the questionable value added with extended lengths of treatment have positioned some insurance companies and health maintenance organizations to limit the number of sessions for which a therapist will be reimbursed.

Therapists are increasingly experiencing pressure, for employers and third-party payers, to not only demonstrate effectiveness but to do so in a cost-effective manner. This emphasis on cost-effectiveness has placed pressure on therapists to control cost via reduction of sessions and improve accountability and outcomes effectiveness. As such, the increased interest in brief, problem-specific approaches to treatment has been, to some degree, the result of therapists' economic realities.

A Rich History and an Inviting Future

Brief therapy has become an attractive method for meeting the increased demand for therapy services in a timely and cost-efficient way. The continuum of care has been augmented by an increasing interest and utilization of brief, time-limited modes of therapy.

Brief therapy provides the clinician with an expanded toolbox, one in which brief modalities can be used as a standalone approach to treatment or as a supplement or prelude to a longer form of therapy. As will be reviewed in the next chapter, brief therapy is *not* time limited by default, nor is it more traditional nontime-restricted therapy "watered down." While the various theories and models of brief therapy to be discussed are unique in many ways, what they share is that they are all planned approaches to treatments designed to produce therapeutic outcomes within a limited time frame.

KEYSTONES

- Brief therapy, as a distinct approach to psychotherapy, is planned and not engaged as a default.
- Brief therapy is unique, not just in the length of services provided but in perspective. Brief therapy de-emphasizes etiology and focuses on current difficulties and resolutions.
- Brief therapy has a rich history and contributions from those practicing in the world of psychoanalysis, including Freud, Adler, Rank, and Ferenczi.
- Significant historical contributors to brief therapy's theoretical underpinnings and actual practice include Milton Erickson, Gregory Bateson, and Jay Haley.
- The Mental Research Institute (MRI) in Palo Alto, California, is recognized as a founding institute for brief therapy.
- The Brief Therapy Center at MRI produced the foundation of a comprehensive model of brief psychotherapy that reflected a paradigm shift to an emphasis on therapists creating actionable change instead of pursuing diagnosis and etiology.

- The success and efficiency of behavioral therapy, the existence of outcome research pointing to the effectiveness of time-limited approaches, and the economic pressures exerted by third-party payers contributed to the development of brief therapy models.

ADDITIONAL RESOURCES

Bale, L. S. (n.d.) *Gregory Bateson, cybernetics, and the social/behavioral sciences*. http://www.narberthpa.com/Bale/lsbale_dop/gbcatsbs.pdf

Budman, S. H., & Gurman, A. S. (1988). *Theory and practice of brief therapy*. Guilford.

Cade, B., & O'Hanlon, W. H. (1993). *A brief guide to brief therapy*. Norton.

Davanloo, D. (Ed.). (1980). *Short-term dynamic psychotherapy*. Jason Aronson.

REFERENCES

Anger, K. (2020). On the shoulders of giants. *Journal of Systemic Therapies, 39*(2), 23–32.

Bale, L. S. (n.d.) *Gregory Bateson, cybernetics, and the social/behavioral sciences*. http://www.narberthpa.com/Bale/lsbale_dop/gbcatsbs.pdf

Bateson, G., Jackson, D., Haley, J., & Weakland, J. (1956). Toward a theory of schizophrenia. *Behavioral Science, 1*, 251–264.

Bauer, G., & Kobos, J. (1995). *Brief therapy: Short-term dynamic intervention*. Jason Aronson.

Bloom, B. L. (1992). Planned short-term psychotherapy: Current status and future challenges. *Applied & Preventive Psychology, 1*(3), 157–164. https://doi.org/10.1016/S0962-1849(05)80137-4

Butcher, J. M., & Koss, M. P. (1978). Research on brief and crisis-oriented therapies. In S. Garfield & A. E. Bergin (Eds.), *Handbook of psychotherapy and behavior change* (2nd ed., pp. 725–768). Wiley.

Center for Substance Abuse Treatment. (1999). *Brief interventions and brief therapies for substance abuse*. Substance Abuse and Mental Health Services Administration.

Corpas, J., Moriana, J. A., Venceslá, J. F., & Gálvez-Lara, M. (2021). Brief psychological therapies for emotional disorders in primary care: A systematic review and meta-analysis. *Clinical Psychology: Science and Practice, 21*(1), 1–13.

de Shazer, S. (1982). *Patterns of brief therapy*. Guilford.

Ferenczi, S., & Rank, O. (1986). *The development of psychoanalysis*. International Universities Press. Original work published in 1924.

Fisch, R, & Schlanger, K. (1999) *Brief therapy with intimidating cases: Changing the unchangeable*. Jossey-Bass; 1999.

Freud, S. (1955). Studies on hysteria. The Standard Edition of the Complete psychology works of Sigmund Freud (Vol. 2, pp. 106–134). Original Work published 1895, translated James Strachey, Hogarth Press.

Guedalia, J. B. (2015). *Neuropsychologist's journal: Interventions and Judaisms*. Urim.

Haley, J. (1976). *Problem-solving therapy*. Jossey-Bass.

Haley, J. (Ed.). (1985). *Conversations with Milton H. Erickson, MD*. Triangle Press.

Haley, J. (1987). *Problem-solving therapy: New strategies for effective family therapy*. Jossey-Bass.

Hoffman, L. (1981). *Foundations of family therapy*. Basic Books.

Jones-Smith, E. (2012). *Theories of counseling and psychotherapy: An integrative approach*. SAGE.

Lambert, M. (2013). The efficacy and effectiveness of psychotherapy. In M. Lambert (Ed.), *Bergin and Garfield's handbook of psychotherapy and behavior change* (6th ed, pp. 168–218). Wiley.

Levenson, H., & Davidowitz, D. (2000). Brief therapy prevalence and training: A national survey of psychologists. *Psychotherapy: Theory, Research, Practice, Training, 37*(4), 335–340. http://dx.doi.org/10.1037/0033-3204.37.4.335

Marmor, J. (1979). Short-term dynamic psychotherapy. *American Journal of Psychiatry, 136*(2), 149–155.

Muran, J. C., Safran, J. D., Gorman, B. S., Samstag, L. W., Eubanks-Carter, C., & Winston, A., (2009). The relationship of early alliance ruptures and their resolution to process and outcome in three time-limited psychotherapies for personality disorders. *Psychotherapy: Theory, Research, Practice, Training, 46*(2), 233–248. http://dx.doi.org/10.1037/a0016085

Nichols, M., & Schwartz, R. (2005). *Family therapy: Concepts and methods* (7th ed.). Prentice-Hall.

Orlinsky, D. E., & Howard, K. I. (1986). Process and outcome in psychotherapy. In S. Garfield & A. E. Bergin (Eds.), *Handbook of psychotherapy and behavior change* (3rd ed., pp. 311–381). Wiley.

Pardes, H., & Pincus, H. A. (1981). Brief therapy in the context of national mental health. In S. H. Budman (Ed.), *Forms of brief therapy* (pp. 7–22). Guilford.

Ray, W. (2007) Bateson's cybernetics: The basis of MRI brief therapy: Prologue. *Kybernetes, 36*(7/8), 859–870. https://doi.org/10.1108/03684920710777388

Rohrbaugh, M. J., & Shoham, V. (2001). Brief therapy based on interrupting ironic processes: The Palo Alto model. *Clinical Psychology: A Publication of the Division of Clinical Psychology of the American Psychological Association, 8*(1), 66–81. https://doi.org/10.1093/clipsy.8.1.66

Short, D. (2019). *Principles and core competencies of Ericksonian therapy: 2019 edition*. The Milton H. Erickson Institute of Phoenix. http://www.iamdrshort.com/PDF/Papers/Core%20Competencies%20Manual

Sluzki, C. E., & Ransom, D. C. (1976). *Double bind: The foundation of the communicational approach to the family*. Grune & Stratton.

Strupp, H. H., & Binder, J. L. (1984) *Psychotherapy in a new key: A guide to time-limited dynamic psychotherapy*. Basic Books.

Stulz, N., Lutz, W., Kopta, S. M., Minami, T., & Saunders, S. M. (2013). Dose–effect relationship in routine outpatient psychotherapy: Does treatment duration matter? *Journal of Counseling Psychology, 60*(4), 593–600. https://doi.org/10.1037/a0033589.supp

Toner, P., Ali, S., & Mikocka-Walus, A. (2021, October 21). Are brief psychological therapies effective for adults experiencing common mental health difficulties in primary care? *Clinical Psychology: Science and Practice, 28*(4), 377–379. http://dx.doi.org/10.1037/cps0000045

Visser, C. F. (2013). The origin of the solution-focused approach. *International Journal of Solution-Focused Practices, 1*, (1), 10–17. http://dx.doi.org/10.14335/ijsfp.v1i1.10

Watzlawick, P. Weakland, J. H., & Fisch. R. (1974) *Change: Principles of problem formation and problem resolution*. Norton.

Weakland, J. H., Fisch, R., Watzlawick, P., & Bodin, A. (1974). Brief therapy: Focused problem resolution. *Family Process, 13*, 141–168.

Wiener, N. (1950). *The human use of human beings: Cybernetics and society*. Riverside Press.

CHAPTER 2

Brief Therapy

More Than "Limited Sessions"

Brief therapy is a state of mind.

Budman & Gurman (1988, p.10)

As previously noted, brief therapy is not traditional therapy watered down, nor simply defined by its limited number of sessions. While historically brief therapy may have been viewed as a "superficial and expedient treatment to be used only in emergency situations until long-term therapy could begin" (Koss et al., 1986, p. 60), the models and approaches employed today reflect a distinct, effective, and efficient mode of psychotherapy. Therapy of short duration does not exemplify brief psychotherapy unless specific therapeutic characteristics are present (Koss et al., 1986).

The current chapter reviews the defining perspective, values, and technical elements that "define" brief, planned psychotherapy. After reading this chapter, you will be able to do the following:

1. Describe the values and principles that distinguish brief therapy from longer forms of psychotherapy.
2. Describe the technical characteristics that appear brief therapies share.
3. Describe factors that may impact the suitability of brief therapy for any one client.

A Common Core: Multiple Presentations

Brief therapy is not a single theory or unitary approach. As will be illustrated in the upcoming chapters, a wide variety of theoretical models and approaches have been configured or, in some cases, reconfigured to reflect the essential components of that called brief therapy. Central to each of these models is the inclusion of time as an integral element in the planning and approach to psychotherapy. Time, however, is not the only, nor sufficient, element defining brief, planned therapy.

Regardless of the uniqueness of strategies employed or theoretical orientation underpinning the therapeutic approach, models that identify as planned, brief therapy reflect a specific perspective and set of values, along with specific technical elements.

Guiding Values and Principles

Psychotherapists engaged in brief therapy approach therapy with a sense of parsimony to their interventions. They begin treatment using the least costly and least complicated or time-committed interventions. They do this with the belief that clients are malleable and continue to develop and that they have resources that can be called forth to address the current situation. With this as a value and perspective, brief therapists "can judiciously allocate his or her time to help the patient maximize the trajectory of change" (Budman & Gorman, 2008, p 14).

Brief therapy differs from the more traditional long-term approach in a number of its guiding principles and values. Budman and Gurman (2008) identified eight major differences in the values and principles guiding brief therapy from those present in long-term psychotherapy (see Table 2.1).

While brief therapists and their operational models may differ and reflect specific philosophical or theoretical focal points, the shared values and perspectives that define brief therapy will, in varying degrees, be evident in their approach. Central to each model or theory of brief therapy is the incorporation of specific technical aspects that reflect a valuing of a client's strengths and developmental potential, as well as the belief that therapeutic change is not limited to therapy or engagement with a therapist and a focus on clients' here-and-now concerns.

Shared Technical Characteristics

While there is uniqueness among the specific brief therapy models, they appear to share several characteristics that connect them as a model of planned brief therapy. The technical characteristics most often cited as the basis upon which to distinguish brief psychotherapies from long-term approaches or even unplanned short-duration therapy include (a) a nonpathologizing perspective, (b) time limitation, (c) a focus on client strength and evidence of change over the client's life span, (d) a collaborative working alliance between counselor and client, (e) therapists' pro-activeness, (f) a focus on outcomes, (g) flexibility of technique, and (h) engaging client systems (Bitter & Nicoll, 2004; Koss et al., 1986; Koss & Shiang,1994; Nicoll et al., 2000).

Nonpathologizing

In general, brief therapies are unique in that they de-emphasize concepts such as ideal health and pathology. Brief therapists generally engage in nonpathologizing, collaborative, and competency-oriented work with clients. They do not approach their work with a client as

TABLE 2.1 DOMINANT VALUES IN BRIEF AND LONG-TERM THERAPISTS

Long-term therapist	Short-term therapist
Seeks change in essential character	Prefers pragmatism, parsimony and the least radical intervention and does not believe in the notion of "cure"
Believes that significant psychological change is unlikely in everyday life	Maintains an adult developmental perspective from which significant psychological change is viewed as inevitable
Sees presenting problems as reflecting more basic pathology	Emphasizes patients' strengths and resources; presenting problems are taken seriously (although not necessarily at face value)
Wants to "be there" as the patient makes significant changes	Accepts that many changes will occur "after therapy" and will not be observable to the therapist
Sees therapy as having a "timeless" quality and is patient and willing to wait for change	Does not accept the timelessness of some models of therapy
Unconsciously recognizes the fiscal convenience of maintaining long-term patients	Fiscal issues are often muted, either by the nature of the therapist's practice or by the organizational structure for reimbursement
Views psychotherapy as almost always benign and useful	Views psychotherapy as being sometimes helpful and sometimes harmful
Sees patients being in therapy as the most critical part of the patient's life	Sees being in the world as more important than being in therapy.

Source: Budman & Gurman (1988, p. 11)

that requiring them to identify symptoms, cluster these into syndromes, and then seek the hypothesized underlying disease or disorder.

Most who employ a brief therapy approach recognize that life presents challenges, and sometimes individuals have difficulty coping with or adjusting to these challenges. A client presenting for therapy is often in just this type of distress. However, the brief therapist does not immediately pathologize the client or the clients' issues. Brief therapists are resistant to moving from what is being presented to identify the underlying pathology.

Here-and-Now Focus

Brief therapists do not deny the presence of psychiatric disorders that have long and deep roots in the client's biology and history. However, they attempt to deal with that which is being presented, in the here and now, feeling that it is neither necessary nor beneficial to conceptualize all the issues presented by one's clients as reflective of an illness—one demanding extended therapy.

The brief therapist focuses on the client's present conditions and preferred future rather than the search for understanding of their past. The brief therapist views current symptoms, problematic relationships, or repetitive patterns of relationships in the client's life as having primary importance. The strategies and the intervention employed target the presenting concern, as well as the concrete goals as reflected at present time (see Case Illustration 2.1).

Rather than the formal analysis of historical causes of distress or the issue under investigation, the primary approach of brief therapy is to help the client to view the present from a broader context and to utilize a more functional understanding of the factors contributing to the presence of this undesirable state (see Case Illustration 2.1).

CASE ILLUSTRATION 2.1[1]

Here and Now

Entering the counselor's office, the student, 16-year-old Alicia, was quick to highlight her long history of getting into trouble. While respecting the client, the school counselor gently refocused the conversation on the current situation.

Alicia: (entering office, very upset) I can't do it; I can't take it anymore. I am a total screw-up and always have been; I don't know what's wrong with me.

Counselor: Alicia, come in, please. Have a seat and take a breath (smiling).

Alicia: No, Really—I'm messed up. You don't understand. I can't make friends; I mean, no one likes me. My parents are ready to disown me. They think I'm a psychopath; my brother is a drug addict. I don't know what to do or where to turn. My life is a mess.

Counselor: Alicia, I am sorry that you are so upset. I can hear how overwhelming and even hopeless that it feels. I wonder if it would help if we could take a moment to talk about what just happened? What happened today that is upsetting you so much and has led you to come to my office?

---

[1] All case illustrations reflect composites of clients and not any one specific individual.

Time Limited

Brief therapies are planned as time-limited processes. There is no set number of sessions or specific session length that defines brief or time-limited therapy. Brief therapy may occur within a single session or be carried for twenty or more sessions. The focus is on keeping therapy short and limited, while effective, rather than specifying the maximum allowed amount of necessary time (Manaster, 1989).

Applying a time limit to psychotherapy may have advantages for the therapy process. By setting targets and a time limit, clients may feel that the therapy does not imprison them but that an improvement of their condition is both insightful and tangible. The deadline can add a sense of urgency and intensity that causes therapists and patients to make the most of their time in therapy. Setting a fixed limit on the number of sessions has value in highlighting the nature of the work, the expectation of positive outcomes, and providing a structure for therapy with a defined beginning, middle, and end. It is believed that setting such time or session limits could cause an acceleration in symptom improvement and lower dropout rates (De Geest & Meganck, 2019; Mann, 1973).

Valuing Client Strengths

Brief therapists hold to the perspective that people are developing, changing, and adaptable. They take a perspective that emphasizes client health and strength rather than illness, pathology, or deficiency. Brief therapists emphasize engagement of the client's resources and minimize client shortcomings.

A classic illustration of this valuing and engagement of client strengths can be found in solution-focused brief therapy (see Chapter 3). Therapists employing this model often attempt to identify experiences that are the exception to the current situation or experiences where the client was more successful at coping with similar demands and challenges. The position taken by a brief therapist is that all clients, regardless of their current difficulties, have either experienced a time when the difficulty was not being experienced or was experienced to a lesser degree. At that time, the client was more successful at coping. By examining these times of exception and times of coping, the therapist and client gain a clearer understanding of a preferred future and identify the competencies that the client employed during those times, which in turn may be engaged in addressing the current situation.

The brief therapist will help the client identify core strengths and resources and help them further develop these resources and use them in service of their desired goals and preferred future. The approach requires the counselor and client to move beyond the identification of specific skills to identifying the underlying set of qualities and aptitudes that enable the person to employ that disposition or skill (see Case Illustration 2.2).

In this case illustration, the therapist working with a client currently struggling in a relationship helps him identify and understand that his ability to listen and enter the experience of his customer, employ open questions, and demonstrate a respect and valuing of that customer are

> ## CASE ILLUSTRATION 2.2
>
> ### Messing Up My Marriage
>
> The client came to the first session upset, confused, and concerned that he would destroy his marriage of 30 years.
>
> **Client:** I love her so much, yet I know how frustrated and exacerbated she is with me. She says that she feels like our marriage or relationship is falling apart and that she is not sure that I know who she is anymore.
>
> **Counselor:** Could you perhaps share a recent example of when you were with her, and she shared her upset?
>
> **Client:** Just today—I could tell that she was unhappy about something at work. I began to give her suggestions, ideas on what she could do, and she got really upset and said: "You don't get it … You're not listening." Doc, I don't get—I was trying to help—I was listening. I mean, I am and have been a very successful sales rep because I'm a good listener and a good problem solver. However, I don't know what to do here?
>
> **Counselor:** A good listener? Could you give me an example of how you listen when engaging with your customers?
>
> **Client:** Well, I have taken many courses on communication, so when I am with a client, I use my knowledge and skills about active listening. I encourage them to share their concerns; I ask open questions, that kind of thing. Now, I am not a therapist, but I know it is good to reflect what you are hearing to let the other person know that you are listening and check if what you are hearing is accurate.
>
> **Counselor:** Wow, that's fantastic; that is an excellent use of attending and communication skills. Is that the approach you use when your wife wants to share her concerns?

the same skills that have value within the current relationship. It is not a matter of limited skill but rather the need for the client to truly value those skills, not just for sales but for developing and maintaining a healthy relationship.

Brief therapists not only value a client's strengths and resiliency and engage these as resources to be employed in addressing the current concern, but they also seek to nurture those strengths. The goal is more than a resolution of this one problem. Brief therapists seek to successfully develop the client's ability to navigate similar challenges in the future. This perspective takes form in the therapist's attempt to reduce thier influence and even support and ultimately remove themself from the client's life.

A Collaborative Working Alliance

As a reflection of their valuing of the client and client strengths, brief therapists seek to develop caring, respectful relationships with clients in which clients are complete and coequal agents in the change process. Brief therapists recognize that the client is the expert on their own experience. While the therapist has expertise with the therapeutic process and thus is an active agent in developing, maintaining, and advancing the relationship, the client brings the expertise on their life, life condition, values, and beliefs. These elements need to be considered when engaging with intervention strategies so that maximum client ownership and engagement can be achieved.

In developing a collaborative, coequal relationship, the therapist will engage in active, reflective listening, checking with the client to ensure accurate understanding and inviting client suggestions and directions.

Therapist: Proactive Agent of Change

While maintaining a collaborative style, therapists in brief therapy are active and directive. While the client is the expert in terms of their lived experience, the therapist brings process expertise to the relationship and thus assumes responsibility for maintaining the therapeutic focus. Brief therapists embrace their role as active, responsible agents in the relationship.

Brief therapists assume responsibility for creating the conditions that assist the client in successfully resolving their problem and achieving their desired goals. To achieve goals in a limited time, therapists engage a higher level activity than may typically be observed in those engaged in longterm psychotherapy approaches.

A primary focus for the brief therapist's efforts is on defining, or at times reframing, the presenting concerns so that a solution can be found. In this process, the therapist will often redirect the interaction from a review of the possible historic roots of the issue to investigate the context in which the problem occurs (and is maintained), the possibility of the engagement of others in the problematic situation, and the various strategies employed by the client in an attempt to resolve the problem.

Brief therapists keep the therapy focused. They are often engaged in making interpretations, formulating plans of action for the client to follow, assigning homework, and teaching problem solving (Koss et al., 1996).

Outcome Focused

Limiting time is one way to make therapy brief. However, it is not just brevity that is sought, but rather effectiveness and outcome achievement. A way of achieving both efficiency and effectiveness is for the brief therapist to limit the focus of the therapeutic endeavor to a specific resolution of an identifiable issue or difficulty. Brief therapists are outcome focused.

Unlike some traditional psychotherapies, where the goals may be as extensive as gaining insight into the psychogenic origins of a client's problem or the reconstruction of one's personality, brief therapy pursues more specific and more concretely defined outcomes. The goals established in brief therapy reflect those of importance to the client. Often goals include a desire to ameliorate some condition or disabling symptoms, or perhaps the reestablishment of a previous emotional state, or the ability to cope with similar challenges in the future.

Brief therapists most often will attempt to not only define the goals in specific, measurable terms but will help the client establish the goals, or perhaps subgoals, in ways that make them manageable, thus increasing the likelihood of the client experiencing success in moving forward (see Case illustration 2.3).

CASE ILLUSTRATION 2.3

Tiny Steps

The client, a college freshman, sought assistance from the counselor because, as she describes, she is falling behind in her assignments and is losing her motivation.

Counselor: I know you are saying that you have lost your motivation, but quite honestly, I'm impressed that you have taken this step to meet with me.

Client: Thanks, but it is getting really bad. I look at everything I have to do, and it is overwhelming. I find the books on my desk, and I ask myself, why bother? It's too much, and so I go play a video game.

Counselor: If I understand you correctly, you are currently trying to complete four major assignments, including a 20-page research paper and three 5- to 10-page literature reviews. Is that correct?

Client: Yeah—and it all has to be done in 4 weeks.

Counselor: As you were describing the things you need to accomplish, the image I got was this was a gigantic mountain of paperwork that is pressing down on you.

Client: That's exactly it: I look or imagine everything that I need to do and go "there is no way hell I can get this done."

Counselor: I get that looking at it as one gigantic task makes it appear undoable. I am wondering, do you think that we could break this massive task down?

Client: I am not sure I understand.

Counselor: Well, I'm wondering, do each of the projects have to be done simultaneously, or could we prioritize?

Client: Oh, yeah. The first thing that needs to get done is a lit review for my neuropsych class. That's about five pages. The big 20-pager isn't due for 5 weeks.

Counselor: Great. I wonder if it would look a little less ominous and overwhelming if we organized four projects and then maybe identify the steps you could take in attacking the first project on the list? You know, take some tiny steps?

Flexibility of Techniques

Brief therapy is often highly strategic, exploratory, and solution based rather than problem oriented. In general, brief therapists do not adhere to one "correct" approach but rather accept that many paths could prove successful in achieving the desired outcomes. While identifying with a specific theory, such as solution-focused, psychodynamic, or cognitive behavioral therapy, a brief therapist will often draw on the strategies and techniques across such traditional theories. This flexibility in approach often takes shape in the use of time as a therapeutic factor.

While traditional therapy may, especially in the early phases, be scheduled as weekly, 50-minute sessions, brief therapists approach scheduling and time with a sense of flexibility and eye toward its therapeutic value. For brief therapy, the number, spacing, and length of sessions are seen as a significant therapeutic element and thus are configured in service of outcome achievement. Every patient or every session need not be weekly, nor 50 minutes. Biweekly, 30-minute sessions, or even daily, 15-minute check-ins will be considered in light of their therapeutic value and utility in facilitating goal achievement.

Engaging Client Systems: Therapy Outside of the Office

While maintaining the focus on goal achievement, brief therapists remain flexible in their intervention strategies. Brief therapists believe that growth can occur outside of the therapist's office. Practitioners of brief therapy believe that some changes can happen through a more rapid process or that a short initial intervention will start an ongoing process of change that does not need the constant involvement of the therapist. While maintaining the focus on goal achievement, brief therapists remain flexible in their intervention strategies.

One strategy that extends the therapy beyond the confines of the therapist's office is the use of homework. Most brief therapists employ liberal use of homework assignments. It is argued that such assignments help maintain a therapeutic focus, strengthen the therapeutic alliance, enhance motivation, and reduce termination difficulties (Macaskill, 2007).

In addition to assigning homework as a means of extending therapy, the brief therapist will often invite the client to engage in "natural" therapeutic experiences, such as engaging in physical exercise, reading, and meditation. The brief therapist often elicits the support of the client's social system, including friends, family, and community-based support and self-help groups (see Exercise 2.1).

EXERCISE 2.1

Therapy Outside the Office Walls

Directions: It is important to be aware of the activities, services, and organizations within your community that provide support and opportunities for personal development. These are resources of therapy encountered outside of a clinician's office.

You are presented with several presenting concerns and goals in the table provided. Your task is to identify natural resources within your community that may augment the therapeutic work of the brief therapist.

You may find value in sharing your data with your colleagues or classmates, and in so doing develop a valuable referral source.

Presenting concern/goal	Resource	Contact information
Problem with overeating, desire to lose 20 pounds		
Problem with social anxiety, desire to meet and make friends		
Unhappy with current employment, would like to identify a career that would be satisfying		
Problem with road rage, would like to be less angry and explosive		
Sad as a result of experiencing a recent death of a loved one, desires to experience joy in life once again		
Arrested from driving under the influence, unsure if he has a problem with alcohol		

A Question of Suitability

There is no consensus among brief therapists on which type of client or presenting concerns are most suitable for these methods. Garfield (1989) suggested that except for very seriously disturbed individuals, brief treatment can be considered for most patients in touch with reality, experiencing some discomfort, and who make an effort to seek help. At the same time, David Malan (1979) posited that only clients with well-adjusted personalities experiencing an acute illness were suitable for brief therapy. For Malan (1979), it was important that "the patient's life problem [] be clearly defined and offer [] a clear-cut theme or focus for therapy" (p. 243).

Most proponents of brief therapy generally agree that it is not indiscriminately suitable for all kinds of psychiatric problems. The brief therapist generally holds that not all patients and diagnoses can be adequately handled in a significantly abbreviated time frame. There are several significant issues to consider when deciding whether psychotherapy of fewer than 20 sessions is likely to be the best approach. It appears that the severity and nature of the issue presented, the client's ability to form a therapeutic alliance, and the client's stage of change are all essential factors when deciding to engage in brief therapy.

Severity and Complexity

The prime considerations when assessing the viability of a brief therapy approach are whether the problems described are long standing or of recent vintage (Dewan et al., 2008). Chronic problems are likely to be embedded in overlearned behavioral and emotional patterns and may require more extended treatment.

A short-term approach is contraindicated if the initial presentation suggests more severe issues or the existence of multiple complex problems are overwhelming the client's ability to function. A high severity level will likely hamper the patient's ability to actively engage in treatment efforts during sessions and assignments between sessions (Hales et al., 2008). Identifying and targeting specific concerns and treatment goals may be difficult and impede progress through brief therapy with multiple complex problems.

Impediments to Therapeutic Alliance

Given the emphasis and value assigned to the development and maintenance of a collaborative therapeutic alliance, it can be assumed that anything that interferes with the formation of such an alliance will slow down treatment progress and thus lengthen therapy. It could be expected that clients with histories of poor interpersonal relationships may have difficulty adapting to the intensity of the therapy relationship and the need to work collaboratively to achieve the desired goals. It is also fair to assume that clients who have had their trust violated and present as highly vulnerable, as may be the case for an abused client, may find it difficult to form a quick therapeutic connection and thus delay the progress of therapy.

Client's Stage of Change

Prochaska and Norcross (2002) have presented a transtheoretical model of change that depicts change as progressing through sequential stages. Clients enter therapy with differing levels of readiness to change. Some clients may lack an awareness of the need and value of engaging in therapy, while others may enter fully invested in the process of making change.

Clients who fail to understand the need or value of therapy might be considered poor candidates for brief therapy. Such clients, who perhaps are engaging at the request or mandate of another, will require the therapist to turn energy and focus on "selling" the therapy and creating a working alliance. The requirement to focus energy on relationship building will interfere with the therapist's ability to move quickly to identify meaningful, concrete goals and engage the client's collaborative participation.

KEYSTONES

- Psychotherapists engaged in brief therapy approach therapy with a sense of parsimony to their interventions. They begin treatment using the least costly and least complicated or time-committed interventions.
- Central to each model or theory of brief therapy is the incorporation of specific technical aspects that reflect a valuing of a client's strengths and developmental potential. Brief therapists believe that therapeutic change is not limited to therapy or engagement with a therapist and focus on the here-and-now concerns of a client.
- The shared technical characteristics most often cited as the basis on which to distinguish brief psychotherapies from long-term approaches or even unplanned short-duration therapy include (a) a nonpathologizing perspective, (b) time limitation, (c) a focus on client strength and evidence of change over the client's life span, (d) a collaborative working alliance between counselor and client, (e) therapist proactiveness, (f) a focus on outcomes, (g) flexibility of technique, and (h) engaging client systems.
- Most proponents of brief therapy generally agree that it is not indiscriminately suitable for all kinds of psychiatric problems.
- It appears that the severity and nature of the issue presented, the client's ability to form a therapeutic alliance, and the client's stage of change are all essential factors when deciding on the suitability of brief therapy for any one client.

ADDITIONAL RESOURCES

Cade, B., & O'Hanlon, W. H. (1993). *A brief guide to brief therapy*. Norton.

Center for Substance Abuse Treatment. (1999) *Brief interventions and brief therapies for substance abuse.* Substance Abuse and Mental Health Services Administration. https://store.samhsa.gov/sites/default/files/d7/priv/sma12-3952.pdf

Dewan, M. J., Steenbarger, B. N., & Greenberg, R. P. (Eds.). (2004). *The art and science of brief psychotherapies: A practitioner's guide*. American Psychiatric Press.

REFERENCES

Bitter, J. R., & Nicoll, W. G. (2004). Relational strategies: Two approaches to Adlerian brief therapy. *Journal of Individual Psychology, 60*(1), 42–66.

Budman, S. H., & Gurman, A. S. (1988). *Theory and practice of brief therapy*. Guilford.

De Geest, R. M., & Meganck, R. (2019). How do time limits affect our psychotherapies? A literature review. *Psychologica Belgica, 59*(1), 206–226. https://doi.org/10.5334/pb.475

Dewan, M. J., Steenbarger, B. N., & Greenberg, R. P. (2008). Brief psychotherapies. In A. Tasman, J. Kay, J. A. Lieberman, M. B. First, & J. A. Maj (Eds.), *Psychiatry* (Vol. 2, 3rd ed., pp 1889–1903). Wiley.

Hales, R. E., Yudofsky, S. C., & Gabbard, G. O. (2008). *The American Psychiatric Association publishing textbook of psychiatry*. APA.

Garfield, S. L. (1989). *The practice of brief psychotherapy*. Pergamon.

Koss, M. P., Butcher, J. N., & Strupp, H. H. (1986). Brief psychotherapy methods in clinical research. *Journal of Consulting and Clinical Psychology, 54*(1), 60–67.

Koss, M. P., & Shiang, J. (1984). Research on brief therapy. In A. E. Bergin & S. L. Garfield (Eds.), *Handbook of psychotherapy and behaviour Change* (4th ed., pp. 664–700). Wiley.

Macaskill, N. (2007). Homework assignments in brief psychotherapy. *British Journal of Psychotherapy, 2*(2), 134–141.

Malan, D. (1979). *Individual therapy and the science of psychodynamics*. Butterworth.

Manaster, G. J. (1989). Clinical issues in brief psychotherapy: A summary and conclusion. *Individual Psychology: The Journal of Adlerian Theory, Research & Practice, 45*(1/2), 243–248.

Mann, J. (1973). *Time-limited psychotherapy*. Harvard University Press.

Nicoll, W. G., Bitter, J. R., Christensen, O. C., & Hawes, C. (2000). Adlerian brief therapy: Strategies and tactics. In J. Carlson & L. Sperry (Eds.), *Brief therapy strategies with individuals and couples* (pp. 220–247). Zeig/Tucker.

Prochaska, J. O., & Norcross, J. C. (2002). Stages of change. In J. C. Norcross (Ed.), *Psychotherapy relationships that work: Therapist contributions and responsiveness to patients* (pp. 303–314). Oxford University Press.

PART II

Theories and Their Applications

CHAPTER 3

Solution-Focused Brief Therapy

Find out what works, and do more of that.
—Steve de Shazer (de Shazer & Berg, 1995)

The observation made by Steve de Shazer is a succinct explication of the solution-focused brief therapy approach. With his quote, de Shazer, founder of the solution-focused brief therapy model, highlights the essence of the approach, which views the client as the expert and encourages individuals to find what is working in their lives and what is not. Those areas where discord between desired goals and actual behaviors exist are addressed, and more productive, goal-oriented behaviors replace the problematic behaviors.

The current chapter reviews the basic tenets, constructs, and strategies employed in solution-focused brief therapy. Upon completion of this chapter, the reader will be able to do the following:

1. Explain how solution-focused brief therapy provides a unique perspective on psychotherapy.
2. Describe the assumptions serving as the foundation for solution-focused brief therapy.
3. Identify the techniques and interventions commonly associated with solution-focused therapy.

History and Contributors

Steve de Shazer and Insoo Kim can undoubtedly be accredited with the origination of solution-focused brief therapy. However, the principles reflected in that model were shaped by the work of Milton Erickson, as well as the early research of the MRI.

Berg and de Shazer, aware of the earlier work of Erickson (see Chapter 1), recognized the need to turn the focus from client problem and the history of problem development to placing energy on finding solutions to these problems. They were particularly interested and aligned with Erickson's basic principles guiding practice: (a) meet clients where they are, (b) help clients gain control by changing their perspectives, and (c) allow for change that meets clients' needs (de Shazer, 1985). These principles served as a foundation for the development of their model of solution-focused brief therapy.

While at the MRI (see Chapter 1), Berg and de Shazer were further influenced by the work of Richard Fisch and associates, who were engaged in researching and studying the effects of short-term interventions for treatment. The work of the Brief Therapy Center at MRI produced a model of therapy that was goal-oriented, pragmatic, and focused in the here and now. Brief therapy at the MRI was based on the interactional view in which problems were seen as happening between rather than within people. The perspective was that problems resulted from individuals responding to life's challenges in ways that made them worse, entrenched problems. With this perspective, the therapist at MRI saw their role as helping the client identify what the attempted solutions were causing rather than solving the problems and then helping the client do something else instead. Inspired by this new approach, de Shazer and Berg created the Brief Therapy Family Center (BTFC) in Milwaukee, Wisconsin, where they continued their research and theory development.

The original members of the BFTC team were Steve de Shazer, Insoo Kim Berg, Jim Derks, Elam Nunnally, Eve Lipchik, and Marilyn LaCourt. Other therapists who became members of the team were Marvin Weiner, Alex Molnar, Wally Gingerich, Michele Weiner-Davis, John Walter, Kate Kowalski, Ron Kral, Gale Miller, Scott Miller, and Larry Hopwood (Visser, 2013). All these people contributed in one way or another to the development of the solution-focused approach.

A Nontraditional Perspective

Solution-focused brief therapy was an apparent deviation from traditional practice. The theory emphasized problem resolution rather than diagnosis and etiology. From this perspective, finding solutions was more important than identifying problems and their contributing factors. The goal, the preferred future, is the focus, not the past.

The solution-focused approach focused not on client deficits nor deficiencies but client strengths. The fundamental belief was that clients were competent, as evidenced by the fact that they had navigated life challenges up to this point. As such, emphasis was placed on the client's resiliency and resources with the intent of reconfiguring these to bring about the desired changes. Those embracing a solution-focused model believe that the diagnosis of a client's problem is not essential nor critical to the therapeutic process and thus can be omitted without affecting the quality of service and outcome. Rather than time spent diagnosing and searching for etiology, the solution-focused therapist turned attention to what works for clients' treatment, as evident by the progress made (de Shazer, 1988).

As is true for all brief therapy models, those employing a solution-focused brief therapy approach were active in structuring and directing the process. Solution-focused brief therapists collaborate with their clients, coconstructing solutions that reflect their strengths, resources, and particular worldviews (DeJong & Berg, 2002).

More Than a Technique

Engaging in solution-focused brief therapy requires more than knowledge of the theory and techniques. To be effective, therapists using this approach must embrace and assimilate the philosophy and fundamental principles underlying these strategies. Therapists must move beyond mastering the skills and techniques of solution-focused therapy and adopt the attitudes and fundamental principles that support this model (Budman et al., 1992; Talmon, 1990).

A review of the model's basic tenets may lead one to assume that accepting and assimilating these into one's professional identity and practice is easy. This may not be the case, particularly for those trained in more "problem-focused" models of therapy. Embracing a solution-focused orienting framework will represent a significant paradigm shift. Resisting the tendency to seek the nature of the problem and its historic roots, shifting to a focus on goals and solutions, may not come quickly.

Assumptions and Principles Guiding Practice

Solution-focused brief therapy reflects a paradigm shift and nontraditional perspective on mental health and therapy. This shift can be seen in the assumptions underlying processes and procedures employed in solution-focused brief therapy (O'Hanlon & Weiner-Davis, 2003).

1. *Clients have resources and strengths to resolve complaints.*

   The reality is that all clients have the strength and resources to navigate life's challenges successfully. Therapists are called on to help clients identify and reengage their strengths and resources to find a pathway for resolving current challenges and achieving desired goals.

2. *Change is constant.*

   While a client may feel stuck, imprisoned in their current situation, the solution-focused therapist beliefs that change is constant and conveys that belief.

3. *The solution-focused therapist's job is to identify and amplify change.*

   Therapists and therapy are not required for clients to change and experience resolution of their difficulties. Therapists, however, can be of value in creating conditions that are conducive to facilitating that change. The solution-focused therapist will be active and directive in helping the client identify goals and their actions that work and those that do not. The therapist can help the client to set reasonable goals and celebrate successes.

4. *It is usually unnecessary to know a great deal about the complaint to solve it.*

   Central to solution-focused brief therapy is the belief that while problems exist and may never be erased or wholly prevented, actions can be taken to minimize their future existence and impact. In solution-focused therapy, the goal is to find new methods or adaption of previously successful methods for solving the current problems. The client and therapist will identify what has worked in the past and attempt to configure that strategy to address the current situation and move the client closer to their desired goals.

5. *It is not necessary to know the cause or function of a complaint to solve it.*

   In contrast to what traditional therapies may suggest or even the commonplace assumptions of our clients, solution-focused therapy posits that understanding the origins of a problem is *not* necessary for engagement with a solution. The position is that one need not spend inordinate amounts of time and energy unearthing a cause for a problem to take steps to move in the direction desired. For example, if one is hungry, it is not necessary to understand the physiology of hunger to find a solution to that hunger. The solution-focused therapist attempts to help clients see that their end result, resolution of the original problem, could be achieved without going back and finding why the problem began in the first place.

6. *A small change is all that is necessary; a change in one part of the system can affect change in another part of the system.*

   Evidence from life span development points to the fact that significant gains start with and are built on small successes. One crawls before they walk. The solution-focused therapist helps clients experience small changes, which can be built on and collectively result in the state of change and outcomes desired by the client.

7. *Clients define the goal.*

   That which works for me or you may not work for another. From a solution-focused perspective, there is no one right or ideal way to live or experience happiness. As such, the solution-focused therapist attempts to assist the client in identifying what it is that they seek. Often the role of therapist involves assisting the client in distinguishing between strategies (e.g., I want to be famous) from actual goals (e.g., I want to feel good about myself, experience self-esteem).

8. *Rapid change or resolution of problems is possible.*

   The very nature of brief therapy reflects the belief that change can occur and in a concise time frame. The solution-focused therapist does not see counseling as needing to be an extended process, and the message conveyed is one of hope and progress toward change.

9. *There is no one right way to view things; different views may be just as valid and may fit the facts just as well.*

    With this as an operational assumption, solution-focused therapists attempt to help clients see that while they may hold to a perspective and approach to their situation, there may be other more economical and beneficial paths to follow. While the directive "if at first, you do not succeed, try again" may have value, perhaps limited value, in some circumstances, when the result with trying again continues to be less than desired, it is time to consider an alternative approach. Thus a student who cuts class in response to not having prepared for the assignments may be invited to look at how well that has worked out. Assuming that such a strategy only compounded the student's distress, an alternative approach may become more desirable.

10. *Focus on what is possible and changeable rather than what is impossible and intractable.*

    With a focus on taking small steps and achieving small changes that build momentum, the solution-focused therapist help clients engage in activities that are likely to succeed with change that is possible. For the solution-focused therapist, identifying that which can be fixed versus that which cannot is key to successful therapy. While an individual may not be able to reverse the reality of a fatal condition, they can attend to prepare for their death and attempt to develop an attitude and perspective that may provide them the most comfort during their final days.

Principles in Action

While there are several specific techniques that will be discussed in the next section of this chapter, it is crucial to understand the fundamental principles that serve as the foundation of the practice of solution-focused therapy/counseling.

Problem Deconstruction Discourse

Clients often present as being overwhelmed, believing their problem is monumental and unsolvable. With a constructed reality, the client may simply want to surrender. Solution-focused therapists engage in problem deconstruction as an initiation to change.

Deconstruction of a problem is a process of taking that which is vague, overly generalized, and absolute and reframing it as concrete and manageable (see Case illustration 3.1).

In reviewing this exchange, it is clear that Roberta's initial worldview was one in which no one liked her, that she was "all alone." If that were true it certainly would be overwhelming. As evident by the discourse that followed, her constructed worldview was not supported by the actual events of her life. The therapist's redefinition of the scope of this issue was a valuable step toward achieving a calmer, more hope-filled construction of her world.

CASE ILLUSTRATION 3.1

Problem Deconstruction

Therapist: Roberta, please sit down (handing her a tissue). What's wrong? Why are you crying?

Roberta: I'm all alone (crying).

Therapist: All alone?

Roberta: Yes.

Therapist: All alone—you have no social relationships? Roberta, maybe you could tell me what happened?

Roberta: I overheard two of my coworkers bad mouth me at the break. They were calling me a loser and didn't ever want to hang with me.

Therapist: So when you say that you are all alone, you are referencing this rejection by your coworkers.

Roberta: (crying again) Yeah, but it's everybody.

Therapist: Roberta, it sounds like their comments really upset you, but when you say you're are all alone, I'm confused. Are there others in your life—or even at work—who are not actively rejecting you?

Roberta: Okay, it may not be everyone; obviously, my family doesn't reject me. We have lots of fun every time we are together, and even though I don't see them every day, Louis and Mary Ellen, who work in another department, will sometimes invite me to lunch.

Therapist: I think I understand. So for some reason, these two coworkers appeared to be really critical. It seems that they don't want to hang with you. However, as you shared, they are not everyone. Your family certainly enjoys your company, and it appears that at work, Louis and Mary Ellen enjoy sharing lunch when they can.

Roberta: Yeah (calmer), and I also spend time with Liz, who works in the cubicle next to me.

Problem-Free Talk

Clients often present with language that focuses on all that they cannot do, all that is wrong in their life, all that is flawed with themselves. Many traditionally trained therapists will follow the client's direction and pursue more information, illustrations, and examples of their "failures."

Solution-focused therapists, as constructivists, posit language as playing an essential role in how we perceive ourselves and the world around us. Thus, when engaging with a client, the

EXERCISE 3.1

Problem or Solution Speak

Directions: Shifting one's mind-set and approach from that targeting problems, diagnosis, and causes to goals and solutions is not easy for many counselors trained in traditional theories of counseling.

Part I: Respond to each of the following:

Scenario 1: A client enters your office. This is the first session, and after gathering basic demographic information you begin the session.

Describe what you do or say to begin the session. _____

_____

Scenario 2: Your client begins to cry. After you provide evidence of your care and empathy, what questions might you have in mind and seek to pursue? (Describe)

Scenario 3: This is your first meeting with this client. The client has been court ordered to see you as a result of driving while under the influence. This is the third time the client has been arrested for DUIs. The client states, "This is bullshit. I don't need to be here. I don't have a drinking problem." Describe your thoughts upon hearing this.

_____

_____

Part II: Review responses to each of the scenarios presented in part I. Does your thinking and anticipated response take the discourse in the direction of problem clarification and analysis, or do you redirect the client to focus on goals, desired outcomes, and positive expectations for the counseling?

---

solution-focused therapist employs language that highlights solutions rather than problems (Metcalf, 1995, 2008).

This elimination of "problem speak" is subtle, yet is a significant difference between more traditional problem-focused models of therapy and that of solution focus. As simple as it may seem, a phrase such as "How can I help you?" or "Can you tell me what is concerning you?" sets the stage for a focus on a client's deficits and problems, not strengths and solutions. For those trained in more traditional approaches to therapy, avoidance of problem speak will not come easily. It is not simply a matter of technique or strategy but rather a reflection of a true paradigmatic shift (see Exercise 3.1).

Collaboration

The therapeutic alliance is essential for the solution-focused therapist. The alliance formed is one of collaboration and cooperation (Watts & Pietrzak, 2000). For the solution-focused therapist, the desire to form a collaborative relationship, where the client is an active participant, a "consumer," takes center stage even during the initial contact (Berg, 1994). The solution-focused school therapist employs all the core elements found in all effective counseling. In addition to the core conditions of warmth, genuineness, and unconditional positive regard, the solution-focused therapist employs encouragement, compliments, and affirmations as they identify and embrace the client's goals.

The solution-focused therapist is clear to convey that it is the client's goals that take precedence, and the competencies, experiences, and resources the client brings to counseling are valued. The therapist truly believes that the client is the expert about their own life (DeJong & Berg, 1998) and brings valuable expertise and insight to the process. This does not imply an abdication of the role and responsibility of the therapist. The therapist accepts responsibility for guiding the process of change.

Not all who engage in counseling come as customers and are ready to collaborate in the therapeutic process actively. Some present as visitors or complainants, and when this is the case, the solution-focused therapist will engage their skills to invite these clients to become customers.

Visitors

The solution-focused therapist wants the client to come to counseling with a clear goal and direction in mind and an eagerness to engage in the process. That is not always the case, especially when clients are mandated to treatment or unclear as to the value or need for therapy. When clients fail to own the value of the therapy, they often present as what Berg and Miller (1992) have termed a "visitor" mode.

The client in visitor mode is in counseling in body only, not in spirit. They arrive without the intention of making any personal changes. The visitor typically does not believe that there are problems that need to be worked on, and the central goal is to end contact with the helping system (Berg, 1994). Solution-focused therapists engaged with a visitor will attempt to create a climate in which the client is comfortable sharing what they would like to see changed as a result of the encounter. The therapist will assume good reasons for the client assuming a visitor position and will not be judgmental. Often, when the client is present due to a referral or another's directive, the therapist may inquire what the client thinks this other person would like to see changed. At the initial stage of transitioning a visitor to a customer, the goal is to have the client share their perspective and engage at least minimally in the process of finding value in the encounter.

Complainants

In a complainant relationship, the client does not see their role or the need to change while experiencing conflict or difficulties. It is their circumstance or others in their life that need to change.

For complainants, time in therapy will be used to complain about others or life in general. While avoiding their role and responsibility in the current situation, they fail to recognize that they can be a part of the solution.

Given that solution-focused therapists value a collaborative relationship, one in which the client shares expertise, moving a complainant to become a customer, an active and hopeful participant, takes center stage. Solution-focused therapists working with complainants will acknowledge complaints while refocusing on the client's competencies. They may, for example, invite the client to share how they manage these situations or identify times when they experienced some improvement in the situation, even if in some small way. The intent of this reframing is to help the client begin to identify an alternative preferred future and the resources they bring to the creation of that future. Walter and Peller (1992) described a solution-focused therapist's strategies that may facilitate engagement by a complainant (see Table 3.1).

Customer

The customer is a hopeful, active participant in the therapeutic process. According to Berg and Miller (1992), a customer is a person who will actively participate in the counseling and appreciate the value of counseling and the resources they bring to the process. O'Connell (1998) suggested the ideal customer would present with a very clear idea of what they want to achieve and come willing to invest effort into the changes needed to be made in order to achieve this outcome.

TABLE 3.1 STRATEGIES FOR ENGAGING A COMPLAINANT

Investigating the hypothetical solution   The therapist may simply invite the client to imagine what would happen if others or circumstances changed in the desired direction and what they would notice different about themselves.
Investigating the future assuming nothing changed   While joining the client in the perspective that things will not change, the therapist invites the client to consider that while others and the situation may not change, they may be able to do things for themselves to improve their experience.
Identifying hoped-for client outcomes   The therapist will address the complainant's examples of being stuck and shift focus from what they were doing or unable to do to help the client identify and articulate what they are hoping to achieve.

The very process of meeting the client at their model of the world—embracing their goals and resources and focusing on what can be, rather than picking at what was or was not—will often prove effective in moving the client to become a customer.

In joining the client, the therapist may choose to employ the ideas, metaphors, even the exact language of the client. The goal is not to affirm their experience as objective reality but to more fully understand their reality as it impacts their lived experience. In the process, the therapist may employ questions of clarification or confrontation to more fully understand while inviting the client to a new perspective. For example, asking "Does it happen all the time?" "Are there ever times that are exceptions, where you feel in control" are queries that can invite clarification for both therapist and client.

Starting With an End in Mind: Goal Setting

The principle of starting with the end in mind directs the solution-focused therapist to assist the client in identifying desirable goals, endpoints. Goals are essential for therapy to be brief; therapy can be aimless and anything but brief without an endpoint.

The therapist with a solution-focused framework values the importance of identifying that which is essential to the client, since it is the client who will serve as the primary source of resources needed to achieve these goals. This is not to suggest that therapists will not be alert to inviting a redefining or reframing of the client's reality as a means of facilitating the identification of additional goals. For example, consider the therapist working with a student who is concerned about the real danger of failing out of school and wants to instead work on his anxiety about being rejected by his group of friends. The solution-focused therapist respects that the student's goal takes priority even if the therapist's perspective is that addressing the issue of failing out should be considered. In this case, the therapist may learn that the student is failing because he is not completing his homework as a result of not taking his text or materials home. The client views this decision not to take the needed materials home as a strategy to maintain his position among his peers, whom he fears will mock or even reject him if caught with taking his text home. While some might suggest that this student get a different group of friends or have the courage to stand up for what he values, the solution-focused therapist, respecting and valuing the student's worldview, will attempt to work within the constructed reality. In this case, the therapist may invite the student to collaborate on finding strategies that will allow him to maintain his peer relationships *and* succeed at school, such as acquiring multiple texts, one for school and one for home. What is essential in developing a strategic path is that it reflects the client's resources and addresses the goals the client values.

Miracle Question

One of the most recognized contributions made by de Shazer is his introduction of the miracle question (Berg, 2005). Inspired by Erickson's crystal ball technique, the miracle question is a technique to facilitate goal identification. As defined by Berg and Miller (1992), the miracle question is a "specially designed interview process ... [that] orients the client away from the past and the problem and toward the future and a solution" (p. 13). It truly is a strategy and concept that is central to a solution-focused approach.

While the term *miracle* may lead one to conclude that the question is designed to encourage the client to place their faith in the occurrence of magic or miracles, this is not the case. The miracle question is simply a future-oriented question that invites the client to envision a future when their world were as they wished it to be. This future-oriented question is helpful with goal setting since it shifts the focus from problems and their genesis to the unlimited range of possibilities when envisioning a preferred future.

While there is no strict formula for constructing the miracle question, the essence of it is conveyed in the following:

> Suppose that while you are sleeping tonight and the entire house is quiet, a miracle happens. The miracle is that the problem that brought you here is solved. However, because you are sleeping, you do not know that the miracle has happened. So when you wake up tomorrow morning, what will be different that will tell you that a miracle has happened and the problem that brought you here is solved? (de Shazer, 1985, p. 5)

The question does not invite conversation on how this is to be done or the resources and challenges one needs to succeed. The purpose here is to begin identifying goals so that the therapist and client can turn attention away from old, unsuccessful, past behaviors toward a future where the problem no longer exists. The question is designed to allow clients to determine what they want from the therapeutic process without contemplating the cause or source of the original problem. With the emphasis on goals and solutions, the solution-focused therapist employs this strategy early in initial interactions and returns to it in subsequent sessions when the client begins to return to a problem-focused orientation.

The goal is to elicit statements that "include some action, some behavior, some new framing, or something clients will say to themselves or others" (Walter & Peller 1992, p. 78). Thus it is not simply asking the miracle question but guiding the client in their development of that preferred future so that the material gathered can be used to concretize the goals and unearth strategies that may help in goal achievement. When clients respond to the miracle question, therapists ensure that the responses are not too vague or general. An example would be a client saying, "I just want to be happy." To achieve the added specificity needed to build change on, therapists may have the client reframe their response by asking, "What does happy look like?" or "Tell me what you would experience to know that you were happy?"

Fast-Forward Questions

With fast-forward questions, the therapist simply invites the client to consider a future time when the problem will no longer exist. The therapist will ask them how they and their life will be different. Clients will be asked to describe how they will act and how their world will seem different. These details help provide the client and therapist with both a sense of what is desired and a standard against which to revisit possible exceptions where such an experience was more of a reality than currently.

Value Small Steps: Scaling

As constructivists, solution-focused therapists value the power of creating and embracing positive expectations. Helping the client see problems as periodic interruptions to their healthy functioning, rather than irrevocable impediments or character flaws, provides the context within which to inspire hope and belief in the possibility of change (Nunnally, 1993). This hope is further affirmed when change is experienced.

A solution-focused therapist will assist the client in identifying approximations of the ultimate goal and employ strategies that help the client achieve these subgoals and experience progress. Small changes are evidence that affirms the expectations of success. As DeJong and Miller (1995) noted, "It is easier to fill out a job application than to get a job" (p. 730). Setting and achieving small goals encourages the client's continued effort and offers markers against which the therapist and client can monitor progress.

Scaling Questions

With a sense of where the client would ultimately like to be, as well as an awareness of where they feel they currently are in relationship to this ultimate goal, a solution-focused therapist may invite the client to develop a "scale" to quantify present feelings, attitudes, motivations, and thoughts in reference to that which is ultimately desired.

The therapist, using a scaling question, may ask, "On a scale of 1 to 10, where 10 reflects a state where you feel as self-confident as you possibly could, and 1 represents a point of feeling absolutely unsure and insecure, where would you say you are at present, as you prepare for your job interview?"

The presentation of the issue along a scale helps to invite the perspective that progress is possible. The development of a scale, where the ultimate goal can now be broken down into smaller achievable subgoals, makes the change process more manageable and increases the client's motivation to change.

It is crucial to reiterate that the solution-focused therapist engages the client in their world. This takes form during the use of scaling in that the therapist does not debate the accuracy or absolute validity of the client's self-assigned score. It is simply a reference from which the therapist and client will want to build. As such, the focus is not on why a 3, but rather what the client needs to do to move up a number on the scale.

The use of this scaling process can be very empowering. Scaling can help make goals concrete and achievable, empower the client to take responsibility for the change, and evaluate their progress (see Exercise 3.2).

The scaling process also provides a structure for considering sequential steps to bring the client closer to their ultimate goal. Thus, in subsequent sessions the therapist and client can

EXERCISE 3.2

Practice With the Miracle Question and Scaling

Directions: This exercise invites you to experience the effect of using the miracle question to identify a life goal and then scaling to focus your attention on that which is achievable.

1. Respond to the following question as it applies to your professional career:
   Assume that when you went to bed this evening, a miracle occurred while you were sleeping. The miracle was such that when you woke you became aware that all your professional goals were achieved. Describe what you are experiencing or observing that lets you know this.
2. Using the following scale, place your description of the miracle state at the right-hand limit of the scale (i.e., 10). Now, using that as reference point, identify where you are in terms of professional career in light of that ultimate goal. Place an "X" at the number.
   1 2 3 4 5 6 7 8 9 10
3. Write down, what it would look like or what will be different when you move one or two spaces.

As you review your scaling, can you think of specific steps that you could employ to move to that next level?

---

review the scale and check where the client currently views themself. If the client reports moving up the scale, it provides a focus for investigating what the client did to make this move and affirm the change taking place.

Finding Solutions

The solution-focused therapist approaches therapy believing that every client is successful. As suggested by Berg and Miller (1992), solution-focused therapists can employ useful mantras:

> *If it ain't broke, don't fix it.*

> *Once you know what worked, do more of it.*

> *If it doesn't work, don't do it again. Do something different.*

Believing in the fundamental competence of the client, the solution-focused therapist will attempt to reframe the discourse to focus on the client's strengths and resources (de Shazer, 1988). The solution-focused therapist valuing efficacy attempts to identify the client's talents, abilities, style, and ways of successfully adapting. Once identified, these successes will be affirmed, and the client will be invited to consider ways to expand their use creatively.

Finding Exceptions: A Source for a Solution

With the belief that the client has experienced success, the solution-focused therapist invites the client to search for those situations in which they experienced more of their desired goal than they are currently experiencing. These are times when the problem was either less intense or did not exist at all, or, conversely, the client experienced more of the goal they desired. These are exceptions to the client's current experience.

In seeking exceptions, the therapist guides the client to identify experiences where there was a slight, incremental difference to that currently experienced. Often the nature of this exception inquiry has the client identifying times when the problem was less severe, less frequent, less intense, or shorter in duration (O'Hanlon & Weiner-Davis, 1989). Identifying and owning the reality that exceptions did exist invites the client to reconstruct their absolute sense of the overwhelming and ever-present problem and thus open space for their authoring a new, hopeful view of their future. This search for exception not only facilitates the client's deconstructing of the problem as immutable but begins to identify transferable solutions (Berg, 1992). Analyses of these times of exception can help the client and the therapist identify client resources and available strategies, which may be called forth to serve at this point (see Case Illustration 3.2).

It is the detailing of the specifics of who, what, when, where, and perhaps most importantly how that led to the creation of this exception that the elements of a successful solution emerge. The therapist will want to highlight the specifics so that they can be crafted into a helpful solution plan and thus may follow up the exception question with a sequence of questions:

- How did you get that to happen?
- What's different about those times?
- What do you ... so differently?
- How would you explain this success? These differences?
- How could more of that happen?

Coping Questions: Identifying Resources

When attempting to identify client resources, which may be of value to the current situation, a solution-focused therapist may employ coping questions. Perhaps the client cannot find an exception to the current situation but may be able to identify a time when even though the problem remained they were better able to adjust or cope with the problem. Inviting them to identify just how they were able to cope can assist them in shifting their focus from the problem to their strengths and resourcefulness (Clark, 1997). A solution-focused therapist may ask the client questions such as "How have you managed to prevent it from getting worse?" or "This sounds hard. How are you managing to cope with this to the degree that you are?" "How do you have the strength to go on?" or "What would others say are the qualities that you have that keep you going?" (Davis & Osborn, 2000, p. 71).

CASE ILLUSTRATION 3.2

Finding Exception

Therapist: If you are like most of us, this was not the only time someone was critical of you or something you were doing.

Roberta: (smiling) You can't grow up in a family of three older brothers without some mocking and teasing.

Therapist: That's interesting; I'm wondering, were there times when your brothers or a brother excluded you … you know let you know that they did not want you to hang with them?

Roberta: My brothers were pretty cool that way, but my best friend growing up was always hot and cold, and when she was with our neighbor, they both would make fun of me and reject me.

Therapist: What did you do at those times?

Roberta: Sometimes, I would cry and run home.

Therapist: Sometimes you would cry and run home, but were there times when you reacted differently? Perhaps were less upset?

Roberta: Yes. Actually, more times than not, I would either go home and play basketball with Elliot, my youngest brother, or even hang out with Shar, a girl who was in my church choir with me.

Therapist: That's great. It seems like you found ways to adapt when your other friend was being less friendly. I wonder, were there ever times when you just found something to do on your own? I mean by yourself?

Roberta: I loved to read and still do, so sometimes I would just go home and read.

Therapist: So it seems that you had quite a few ways of dealing with rejection. I mean, you entertained yourself, or you found other social outlets. That is super. But how did you do this? I mean, your friend was mean and rejecting, and yet you didn't fall apart but instead found something else to do? That is quite a skill.

Roberta: (smiling) It's funny; in thinking about those times, I realize I would say what my mom would always say "Well, that's their loss."

Therapist: Fantastic! It seems like that attitude and perspective helped you deal with rejection without falling apart or believing that you were all alone. I wonder if it would have a similar effect if applied to your coworkers? You know … "their loss"?

Relationship Questions

Often people get stuck in a problem, and they cannot identify an exception or even generate alternatives to their current way of behaving. In this situation, a solution-focused therapist may invite the client to step into an alternative perspective by asking a *relationship question*. A question such as "What would your spouse say needs to happen in our work together to know that our time has been successful?" allows the client to get unstuck from their viewpoint and observe their experience with new eyes and new perspective of another (DeJong & Berg, 2002). From this different viewpoint, the view of an outsider, the client may be able to identify that which can be changed to more fully experience their desired future.

Task Development

A significant element to strategy discourse is engaging the client in identifying and applying a small task that will move them closer to their goal. In ending a session, the solution-focused school therapist will summarize the strengths and resources identified in the session and compliment the client for all the excellent work they did in identifying strategies for moving closer to the goal. Following this summary, the therapist will then invite the client to identify a specific task they could try before the next session. The therapist might ask, "What one small thing could you try to move you closer to your goal?" or, "I wonder what would happen if you … ?"

The goal of this task development is to move the client away from simply thinking about and discussing small steps to engaging in steps toward solving the problem. This homework would then be discussed in the upcoming session, and whatever data gathered would be analyzed as providing valuable information for further strategy formation.

Supportive Research

The early history of SFBT found little empirical support but extensive clinical and anecdotal reporting of its effectiveness (DeJong & Berg, 2002; Seligman & Reichenberg, 2010). Since its inception, this solution-focused approach has been reported as an effective intervention for various presenting concerns (Kim, 2008; Kim & Franklin, 2009).

More recent studies have demonstrated the efficacy of this therapeutic model (e.g., Gingerich & Eisengart, 2000; Kim, 2008; Kim & Franklin, 2009; Stams et al., 2006). Beyond anecdotal and clinical reports of effectiveness, research supports the use of this approach with chronic and severe mental illness (e.g., Chung & Yan, 2003), abuse (e.g., Ray & Pierce, 2008), and with a variety of behavioral and emotional childhood difficulties (e.g., Bond, 2013; Cepukiene & Pakrosnis, 2010; Daki & Savage, 2010).

Suitability

Gingerich and Peterson (2013), following their review of 43 studies, concluded that solution-focused brief therapy was an effective treatment for a wide variety of behavioral and psychological. Two meta-analyses carried out by Corcoran and Pillai (2009) and Kim (2008) document its application to interventions for the following difficulties or populations: substance abuse; chronic schizophrenia; incarcerated prisoners; adult psychiatric patients; psychiatric inpatients; anger and aggression problems; behavior problems; academic and emotional difficulties; physical abuse; bullying; somatoform disorders; children with incarcerated parents; adolescent mothers; perpetrators of domestic violence; depression; anxiety; self-harm; gambling; obesity; diabetes; truancy; obsessive-compulsive disorder; psychiatric symptoms; stress and coping; young offenders; adults on long-term sick leave; fatigue in Crohn's disease patients; older adults; and children, families, and adults with a developmental delay. In each of these situations it can be assumed that the major challenge is moving the client in treatment to the position of being a customer.

KEYSTONES

- Solution-focused brief therapy, developed by de Shazer and others, is a treatment model that emphasizes client strengths, resources, and abilities.
- Solution-focused brief therapy was influenced by the work of Milton Erickson, those at the MRI, as well as the philosophies of social constructivism.
- Describe the basic tenets of a solution-focused model of counseling.
- Collaboration between the client and therapist is essential, and three types of relationships, including the customer, complainant, and visitor, may develop between the therapist and client.
- Strategies, such as the miracle question and goal scaling, the identification and use of exceptions, and client coping mechanisms, help to move clients toward their preferred future states.

ADDITIONAL RESOURCES

de Shazer, S., & Dolan, Y. (2007). *More than miracles: The state of the art of solution-focused brief therapy.* Haworth.

DeJong, P., & Berg, I. K. (2012). *Interviewing for solutions.* Brooks/Cole.

Kim, J. S. (2013). *Solution-focused brief therapy: A multicultural approach.* SAGE.

Lutz, B. A. (2013). *Learning solution-focused therapy: An illustrated guide.* APA.

Parsons, R. D. (2009). *Thinking and acting like a solution-focused school counselor.* Corwin.

REFERENCES

Berg, I, K. (1992). *Miracle picture: A vision of solutions in couple therapy* [Presentation materials]. Special Problems in Marital and Couples Therapy: Dealing Effectively with Difficult Couples Conference, Portola Valley, CA.

Berg, I. K. (1994). *Family-based services: A solution-focused approach*. Norton.

Berg, I. K. (2005). The state of miracles in relationships. *Journal of Family Psychotherapy, 16*, 115–118. https://doi.org/10.1300/J085v16n01_11

Berg, I. K., & Miller, S. D. (1992). *Working with the problem drinker: A solution-focused approach*. Norton.

Bond, C., Woods, K., Humphrey, N., Symes, W., & Green, L. (2013). Practitioner review: The effectiveness of solution-focused brief therapy with children and families: A systematic and critical evaluation of the literature from 1990-2010. *The Journal of Child Psychology and Psychiatry, 54*(7), 707–723.

Budman, S., Hoyt, M. F., & Friedman, S. (Eds.). (1992). *The first session in brief therapy*. Guilford.

Cepukiene, V., & Pakrosnis, R. (2010). The outcome of solution-focused brief therapy among foster care adolescents: The changes of behavior and perceived somatic and cognitive difficulties. *Children and Youth Services Review, 33*, 791–797.

Chung, S. A., & Yang, S. (2004). The effects of solution-focused group counseling program for the families with schizophrenic patients. *Taehan Kanho Hakhoe chi [Journal of the Korean Academy of Nursing], 34*, 1155–1163.

Clark, M. (1997). Interviewing for solutions. *Corrections Today, 59*(3), 98–102.

Corcoran, J., & Pillai, V. (2007). A review of the research on solution-focused therapy. *British Journal of Social Work, 39*(2), 234–242.

Daki, J., & Savage, R. (2010). Solution-focused brief therapy: Impacts on academic and emotional difficulties. *Journal of Educational Research, 103*, 309–326.

Davis, T., & Osborn, C. (2000). *The solution-focused school therapist: Shaping professional practice*. Edwards Brothers.

de Shazer, S. (1982). *Patterns of brief therapy*. Guilford.

de Shazer, S. (1985). *Keys to solutions in brief therapy*. Norton.

de Shazer, S. (1988). *Clues: Investigating solutions in brief therapy*. Norton.

de Shazer, S. (1991). *Putting difference to work*. Norton.

de Shazer, S., & Berg, I. K. (1995). The brief therapy tradition. In J. Weakland & W. Ray (Eds.), *Propagations: Thirty years of influence form the Mental Research Institute* (pp. 249–252). Haworth.

DeJong, P., & Miller, S. D. (1995). How to interview for client's strengths. *Social Work, 40*(6), 729–736.

DeJong, P., & Berg, I. K. (2002). *Interviewing for solutions* (2nd ed.). Brooks/Cole.

Gingerich, W. J., & Eisengart, S. (2000). Solution-focused brief therapy: A review of the outcome research. *Family Process, 39*, 477–498. https://doi.org/10.1111/j.1545-5300.2000.39408.x

Gingerich, W. J., & Peterson, L. T. (2013). *Effectiveness of solution-focused brief therapy: A systematic qualitative review of controlled outcome studies.* https://www.ncbi.nlm.nih.gov/books/NBK138422/

Kim, J. S. (2008). Examining the effectiveness of solution-focused brief therapy: A meta-analysis. *Research on Social Work Practice, 18*(2), 107–116. https://doi.org/10.1177/1049731507307807

Kim, J. S., & Franklin, C. (2009). Solution-focused brief therapy in schools: A review of the outcome literature. *Children and Youth Services Review, 31*, 464–470. https://doi.org/10.1016/j.childyouth.2008.10.002

Metcalf, L. (1995). *Counseling toward solutions: A practical solution-focused program for working with students, teachers, and parents.* Jossey-Bass.

Metcalf, L. (2008). *A field guide to counseling toward solutions.* Jossey-Bass.

Nunnally, E. (1993). Solution focused therapy. In R. A. Wells & V. J. Giannetti (Eds.), *Casebook of the brief psychotherapies* (pp. 271–286), Plenum.

O'Connell, B. (1998). *Solution-focused therapy.* SAGE.

O'Hanlon, W. H., & Weiner-Davis, M. (1989). *In search of solutions.* Norton.

O'Hanlon, W. H., & Weiner-Davis, M. (2003). *In search of solutions: A new direction in psychotherapy,* Guilford.

Seligman, L., & Reichenberg, L. W. (2010). *Theories of counseling and psychotherapy: Systems, strategies, and skills* (3rd ed.). Pearson.

Smock, S. A., Trepper, T. S., Wetchler, J. L., McCollum, E. E., Ry, R., & Piercem K. (2008). Solution-focused group therapy for level 1 substance users. *Journal of Marital and Family Therapy, 34*, 107–120.

Stams, G. J., Dekovic, M., Buist, K., & de Vries, L. (2006). Efficacy of solution-focused brief therapy: A meta-analysis. *Gedragstherapie {Behavior Therapy], 39*(2), 81–94.

Talmon, M. (1990). *Single session therapy: Maximizing the effect of the first (and often only) therapeutic encounter.* Jossey-Bass.

Visser, C. F. (2013). The origin of the solution-focused approach. *International Journal of Solution-Focused Practices, 1*(1), 10–17. http://dx.doi.org/10.14335/ijsfp.v1i1.10

Walter, J. L., & Peller, J. E. (1992). *Becoming solution-focused in brief therapy.* Brunner/Mazel.

Watts, R. E., & Pietrzak, D. (2000). Adlerian "encouragement" and the therapeutic process of solution-focused brief therapy. *Journal of Counseling & Development, 78*, 442–447.

CHAPTER 4

Time-Limited Dynamic Psychotherapy

Psychoanalyses is like music lessons, for 5 year you do not notice any progress and suddenly you can play the piano.

—Woody Allen

The change process envisioned in traditional psychodynamic therapy typically requires years of sessions. This extended length of treatment was due, at least in part, to its focus on promoting change in an aspect of one's identity or personality. Time-limited dynamic psychotherapy has not only challenged the need and value for such extensive engagement but, in the process, has renounced and reformulated many of the original tenants of psychoanalysis. The evolution, or perhaps more appropriately, the history of the emergence of dynamic, time-limited psychotherapy, has been described as "a story of progressive taboo-breaking ... with each step, a different psychoanalytic taboo must be confronted and broken" (Fosha, 1995, p. 297). Practitioners of brief psychodynamic therapy believe that some changes can happen through a more rapid process or that a short initial intervention will start an ongoing process of change that does not need the constant involvement of the therapist. The current chapter reviews the history of time-limited dynamic psychotherapy (TLDP) and the principles and assumptions guiding the contemporary practice of this brief therapy model. Upon completion of this chapter, the reader will be able to do the following:

1. Identify key figures and their contribution to the emergence of time-limited dynamic psychotherapy.

2. Describe the various ways time-limited dynamic psychotherapy differs significantly from the more classic form of psychodynamic therapy.

3. Explain what is meant by the concept of maladaptive relationship patterns and its value in guiding case conceptualization and treatment planning.

4. Explain what is meant by time-limited dynamic psychotherapy being process-oriented.

5. Describe factors that should be considered when determining a client's suitability for time-limited dynamic psychotherapy.

History and Contributors

The practice of brief or time-limited dynamic psychotherapy has its roots in the work of Sigmund Freud. Bauer and Kobs (1987) suggest that it was with the renouncement of hypnosis as an effective treatment technique that Freud, using education, suggestion and catharsis, began to assist clients with their presenting concerns in a limited number of sessions. However, with the increasing complexity of his theory and the development of techniques such as free association, which placed the analyst in a very passive role, the process of psychoanalysis and the required length of treatment became extended.

Sandor Ferenczi

This emphasis on the "passivity" of the therapist was directly challenged by Sandor Ferenczi (1920/1950). Ferenczi encouraged increased activity on the part of the therapists, feeling that waiting for the appropriate time to employ interpretation was simply ineffective. For Ferenczi, it was important for the therapist to be frank and direct while also exhibiting empathy (Rachman,1988). Ferenczi's emphasis on the therapist's active engagement has become an established principle of time-limited dynamic therapy, one that is "evident throughout all phases of treatment from assessment to termination" (Tosone, 1997. p. 36).

Otto Rank

The transformation of psychoanalysis into a more active, directive and time-limited form of therapy was further aided by the work of Otto Rank (1929/1936). Rank highlighted the importance of assessing clients' motivation to change not only as a negative, as would be the case of Freud's view of resistance, but as a strength of the individual's will. Rank also emphasized the need to set time limits on therapy.

Alexander and French

While both Ferenczi and Rank played vital roles in moving psychoanalysis from treatment without end, a process in which the therapist was passive and emotionally distant, Alexander and French (1946/1974) pushed the boundaries of traditional psychoanalysis, moving it closer to what now takes shape as time-limited dynamic therapy. Specifically, Alexander and French (1946/1974) challenged a number of the classic psychoanalytic positions by arguing the following:

> (1) that the depth of therapy is necessarily proportional to the length of treatment and the frequency of the interviews;

(2) that therapeutic results achieved by a relatively small number of interviews are necessarily superficial and temporary, while therapeutic results achieved by prolonged treatment are necessarily more stable and more profound; and

(3) the prolongation of analysis is justified because the patent's resistance will eventually be overcome, and the desired therapeutic results will be achieved. (p. vi)

The increased attention and interest given to time-limited forms of psychotherapy was in part a response to the zeitgeist of the time. This was during a time when veterans were exhibiting the psychological impact of war stress, and trauma required short-term treatment. In their book, *Psychoanalytic Therapy: Principles and Applications*, Alexander and French (1946/1974) encourage analysts to move from an emphasis on exposing repressed memories and instead structure the therapy in a way that provides clients with a *corrective emotional experience*. The process often involved having clients reexperience some unbearable emotional situations but under conditions of therapist support and more successful resolution.

The therapist's task is to assess transference, even at the initial point of contact, to incorporate these transferential issues into the emotional conflict, the corrective emotional experience as the treatment strategy. The corrective emotional experience allows the client to express emotions in the transference, that is, the process of transferring prominent characteristics of unresolved conflicted relationships with significant others, onto the therapist. The data presented in the transferential process is then interpreted in light of the connection of the actual life situation. It was felt that such an active process of presenting conditions of emotional conflict, followed by transference and interpretation, would effectively mobilize the unconscious process (Magnavita, 1993).

Brief Dynamic Therapy

Between the period of 1960 through the 1980s, a series of books, Malan (1963), Mann (1973), and Sifneos (1987), brought attention to brief treatment from an analytic perspective.

While recognizable as "dynamic" and with roots in psychoanalysis, contemporary brief dynamic therapy has undoubtedly broken the chains that bound therapist and client in the classic psychodynamic therapy model. As noted by Levenson (2017), brief dynamic models "broke the taboo of theoretical and strategic purity" (p. 28). Models of brief dynamic therapy are more integrative in assumptions and approaches employed, as evident by the fact that many incorporate information gleaned from neuroscience and strategies employed in other theoretical models, such as behavioral and cognitive therapy.

A Shift in Perspective

The adoption of brief, time-limited models to psychotherapy has not been easy for many who have been trained and practiced in dynamic psychotherapy or psychoanalysis (Tosone, 1997). The challenge rests not so much in acquiring new skills but rather in adjusting one's perspective and professional assumptions.

From Intrapsychic to Interpersonal

Those employing time-limited dynamic therapy (TLDT) continue to focus on the client's core conflict will block the client's attempts to engage defenses to divert from these issues. However, starting with therapists such as Schacht, Strupp, and Binder (1984) and Lester Luborsky (1984), the emphasis and focus shifted from intrapsychic to interpersonal. This shift in perspective resulted in a less drive-oriented and more relational-focused dynamic approach.

Time-limited dynamic therapists, valuing the interpersonal nature of therapy, shift attention from the intrapsychic working of one person, the client, to the interpersonal processes occurring between two persons, the client and the therapist. The rationale was that regardless of the intrapsychic conflict, it would take form and be expressed in relationships, including the relationship with the therapist.

Emphasis on the client–therapist relationship meant that the therapist no longer acts passively, like a blank screen, but is now an active, coparticipant, shaping the transference.

Here-and-Now Attachment

The shift in focus from that which was intrapsychic to that which was interpersonal invited more consideration of the here-and-now attachment exhibited within the therapy. John Bowlby (1988) highlighted the significance of the emotional quality of early childhood attachments for understanding psychopathology. While the focus on the importance of attachment initially centered on the mother–child relationship, Bowlby's work (1988) made it clear that attachment needs and behaviors manifest throughout life, especially at times of stress.

Therapists employing a time-limited dynamic approach value the relevance of attachment theory to the dynamic and processes of the therapeutic relationship. As stated by Bowlby (1988), therapists can explore their client's

> representational models of himself and his attachment figures with a view to reappraising and restructuring them in light of the new understanding he acquires and the new experiences he has in the therapeutic relationship. (p. 138)

Bowlby's work provided the time-limited dynamic therapist with the rationale for targeting the processing of transference and countertransference in the here and now as the focus of therapy. The shift in perspective was from focusing and delving into the client's past to exploring the here-and-now relationship with the therapist and others in the client's interpersonal world.

Experiential–Affective Theory

Targeting the expression or repression of emotions is not new to dynamic therapy (Hilsenroth, 2007). However, for those who engage in TLBD, there is a greater emphasis on assisting clients to become aware of, experience and process their emotions (Greenberg, 2012).

There is a shift in focus and emphasis for those identified as time-limited dynamic therapists. While engaging therapist interpretation is still seen as a valuable therapeutic process for increasing client awareness, more emphasis is placed on the client gaining insight and understanding through directly experiencing emotions (Diener et al., 2007). The goal, according to Greenberg (2004), is to help clients "become aware and make productive use of their emotions" (p. 3).

Assumptions and Principles Guiding Practice

While it is true that time-limited dynamic therapy is not that of classic Freudian analysis nor is even "your grandfather's brief dynamic psychotherapy" (Levenson, 2017, p. 29), the contemporary practice continues to place value in many of the more traditional concepts, including the unconscious, transference, and anxiety regulation. However, as noted, for TLDT, emphasis shifts from the intrapsychic to the interpersonal, from the past and historical foundations of current concerns to the here and now, and from understanding to experiencing. In addition to this shift in perspective, time-limited dynamic psychotherapy (TLDP) is guided by several fundamental principles (Levenson, 2017).

Emphasis on Attachment and Relationships

TLDP posits that people are innately motivated to search for and maintain human relatedness (Levenson & Strupp, 2007). The formation of a secure interpersonal base is central to one's development. As such, emphasis on issues and experience of attachment and the client's processes of searching for and maintaining relationships is fundamental to TLDP.

Maladaptive Patterns Schematized

TLDP posits that the early formation of maladaptive relationship patterns, especially with caregivers, become schematized (see Case Illustration 4.1). These early experiences result in mental representations (schemata) or working models of the individual's interpersonal world. These experiences thus set the stage for the individual's assumptions about human relatedness and what is required to maintain emotional connectedness to others. When these patterns are maladaptive, they serve as the basis for the client's current struggles and presenting complaints.

Circular Causality

Relationship patterns, with attendant emotions, are "consistent with a person's sense of self, and others" (Levenson, 2017, p. 49). The faulty interpersonal models and the patterns of relationships that have developed and have been schematized persist as a result of being maintained in current

CASE ILLUSTRATION 4.1

Fade Into the Background

Maria came to therapy because of what she described as social anxiety and the inability to make or maintain friendships. When engaging with the therapist, she avoided eye contact, spoke in a very low and soft voice, and employed a body posture that felt like she was trying to disappear to the therapist.

In gathering background information, the interpersonal style took on more, somewhat reasonable, meaning. Maria's back story was that an abusive mother raised her. The mother would verbally attack and ridicule her children, especially when she was drinking and the children appeared to be having fun and ignoring her. In this context, Maria learned that the most effective strategy to employ to avoid such verbal attacks was to "fade into the background." It was a pattern she employed throughout her life, and it was the pattern currently being observed by the therapist.

---

relationships. While having origins in early childhood, the dysfunctional interactive styles are maintained through ongoing utilization in the client's adult life (see Case Illustration 4.2).

In Case Illustration 4.2, Maria's early style of avoiding verbal abuse was effective, and as a style of interaction, it became schematized. While perhaps useful as a defensive strategy in her childhood, this pattern of withdrawing is now a source of further distancing, if not outright rejection, by others.

Clients as Stuck, not Sick

TLDP views the client's struggle and current conflicts as reactions to components of their system rather than the manifestation of a pathology residing within the individual. There is a de-pathologizing of the client. Clients are viewed as stuck in a vicious cycle, in a rut, one

CASE ILLUSTRATION 4.2

Self-Fulfilling Prophecy

Maria (see Case Illustration 4.1) decided to engage in therapy in response to her increasing feelings of isolation and aloneness. As she described it, people at work, and some of her old friends from school, "make fun of me and think I'm weird." "They are always criticizing me and telling me to speak up. Join the party. They tease me and say things like, 'Oh, I didn't know you were sitting here' even though I am sitting right beside them." It hurts when they make those comments so why, bother? It is easier to stay home or, when at work, just keep to myself and eat my lunch at my desk."

created out of a need for self-protection rather than being "sick." Again this becomes clear in reviewing the case of Maria (see Case Illustrations 4.1 and 4.2).

Goals

The focus for TLDP is on helping the client "affectively and cognitively shift well-established (but dysfunctional) ways of relating to self and other" (Levenson, 2017, pp. 51–52). With this as a focus, TLDP therapists seek to provide the client with a more functional interpersonal experience and encourage and assist them in engaging in a new manner of interacting (Levenson & Strupp, 2007).

TLDP Is Process Oriented

TLDP shifts the focus from client symptoms or even the specifics of presenting concerns to investigating intrapersonal and interactive processes maintained by problematic affect or affect regulation difficulties. While the content of the client's story is still valued, it is the interpersonal process of the client–therapist interaction that is central to the therapy.

Thus, the therapist working with Maria (see Case Illustrations 4.1 and 4.2) might invite her to consider how her "fading into the background" may have made her feel safe while now creating a condition that appears to be inviting the feared rejection or verbal abuse. The therapist may even share the impact of her interpersonal style on his thoughts, feelings, and behaviors.

TLDP Is Focused

A central concept in time-limited dynamic psychotherapy is that there should be one primary focus for the therapy. The emphasis in TLDP "is on discerning a client's most pervasive and problematic style of relating" (Levenson, 2017, p. 56). The focus is on a "specific intrapsychic conflict, or developmental impasse, a maladaptive conviction about the self, an essential interpretive theme, or a persistent interpersonal dilemma or pattern of maladaptive activity" (Schacht et al., 1984, p. 66).

This focused perspective is in direct contrast to the more traditional psychoanalytic practice of allowing the client to associate freely and discuss unconnected issues (Malan, 1976). The central focus singles out the most critical issues and thus identifies a goal for the treatment. As applied to the case of Maria (see Case Illustration 4.1 and 4.2), the therapist may attempt to focus their concerns on what was presented initially, which was "feeling alone and isolated."

Therapist as Active

The therapist engaging in TLDP will assume responsibility for providing the client with a new human experience. In the context of that experience, the therapist will attempt to effect changes in the client's previous, faulty learning (Strupp & Binder, 1984). Therapists engaged in TLDP are active participants employing multiple roles (e.g., coach, teacher, observer–participant). The therapist is also expected to be active in keeping the session focused on the main issue. Having a clear focus makes it possible to do interpretive work relatively quickly because the therapist only addresses the circumscribed problem area.

Change Outside of Therapy

The goal in TLDP is "to interrupt the client's ingrained, repetitive, dysfunctional cycle (Levenson & Strupp, 2007, p. 167). As such, a focus is on promoting healthier behavior, which would position the client to experience more satisfying relationships.

The process of change is believed to begin in therapy but finds value in its continuation outside of the therapeutic relationship. Therapy sessions end, "but the therapeutic work needs to continue for the rest of the person's life in the outside world" (Levenson, 2017, p. 57). Thus, for the therapist working with Maria (see Case Illustration 4.1 and 4.2), the treatment plan might include encouraging her to enroll in an assertive training course or even taking steps to interact with those at work.

Principles in Action

The length of therapy is usually related to the ambitiousness of the therapy goals. Most therapists are flexible in the number of sessions they recommend for clinical practice. While structuring sessions' frequency, length, and number will reflect the client's characteristics, goals, and the issues deemed central by the therapist, TLDP is typically considered to be no more than 25 sessions (Bauer & Kobos, 1987). The particulars of any one therapeutic relationship will reflect the uniqueness of the client and therapist but will, in general, include the following steps (see Table 4.1). It is important to note that while the steps presented in Table 4.1 appear as a linear sequence, assessment, case conceptualization, and treatment planning are fluid and that as new data are presented, the therapist will recycle through the steps.

Case Conceptualization

As a general theme, those engaged in TLDP target the client's inflexible and self-defeating patterns as the core of their case conceptualization. The focus is on identifying the client's "cyclical maladaptive pattern" (CMP; Schacht et al., 1984).

Whereas traditional approaches to therapy often search for a linear connection between some event, usually that of a historical nature and the presenting issue, TLDP emphasizes that which is presently enacted as "self-propagating vicious circles" (Schacht et al., 1984. p 73).

The cyclical maladaptive pattern (CMP) is an idiosyncratic cycle of maladaptive interactions that a client employs when in relationships with others. These patterns involve self-perpetuating behaviors, self-defeating expectations, and negative self-appraisals that lead to dysfunctional interactions with others (Butler et al., 1993) (see Case Illustration 4.3). The self-confirming patterns of repetitive social interchange "serve to verify patients' maladaptive views and to validate and reinforce their problematic actions" (Schacht et al., 1984. p 73). Even though these patterns may have their origins in the past, their current employment is the source of the problem. As such, the theorist operating from a TLDP orientation will be less focused on the influence of the past and more attentive to the operation of cyclical maladaptive patterns in the present, including in the interaction with the therapist.

TABLE 4.1 STEPS IN TIME-LIMITED PSYCHOTHERAPY FORMULATION

Assessment

1. The therapist allows the client to tell their own story in their own words and manners. This is in contrast to a structured approach that focuses on specific categories of information (e.g., developmental history). While the data is essential, the client's style in relating these data provides the therapist with insight into the client's interpersonal style.
2. The therapist conducts and anchored history exploring the interpersonal context of the presenting concern. The therapist might ask questions such as "When did the problems begin?" or "What else was going in your life and relationships?"
3. The therapist attends to the emotional flavor of the story (including nonverbal signs). The data are important, but the manner in which they are shared provides insight into the client's interpersonal style.
4. The therapist and client explore the emotional–interpersonal context related to symptoms or problems.
5. The therapist uses CMP categories to gather, organize, and probe for information. The therapist will begin to develop a picture of the client's view of self and expectations of others.

Conceptualization

6. The therapist listens for themes in the client's transactional behaviors and concomitant emotions (in the past and present relationships as well as with the therapist).
7. The therapist is aware of their reciprocal behavioral and emotional reactions (counter-transferential pushes and pulls). The therapist is vigilant in identifying reenactments of dysfunction interactions in the therapeutic relationships
8. The therapist will begin to develop a narrative of the client's idiosyncratic primary CMP, describing the client's predominant dysfunctional emotional–interactive pattern.

Treatment Planning (Formulating Goals and Strategies)

9. The therapist uses the CMP to formulate what new experiences (intrapersonally and interpersonally) might subvert or interrupt the client's maladaptive interactive style and lead to more adaptive relating (goal 1).
10. The therapist uses the CMP to formulate new understandings (intrapersonally and interpersonally). The therapist assists the client in examining the here-and-now interactions with the therapist. The therapist may share their formulation of the meaning and value of the client's interactional pattern and invite the client to begin to formulate a new life narrative and employ more adaptive relating (goal 2). The therapist will also assist the client in de-pathologizing current behaviors by placing them within a historical context.
11. The therapist revises and refines the CMP throughout the therapy. The revisions reflect the additional data on the client's interactional style.
12. For each of the preceding steps, the therapist considers the influence of cultural forces.

Adapted from Hanna Levenson, *Brief Dynamic Therapy*, p. 74. Copyright © 2017 by American Psychological Association.

CASE ILLUSTRATION 4.3

Max: Need to Show Them

Max came to therapy due to a court order following his arrest for an incident of road rage. This was the fifth situation in which explosive anger brought Max to the attention of law enforcement. In the initial interview, the therapist attempted to understand better the nature of Max's cyclical maladaptive pattern of rage.

> "Yeah, so I smashed the guy's car window with a baseball bat. I know it sounds crazy, but you have to understand, he threw the finger at me. This guy was trying to humiliate me. I can't sit there and take that; I would hate myself if I did. I mean who wants to be a wimp and take that? So, I saw him stop at the red light, and I went off.
>
> Boy, was I boiling! I mean, I kept saying to myself that son of bitch can't do that to me; I can't let him get away with that. If I ignore him, he wins. He would think he's better than me.
>
> I mean I was sitting there feeling like a real, ah wimp. I hate that feeling. My older brothers used to make me feel like that all the time. When they did that, it made me furious. I used to get into a fight with them all the time. I showed them I was no wimp. I showed him, too. No one is going to treat me like I am nothing."

As illustrated in Case Illustration 4.3, a therapist working with Max would employ the construct of the cyclical maladaptive pattern to organize the client's information and thus understand the client's thoughts, feelings, and behaviors regarding their actions in terms of relationships ("I was boiling"); their expectations of how others will respond to them ("he would think he's better than me"); their observations about the actions of others ("he was trying to humiliate me"); and, the specific ways the client acts toward themselves ("I can't sit there and take that, I would hate myself if I did"). Exercise 4.1 invites you to reflect on your own experience engaging in the cyclical maladaptive pattern (CMP).

The time-limited dynamic therapist will employ open-ended questions to invite the client to share their narrative story. While encouraging the client to share, the therapist will attempt to focus the client on their relationships with others, their thoughts and feelings often associated with their interactions. This reflection will include disclosure by the client regarding their experience with the therapists and their expectations about what the therapist may be thinking or feeling about them. Such a focus on the therapist and therapeutic encounter can serve as a microcosm of that encountered outside in the client's daily interactions.

With these data, the therapist can develop their case formulation, and out of that identify the goals and intervention strategies relevant to this client.

EXERCISE 4.1

Experience With Cyclical Maladaptive Pattern

Directions: While technically not a CMP, most individuals have had experiences that self-perpetuating behavior, self-defeating expectations, and negative self-appraisals that result in dysfunctional interactions with another.

1. Identify a recent interpersonal exchange that did not go as well as you had hoped.
2. How were you feeling at the moment? _____
   What were you thinking at that moment? _____
   How were you behaving? _____
3. What was your expectation about how the other person would respond to you or think about you?
   _____
4. What were you feeling about yourself, at that moment? _____

Reflection:

a. In reviewing the data can you see any interaction or reciprocal involvement of any of the factors noted?
b. If you considered these questions in light of another less than desirable interaction, either with the same person or another, would any of the factors have been active?

Experiential Learning

TLDP emphasizes the value of experiential learning as a way of challenging a client's maladaptive patterns. Again, the position in contrast to the more classical psychodynamic approach is that clients need more than interpretation, descriptions, or explanations; they need an experience.

The experiences presented are not formulaic or generic but instead tailored to the uniqueness of each client. Therapists working from a TLDP will often employ strategies reflecting other theoretical models.

The therapist attempts to structure the therapy to provide the client with new experiences that increase the client's awareness of their emotional and relational experiences. The therapist will use their understanding of the client's maladaptive patterns to shape the therapeutic encounter in a way that offers the best chance for undermining the client's maladaptive pattern (see Case Illustration 4.4). The intent of the therapist is to "subvert the patient's maladaptive interactive style" (Levenson & Strupp, 2007, p. 168). Should the experience effectively subvert the previous style, the client may become upset and experience tension and disequilibrium. TLDP sees this tension, this disequilibrium, as the elements facilitating the therapeutic process. It is believed that through these experiences, the client can develop a new, more functional internalized working model of relationships.

> ### CASE ILLUSTRATION 4.4
>
> **How Does That Work?**
>
> The client, a 44-year-old single female, because of what she diagnosed as depression. The following exchange occurred during the second session, during which the therapist employed a reflection and then a simple question, *"How does that work?"*
>
> **Client:** I don't know why I bother; nothing is going right, and it is my fault.
>
> **Therapist:** Nothing?
>
> **Client:** I try to do things, I try to clean the house, cook, do something productive, but I screw up everything. I can't manage on my own. I am such a loser.
>
> **Therapist:** Could you give me an example of something that happened recently?
>
> **Client:** There are so many examples. I mess everything up. Everything! I am such a waste, such a loser.
>
> **Therapist:** But perhaps you could talk about one experience that you have had recently?"
>
> **Client:** (looks down) Well … well … oh, I don't know. Look at me I so screwed up, such a loser I can't even think of a "good example."
>
> **Therapist:** I can see that is difficult for you to identify a good example, but you have shared that you have had problems with the house cleaning, cooking, and doing productive things. Beyond that I notice that each time you identified such an issue or challenge you use it to blame yourself and to label yourself as a loser. I'm wondering how that works for you?

In this case (Case Illustration 4.4), the therapist is inviting the client to consider what, if anything, is to be gained by conveying to the therapist that she is a "loser." Does such self-denigration result in some self-protection? Is such a self-evaluation in some way a reflection of her anticipation about what others, in this case, the therapist, maybe thinking? Is this a reflection of her interpersonal and/or intrapersonal schemata? Therapists employing TLDP will attempt to engage experiences that disconfirm the client's interpersonal and intrapersonal schemata.

From Experience to Understanding

In addition to providing clients with correctional inter- and intrapersonal experiences, experiences that target affect and behavior, the therapist engaged in TLDP will help the client process their experience and find new meaning in these emotional and relational encounters. The therapist will help the client understand the connection of this repetitive pattern, as perhaps embodied in the here and now, therapist–client interaction, to their historic roots with past significant others and its continuation in current relationships. This understanding positions the client for change.

As an active participant in the therapeutic process, the therapist will call attention to the client's interactive patterns, especially repetitive ones. The therapist will invite the client to remain in the moment of feelings and together search for relevance and meaning in their emotional experience. It is believed that "inquiring about how one feels about oneself during certain interpersonal behaviors (especially those that are attachment-related) links one's sense of self with transactions with others" (Levenson, 2017, p. 88). Often the therapist will employ homework as part of their approach. Clients may be invited to take their new awareness outside the confines of the therapist's office to see if, and where, these patterns may occur in their daily interactions.

The therapist engaged in TLDP will use reflection, confrontation, and interpretation to help the client gain insight and understanding. The use of interpretation has been described as the most important technical tool in dynamic therapy (Strupp & Binder, 1984). Interpretation is used to heighten the client's awareness of their current psychological state and "restructure the meanings of the current experience to the end of making it more congruent with present-day reality" (Strupp & Binder, 1984, p. 165). It is suggested that when making interpretative interventions, the therapist anchors the intervention in data that both the client and therapist have developed (Strupp & Binder, 1984).

Experience, Understanding, Change

Throughout therapy, the therapist structures experiences in which the client gains a different perspective and appreciation on themselves, the therapist, and their interaction. These new experiences provide the basis for learning new patterns that can replace the old, dysfunctional patterns. Assuming that the client adjusts their schemata, and as a result, feels differently, it is anticipated that they will consequently begin to act differently.

Often a TLDP therapist may provide an experience that promotes positive emotional states. Greenberg and Pascual-Leone (2006) posited that introducing a new feeling, one that is incompatible with the troubled state, can help alter the client's old feelings and responses to that which is more adaptive. The example they provide is of an individual whose fear and tendency to flee a situation can be transformed by assisting the client in accessing anger, which positions them to move forward against what has been feared rather than flee.

This in vivo learning is a critical component in the practice of TLDP. Clients have the opportunity to actively try out new behaviors in the therapy, see how they feel, and notice how another, in this case the therapist, responds. This experience provides the data that challenges the client's previous interpersonal schemata regarding the dictates of how they should act and what they can expect from others.

Strategies

As is true for all therapeutic approaches, developing and maintaining a therapeutic alliance is central to therapeutic outcomes for those engaged in TLDP. As a relationally based approach, the alliance and the dynamics occurring within the therapeutic relationship take on a particular value for those engaged in time-limited dynamic psychotherapy. With the perspective that a human relationship created the problem, the assumption moving forward is that a new relationship, in this case the therapeutic relationship, can be structured in a way to "remedy the ill effects of the previous experiences (Strupp & Binder, 1984, p. 136).

In TLDP, this alliance must be established as soon as possible. Thus the time-limited dynamic therapist must establish a trusting relationship with their clients in a short time. TLDP therapists will employ relationship-building skills, such as exhibiting genuineness, unconditional valuing, and empathy while affirming client feelings, perceptions, strengths and challenges.

Strategies employed in TLDP tend to be direct and certainly relational. The therapist employing TLDP will consider the application of any intervention (regardless of model or theory of origin) if it is felt to facilitate the goals of providing a new experience and new understanding. TLDP employs active-empathic listening and reflection, open questions, summarizations, confrontations, and interpretations as "techniques" to focus clients on their internal experiences and assist them in gaining an understanding of their interpersonal patterns, especially those which are cyclical maladaptive patterns. In addition, therapists practicing TLDP will engage strategies that promote the client's change in the identified cyclical maladaptive patterns. These interventions often take the form of assignments or homework to be completed outside of the session. For example, in working with a client, who is socially anxious and somewhat socially avoidant, as is the case with Case Illustration 4.1 and 4.2, the therapist may suggest enrollment in an assertiveness training course or help the client develop a plan to join a coworker at lunch.

Supportive Research

Support for the effectiveness of brief therapy is found in the work of Barber et al. (2013); Hilsenroth et al. (2006); Knekt et al. (2008); and Leichsenring et al. (2015). Hilsenroth et al. (2006), for example, reported on the effectiveness of brief dynamic psychotherapy in increasing a client sense of well-being and improving social functioning. Research (e.g., Barber et al., 2013; Leichsenring et al., 2015) has found dynamic therapies to be effective in cases of depressive disorders, anxiety disorders, anorexia nervosa, and borderline personality disorder.

While some have reported value and benefit to intensive short-term dynamic psychotherapy for personality disorders (e.g., Abbass et al., 2008), others suggest that longer term treatment may be needed, especially with severe cases (Messer & Kaplan, 2004).

Suitability

Time-limited dynamic therapy is not a panacea nor appropriate for all clients and presenting concerns. The nature of time-limited dynamic therapy is one of high emotional intensity and thus clients with ego resources and who are "highly motivated, capable of insight, and able to establish a collaborative relationship with the therapist" (Tosone, 1997, p. 38) present as suitable candidates.

With emphasis placed on experiential learning, TLDP may be a challenge for individuals who have limited ability to engage in introspection or self-reflection and thus may find it challenging to make sense and find meaning in the experiences being provided. It is possible that individuals with severe depression, who are experiencing psychotic episodes, or who are presenting with characterological issues may require alternative interventions (e.g., pharmacological) and/or extended psychotherapy.

KEYSTONES

- Classical Freudian psychodynamic therapy saw changes at the hands of the likes of Sandor Ferenczi, Otto Rank, and Franz Alexander.
- Time-limited dynamic psychotherapy challenged the classical psychoanalytic positions on the need for depth therapy, the requirement of therapist passivity, and the pursuit of the past.
- TLDP invites therapists to focus attention on the interpersonal world of the client and the here-and-now dynamics of the relationship of client and therapist.
- A focus for those employing TLBD is to provide clients with corrective emotional experiences, those that will undermine the client's faulty interpersonal patterns.
- TLDP posits that early experiences of maladaptive relationship patterns become schematized and continue to be lived out in the here and now and serve as the source of the client's difficulties.
- While clients are "stuck" in engaging these maladaptive patterns, they are not "sick."
- TLDP is process oriented, with the therapist actively engaged in structuring corrective emotional experiences.
- TLDP is focused on the client's most pervasive and problematic style of relating.
- Central to case conceptualization and treatment planning for time-limited dynamic psychotherapy is the identification of the client's cyclical maladaptive pattern.
- Therapists employing TLDP rely heavily on relationship-building skills and communication within the session. They will also utilize strategies from varied theoretical models in service of creating a corrective emotional experience for the client.
- Research supports the effectiveness of TLDP with clients who are highly motivated, capable of insight, and able to establish a collaborative relationship with the therapist.

ADDITIONAL RESOURCES

Binder, J. L. (2004). *Key competencies in brief dynamic psychotherapy: Clinical practice beyond the manual.* Guilford.

Levenson, H. (2017). *Brief dynamic therapy* (2nd ed.). American Psychological Association.

Levenson, H., & Strupp. H. D. (2007). Cyclical maladaptive patterns: Case formulation in time-limited dynamic psychotherapy. In T. D. Eels (Ed.)., *Handbook of psychotherapy case formulation* (2nd ed., pp. 164–197), Guilford.

Tosone, C. (1997) Sändor Ferenczi. *Journal of Analytic Social Work, 4*(3), 23–41.

REFERENCES

Abbass, A., Sheldon, A., Gyra, J., & Kaplan, A. (2008). Intensive short-term dynamic psychotherapy for DSM-IV personality disorders: A randomized control trial. *Journal of Nervous and Mental Disease, 196*, 211–216.

Alexander. F., & French, T. M. (1974). *Psychoanalytic therapy: Principles and applications.* University of Nebraska Press. (Original work published 1946)

Barber, J. P., Muran, J. C., McCarthy, K.S., & Keefe, J. R. (2013). Research on dynamic therapies. In M. J. Lambert (Ed.), *Handbook of psychotherapy and behavior change* (pp. 443–494). Wiley.

Bauer, G. P., & Kobos, J. C. (1987). *Brief therapy: Short-term psychodynamic intervention.* Jason Aronson.

Bowlby, J. (1988). *A secure base: Clinical applications of attachment theory*. Routledge.

Butler, S. F., Strupp, H. H., & Binder, J. L. (1993). Time-limited dynamic psychotherapy. In S. Budman, M. Hoyt, & S. Friedman (Eds.), *The first session in brief therapy* (pp. 87–110). Guilford.

Diener, M. J., Hilsenroth, M. J., & Weinberger, J. (2007). Therapist affect focus and patient outcomes in psychodynamic psychotherapy: A meta-analysis. The American Journal of Psychiatry, 164, 936–941. http://dx.doi.org/10.1176/ajp.2007.164.6.936

Ferenczi, S. (1950). Technical difficulties in the analysis of a case of hysteria. In J. Rickman (Ed.), *Further contributions to the theory and technique of psychoanalysis* (pp. 189–198). Hogarth. (Original work published 1920)

Fosha, D. (1995). Technique and taboo in three short-term dynamic psychotherapies. *The Journal of Psychotherapy Practice and Research*, 4, 297–318.

Greenberg, L. S. (2012). Emotions, the great captains of our lives: Their role in the process of change in psychotherapy. American Psychologist, 67, 697–707. http://dx.doi.org/10.1037/a0029858

Greenberg, L. S., & Pascual-Leone, A. (2006). Emotion in psychotherapy: a practice-friendly research review. *Journal of clinical psychology, 62*(5), 611–630. https://doi.org/10.1002/jclp.20252

Greenberg, R. P. (2004) Psychoanalytic trials and tribulations: a review of outcomes of psychoanalytic treatment. *Contemp Psychol. 49*:145–147.

Hilsenroth, M. J. (2007) A programmatic study of short-term psychodynamic psychotherapy: Assessment, process, outcome and training. *Psychotherapy Research*, 17, 31–45.

Hilsenroth, M. J., Defife, J. A., Blagys, M. D., & Ackerman, S. J. (2006). Effects of training in short-term psychodynamic psychotherapy: Changes in graduate clinicians technique. *Psychotherapy Research*, 16, 293–305.

Knekt, P., Lindfors, O., Härkänen, T., Välikoski, M., Virtala, E., Laaksonen, M. A., Marttunen, M., Kaipainen, M., Renlund, C., & Helsinki Psychotherapy Study Group (2008). Randomized trial on the effectiveness of long-and short-term psychodynamic psychotherapy and solution-focused therapy on psychiatric symptoms during a 3-year follow-up. *Psychological medicine*, 38(5), 689–703. https://doi.org/10.1017/S003329170700164X

Leichsenring, F., Leweke, F., Klein, S., & Steinert, C. (2015). The empirical status of psychodynamic psychotherapy—an update: Bambi's alive and kicking. *Psychotherapy and Psychosomatics, 84,* 129–148.

Levenson, H. (2017). *Brief dynamic therapy* (2nd ed.). American Psychological Association.

Levenson, H., & Strupp. H. D. (2007). Cyclical maladaptive patterns: Case formulation in time-limited dynamic psychotherapy. In T. D. Eels (Ed.)., *Handbook of psychotherapy case formulation* (2nd ed., pp. 164–197), Guilford.

Luborsky, L. (1984). *Principles of psychoanalytic psychotherapy: A manual for supportive-expressive treatment.* Basic Books.

Magnavita, J. J. (1993). The evolution of short-term dynamic psychotherapy: Treatment of the future? *Professional Psychology: Research and Practice, 24*(3), 360–365.

Malan, D. H. (1963). *A study of brief psychotherapy*. Tavistock.

Malan, D. H. (1976). *The frontier of brief psychotherapy*. Plenum.

Mann, J. (1973). *Time-limited psychotherapy*. Harvard University Press.

Messe, S. B., & Kaplan, A. H. (2004). Outcomes and factors related to efficacy of brief psychodynamic therapy. In D.P. Charman (Ed.) *Core processes brief psychodynamic psychotherapy* (pp. 103–118). Erlbaum.

Rachman, A. W. (1988). The rule of empathy: Sandor Ferenczi's pioneering contributions to the empathic method in psychoanalysis. *Journal of the American Academy of Psychoanalysis, 16*, 1–27.

Rank, O. (1936). *Will therapy* (J. Taft, Trans.). Knopf. (Original work published in 1929)

Schacht, T. E., Binder, J. L., & Strupp, H. H. (1984). The dynamic focus. In H. H. Strupp & J. L. Binder (Eds.), *Psychotherapy in a new key* (pp. 65–109). Basic Books.

Sifneos, P. E. (1987). *Short-term dynamic psychotherapy: Evaluation and technique*. Plenum.

Strupp, H. H., & Binder, J. L. (1984). *Psychotherapy in a new key: A guide to time-limited dynamic psychotherapy*. Basic Books

Tosone, C. (1997) Sándor Ferenczi. *Journal of Analytic Social Work, 4*(3), 23–41.

CHAPTER 5

Brief Cognitive Behavior Therapy

Men are disturbed not by things but by the view which they take of them.
—Epictetus

The chapter's opening quote, attributed to the ancient Greek philosopher Epictetus (Long, 2002), succinctly depicts the keystone of a cognitive behavioral therapeutic approach. It could be argued that the philosophic origins of a cognitive approach to psychotherapy started with the Stoic philosophers, including Epictetus and Marcus Aurelius. CBT, or in the case of this chapter, brief cognitive behavioral therapy, is not a singular theory but an approach that is guided by shared assumptions and principles. As described by Judith Beck (2001), CBT is defined not by the types of techniques the therapist uses but rather by the therapist's planning and implementing treatment according to a cognitive formulation and conceptualization.

The current chapter reviews the evolution of brief CBT and the basic tenets, constructs, and strategies that form this psychotherapy approach. Upon completion of this chapter, the reader will be able to do the following:

1. Identify the major historical contributors to the development of (brief) CBT.
2. Describe the assumptions underlying the cognitive behavioral model of therapy.
3. Describe the major tenets of a cognitive behavioral model of psychotherapy.
4. Explain how the utilization of construct such as schemata, cognitive distortion, and cognitive dissonance are employed in cognitive behavioral psychotherapy.

History and Contributors

As reflected in the quote used to open this chapter, one could argue that modern cognitive behavior therapy has its roots in the Greek Stoic philosopher Epictetus (50–135 AD). However, it is both more accurate and useful to attribute the emergence of CBT to the 20th-century work of behaviorists such as Joseph Wolpe (1958) and cognitive therapists such as Albert Ellis (1957, 1958) and Aaron Beck (1970, 1975).

CBT results from the integration of a behavioral orientation, one that focuses on classical conditioning and operant learning, social learning theory, and the influence of modeling; cognitive theory and its focus is on the role of thoughts and beliefs and attributions. This integration sets the foundation for CBT's interest and focuses on cognition as a mediator between experience or antecedent events and the resulting feelings and behaviors.

Behavioral Therapy

With a focus on learning and learning experiences as the foundation for developing behavior, behavioral therapists did not pathologize the client. Instead, they assessed the adaptive quality and function of their actions. When the individual's behavior was seen as dysfunctional, techniques would be engaged to reduce the dysfunctional behavior and/or increase the frequency of alternative, functional behaviors. Specifically, behavioral therapists would employ interventions that targeted (a) the modification and manipulation of antecedent conditions and events and/or consequences associated with the behavior of concern, (b) provide alternative response training, or (c) modify the environment to elicit the desired behavior.

Joseph Wolpe

One behavioral strategy that demonstrated both efficiency and effectiveness was systematic desensitization. Rooted in the principles of respondent conditioning (i.e., Pavlovian conditioning), systematic desensitization established itself as an effective treatment for clients experiencing anxiety.

The treatment involved the process of reciprocal inhibition, wherein a client would experience the source of their anxiety while in a state of relaxation (Wolpe, 1976). The presentation of a feared stimulus to a client who was relaxed resulted in counterconditioning of the fear signal. This process neutralized the fear signal such that it no longer elicited a fear response.

Wolpe's (1990) technique, while behavioral, deviated from the more classic behavioral interventions, which restricted focus to overt and directly observable behavior. Wolpe often employed imaginal exposure of the fear stimuli. That is, rather than presenting the fear signal in real-time (in vivo), the therapist would have the client repeatedly imagine the feared stimuli while practicing relaxing (Vinograd & Craske, 2020; Wolpe, 1980). Such imaginal exposure was not only effective but moved behavioral intervention from that which was extra personal to the engagement of the client's mental operations.

Through its employment of techniques such as exposure and response prevention, systematic desensitization, and operant conditioning, behavioral therapy established itself not only as an effective treatment modality but also economical, in terms of a utility even with limited sessions.

Cognitive Therapy

The early 1970s witnessed an increased level of interest in the relationship of thoughts, beliefs, interpretations, and images with emotions and behaviors. Individuals such as Albert Ellis and Aaron Beck began to center their research and theory development on the role of cognition in the creation and maintenance of emotional disturbances. Ellis's (1957) rational emotive behavior therapy (REBT) and Aaron Beck's (2015) cognitive therapy (CT) serve as the two main pillars of current cognitive behavioral therapies (David et al., 2017).

Albert Ellis

Ellis, who was initially trained as a psychoanalyst, began working on his therapeutic approach in the 1950s. By 1955 Ellis (1957, 1958) had "abandoned psychoanalysis entirely, and instead was concentrating on changing people's behavior by confronting them with their irrational beliefs and persuading them to adopt rational ones" (David et al., 2010, p. XI). His theory was introduced with the name of rational psychotherapy (RT); later, to emphasize its focus on emotional outcomes, it was named rational emotive therapy (RET). In the 1990s, Ellis (1995) changed its name into rational emotive behavior therapy because behavioral factors constitute a fundamental component of this treatment approach.

REBT is an action-oriented approach to managing cognitive, emotional, and behavioral disturbances. While recognizing the impact of previous experience and learning, REBT emphasizes the present (Ellis, 1995). In REBT, clients are taught how to examine and challenge faulty, irrational, and thus unproductive thinking. This irrational thinking is posited as the source of a client's unhealthy emotions and self-defeating/self-sabotaging behaviors (David et al., 2010). The focus of treatment is on changing irrational beliefs into rational beliefs, intending to change dysfunctional emotions and maladaptive behaviors into functional and adaptive ones.

Aaron Beck

Beck, who is often identified as the father of cognitive therapy (Folsom et al., 2016), was trained in psychodynamic theory like Ellis. Oatley (2004) reported that during a session in which Beck was conducting free association, he noticed that the client's thoughts were not as unconscious as he was trained to believe and that some of these thoughts appeared intricately tied to the emotional distress the client was experiencing.

These early experiences led him to develop his cognitive therapeutic approach. By the late 1970s, cognitive therapy established its foothold as an effective form of psychotherapy (see Beck et al., 1979; Rush et al., 1977).

The Blending of Cognition and Behavior

While classic behavioral theorists rejected the focus on that which was mental or nonobservable, the work of David Clark (1986) and David Barlow (1988) around the treatment of panic disorders demonstrated the effectiveness of merging cognitive and behavioral techniques (Rachman,

1997). Over the succeeding years, behavioral and cognitive therapies grew together. They influenced each other to such an extent that the resulting amalgam is now most commonly known as CBT.

Brief CBT

It could be argued that CBT is brief by definition and origin. While the number of sessions will depend on the nature of the issue being addressed and the uniqueness of the client, CBT adheres to the fundamental goals of planned brief therapy lasting from 12 to 20 weeks (Freeman et al., 1990).

Brief CBT reflects a further shortening or compression of the number of sessions. In brief CBT, which typically extends over four to eight sessions, concentration is on specific treatments for a limited number of client issues (Cully & Teten, 2008). While all CBT elicits the client's active participation both within the counseling sessions and outside of the counseling office via homework assignments, brief CBT is even more focused on using reading materials and homework to facilitate client progress.

Perspective

Brief cognitive therapy, as is true for its more traditional presentation of CBT, combines cognitive and behavioral strategies to increase client awareness of their thoughts, beliefs, and fundamental assumptions that serve as the basis for the current emotional distress. The perspective is that there is no direct link between life events and one's emotional reaction to those events. Instead, it is one's thoughts, beliefs, attitudes, and perceptual biases that is the meaning one assigns to an experience that crafts the emotional response (Parsons, 2019).

The basic premise of CBT is that emotions are difficult to change directly, so CBT targets emotions by changing thoughts and behaviors contributing to the distressing emotions (Cully & Teten, 2008). This perspective is an apparent deviation from those models that emphasize intrapsychic conflict and the unconscious meaning behind the behavior.

CBT involves problem-focused and action-oriented engaging strategies to assist clients in replacing dysfunctional thoughts and behaviors with new information-processing skills and coping behaviors (Beck, 2011). Brief CBT is active and collaborative with a focus beyond that of facilitating client insight and understanding to the development and acquisition of skills.

Assumptions and Principles Guiding Practice

CBT can be viewed as an umbrella for various distinct approaches to psychotherapy. While diversity and variation in specific techniques and philosophies characterize the numbers models of CBT, the one consistency binding each of these approaches is the emphasis given to the role that cognitive processes play as the foundation for human feeling and action.

Therapists operating from a cognitive orienting framework emphasize cognitions as vital mediators in the creation and modulation of emotions and behaviors and generally embrace the following principles and assumptions.

Humans Are Meaning Makers

Humans attempt to create meaning and adapt to life experiences by creating assumptive systems and schemata about self, others, and the world (Piaget, 1985). These schemata and assumptive systems become organized into attitudes with cognitive, affective, and behavioral components (Rokeach, 1968). These cognitions constitute a person's stream of consciousness, which reflects how a person configures a view of self, the world, the past and the future (Beck et al., 1979).

To successfully function and adapt to the demands of one's life, a person's assumptive world must correspond to conditions as they are, thus providing the individual with a sense of reality that is functional. However, our assumptive systems and the cognitions we employ to make meaning of our experiences are not always adaptive and functional. The goal of CBT is to assist clients in modifying assumptive systems to increase adaptability and functionality.

Cognitions as Mediator

Central to a cognitive behavioral model is the assumption that thoughts, beliefs, attitudes, and perceptual biases influence what emotions will be experienced and the intensity of those emotions. An individual's affect and behavior are primarily determined by how they structure or give meaning to their experiences.

For example, a client may present a story that highlights a specific event or experience, such as being served divorce papers, as the source of his distress. The cognitive behavioral therapist believes that it is not this activating event of life (point A) that is the direct cause of the client's distress. Instead, as is actual for all experiences, this event must be interpreted or assigned meaning if it is to have an impact on one's feelings and actions. The specific meaning that this client is assigning to this event serves as the foundation for their current emotional and behavioral experience. The power of perspective and the meaning assigned is demonstrated in Exercise 5.1.

Cognitions Operating at Varying Levels of Awareness

Our thoughts our beliefs appear to reside at various levels of conscious awareness. Most often, those that are the source of our emotional reactions are operating at a less than entirely conscious level, and thus it will take practice to begin to identify them.

One model for discussing these various levels of thoughts describes them as *voluntary* and *automatic* and those that serve as our *core beliefs* (Beck & Weishaar, 1989). The voluntary thoughts are readily accessible to one's awareness and generally reflect the person's conscious processing of the momentary experience. Thus, as you read this text, you may be aware that you are thinking about what to eat for lunch or do later in the day. These are thoughts that

EXERCISE 5.1

It Is All a Matter of Perspective

Directions: While we often attribute the source or cause for our emotional responses to some outside force or event, CBT posits that our emotions are the result of the meaning, the perspective, we give to these external events. The following exercise invites you to consider the role of perspective in the experience of emotions.

Part A:

Event	Feelings/Emotions	Actions/Behaviors
You are driving on the highway and an individual in a pickup truck cuts in front of you, and you jam on your breaks.		
Your boss calls you in and, without any warning or notice, fires you.		
A person you are dating sends you a text message stating that they are ending the relationship.		
You realize that the lottery ticket you bought last night was a million-dollar winner.		

Part B: Review the additional information regarding the events listed in part A. Again, identify your feelings and your actions.

Event	Additional Information	Feelings/Emotions	Actions/Behaviors
You are driving on the highway and an individual in a pickup truck cuts in front of you and you jam on your breaks.	As the truck passes, you can see in the back bed a man holding a little boy in his lap, and the boy is visibly bleeding from his head.		

(Continued)

EXERCISE 5.1 (Continued)

Event	Additional Information	Feelings/Emotions	Actions/Behaviors
Your boss calls you in and, without any warning or notice, fires you.	Your plan this day was to tell your boss you were quitting since you just got a job offer and twice the salary.		
A person you are dating sends you a text message stating that they are ending the relationship.	You have been struggling for more than a week trying to figure out how to end this relationship.		
You realize that the lottery ticket you bought last night was a million-dollar winner.	The ticket you bought you gave as a Christmas gift, that very morning, to your trash hauler.		

are accessible to your consciousness and can be easily replaced by other thoughts at any one moment. Automatic thoughts are ways of processing information that are spontaneous and require little to no conscious reflection. Thus, while individuals may be aware of thinking "that's a gun," they may be less aware of what followed in their thinking: "Oh, my God, I'm going to die!" It appears that thoughts at this level are those we have employed, in some form or another, often to make them spontaneous assessments of particular events. The final level of our thinking is our core beliefs, assumptions, or philosophical perspectives that serve as a foundation for the views and expectations we hold about ourselves, others, and the world. Thus, should an individual experiencing another person cutting them off on the highway have a core belief such as "There are evil, horrible people in this world who must be punished," such a core belief may give rise to an automatic thought, such as "This guy is a real a**hole. I will show him." With that interpretation, the individual may find themselves in a state of road rage.

While developing core beliefs that are more reflective of reality and supportive of adaption and functionality, modifying such core beliefs may be beyond the scope of brief CBT. Automatic thoughts, which can be addressed in a time-limited CBT, are central to CBT. They are viewed as that which exerts direct influence over our mood at any point in time.

Cognitions Can Be Functional and Dysfunctional

The beliefs, cognitions, and schemata one employs to give meaning to life experiences can be rational and functional and thus result in emotional and behavioral consequences (at point C) that help the individual respond to the activating events effectively. From the cognitive behavioral perspective, it is also true that individuals can distort the meaning of life events, and with such distortion create feelings and behaviors that are not the most effective and functional in that particular situation.

Maultsby (1984) provided the following as criteria for discerning thinking that is rational and functional from that which is distorted and dysfunctional:

1. Rational thinking is based on obvious facts.
2. Rational thinking best helps people protect their lives and health.
3. Rational thinking best helps people achieve their own short-term and long-term goals.
4. Rational thinking best helps people avoid their most unwanted conflicts with other people.
5. Rational thinking best helps people feel emotionally the way they want to feel without using alcohol or other drugs.

Schemata Are Resistant to Change

When an individual's distress results from dysfunctional and distorted beliefs and schemata, changing those beliefs becomes the target for a cognitive behavioral therapist. While changing or modifying a client's maladaptive schemata seems like a reasonable goal, it is not a goal that is easily or readily accomplished.

Jean Piaget (1985) highlighted the process by which an individual takes new experiences and makes meaning by either incorporating the new experience into an existing schema, in a process called *assimilation*, or by creating an entirely new structure or schema or dramatically adjusting an existing one (i.e., *accommodation*). This second process, of modifying old schemata or creating new ones, requires more psychic energy, and, as such, it is not the first choice as we try to adapt to new circumstances.

We tend to resist accommodating to new experiences, embracing information that confirms our assumptions and schema, and either ignoring or distorting those data that are nonconfirmatory. It is not that a client who is depressed wants to be depressed; instead, the belief that life is hopeless and they are helpless is so firmly entrenched as their truth, their reality, that it is not readily surrendered.

Cognitions Can Be Modified

Cognitive behavioral therapists understand that even though a client may resist modifying their schemata, choosing instead to modify experience so that it fits (assimilates) existing schemata, the truth is that cognitions can be modified (Ellis, 2002). In situations where clients cannot simply adjust the world to fit their assumptions, they will be motivated—by the cognitive dissonance (tension) that they experience—to reexamine their basic assumptions and embrace more reliable and functional cognitions. Cognitive behavioral therapists believe the following:

1. Clients can become aware of their dysfunctional thoughts and cognitive distortions.
2. Clients can be taught to shift from self-defeating, dysfunctional thoughts and attitudes to self-enhancing, functional thoughts.
3. Correction of these faulty dysfunctional constructs can lead to more adaptive and functional ways of responding to the lived experience.

Cognitive Change Requires Work!

CBT focuses on the here and now, with an emphasis on identifying, challenging, and reformulating client dysfunctional thinking both in session and between sessions (Beck et al., 1979). Cognitive behavioral therapists believe that while changing one's schemata and cognition is possible, it requires work, both on the part of the therapist and the client. The therapist with a cognitive orientation is active and deliberately interactive with the client in challenging and reformulating beliefs and perceptions. CBT requires clients to develop a new way of processing information, a new fundamental philosophy of life, and, as such, it takes work.

Principles in Action

Cognitive behavioral therapists will employ directive or reflective modes, implement scientific-didactic principles or empathic, nondirective methods, and call on a variety of educational materials, including readings and videos, in their efforts to assist clients in the identification and correction of distorted and dysfunctional belief systems. While the approach reflects the uniqueness of each client and the specifics of the case formulation, CBT typically includes (a) assisting the client in understanding and embracing the reality of the connection between thoughts and feelings; (b) monitoring and recognizing specific forms of cognitive distortions and dysfunctional thinking; (c) testing the logic, validity, and adaptiveness of the identified cognitions; and (d) reformulating cognitions and underlying beliefs so that they result in a more functional, adaptive processing of life experiences (Beck et al., 1979).

Connecting Thoughts and Feelings

Often during the first session, a therapist working from a brief CBT orientation will introduce the client to the connection of thoughts to feelings and actions. Given the specifics of the presenting concern, the therapist, using attending skills, reflection, and often confrontation, will help the client begin to understand the beliefs and thus interpretive perspective that they bring to the situation. The therapist will use a variety of techniques to not only raise the client's awareness of the connection of thoughts and feelings but also to help the client experience an actual "ah-ha" moment, one giving evidence that they have assimilated the principles and see the application to their situation (see Case Illustration 5.1).

CASE ILLUSTRATION 5.1

Connecting Thoughts and Feelings

The client, in this case, came to therapy because of feelings of anxiety. The following brief interaction of client and therapist demonstrates an approach that one therapist used to help the client see the connection of thoughts and feelings, targeting the experience of anxiety.

Therapist: Tina, I know you shared that you have a 4-year-old daughter, Emily; is that correct?

Client: Yes. She is something special.

Therapist: If you will allow me, I would like to use Emily to demonstrate the point I was attempting to make regarding the connections of our thoughts to our feelings. Would that be okay?

Client: Sure.

Therapist: Thanks. So, let's imagine that you just put Emily to bed, and it is one of those windy, rainy nights like we had last night. Now, 10 minutes after you left her room, you hear her crying and calling for you.

Client: Actually, that happened last week.

Therapist: Well, I assume you went to her right away.

Client: I did, and she was sitting up scared.

Therapist: Did she tell you what it was that frightened her?

Client: She said her night-light went off and that she's afraid of the dark.

Therapist: Hmmm ... that sounds like something a young child would say, but I wonder if that is really the source of her fear?

Client: I'm not sure what you mean. Aren't children afraid of the dark?

Therapist: Great question. My answer may not be what you expect. Actually, no one is afraid of the dark. Let's think about that. If Emily was afraid of the dark, wouldn't she be afraid every night? Or, like last week when you took her to movies, wouldn't she be frightened upon entering the darkened theater?

Therapist: I wonder, is it possible that as she was falling off to sleep, she heard something, and her thoughts went to wondering what it was, maybe actually saying, "What's that?"

Client: Probably. I know that is what I would be thinking.

(Continued)

> ## CASE ILLUSTRATION 5.1 (*Continued*)
>
> **Therapist:** Okay, but I wonder if perhaps she not only asked the question "What's that?" but drew a conclusion in response. I mean, I wonder if her interpretation and thus belief about what was happening was that it was "a monster."
>
> **Client:** Actually, that's what she said. She wanted me to check the closet for a monster!
>
> **Therapist:** So, thinking it was a monster created her fear. I wonder since it is close to Christmas, and I know you celebrate that holiday, if when she heard the noise, and then wondered "What was it?" how she would have felt and reacted if her answer was "It's Santa!"
>
> **Client:** She would have been out of bed ASAP!
>
> **Therapist:** Interesting. Same dark, same noise … different interpretation—and as a result different emotional and behavioral outcomes. That's what I meant when I talked about the thinking-feeling/behaving connection.
>
> **Client:** (smiling) I guess I'm doing a little monster-making myself?

Recognizing and Monitoring Cognitive Distortions

A second target for therapist action is on assisting the client in identifying the nature of cognitive distortions and those situations in which the client may be employing such distortions to process an experience. Therapists will employ various techniques to educate clients about the forms of dysfunctional thinking (see Table 5.1), including assigning readings, direct instruction, and most importantly, the analyses of clients' raw data reflecting their life experience.

TABLE 5.1 ABBREVIATED LIST OF COGNITIVE DISTORTIONS

All-or-nothing thinking	A person engaging in this type of thinking sees things as only black or white. Things are seen in terms of extremes: You are either perfect or a total failure. This would be the case of the person determined to lose weight and who, following one slip off her diet, decides, "What the hell? That diet is blown, so I might as well order a second dessert."
Overgeneralization	In this case, a person takes a single adverse event and concludes that all similar situations will be the same. This would be the case of a person whose application to grad school has been rejected and concludes that it is no use to apply to other schools. The use (and belief) in words such as "always" and "never" may provide a clear indication that overgeneralization is being engaged to find meaning at that moment.

(*Continued*)

TABLE 5.1 *(Continued)*

Mental filters/ selective abstraction	When using this form of dysfunctional thinking, a person pulls out only the adverse events in their lives, overlooking the positives. It is like they have a filter that allows some information in (negative details) and excludes any contradictory positive information. The result is that the person's view of reality becomes tinted by that negativity. For example, imagine that a person just received a printed assessment of their job performance. Assume that the actual evaluation contained seven areas identified as highly proficient and one identified as needing improvement. If the individual began to obsess about the one area needing improvement, even to the point of concluding that they were messing up at their job, they would be employing selective abstraction.
Jumping to conclusions	As suggested by the title, this error in information processing occurs when a person draws a grand conclusion based on insufficient information. This may be the source of anxiety for an individual who is unexpectedly called in to the boss's office. If the conclusion is "I'm in trouble," based just on this unexpected request, the anxiety would be the result of a cognitive distortion, jumping to a conclusion.
Magnification (catastrophizing)/ minimization	With this form of cognitive error, a person exaggerates the significance of an event or piece of information. The individual who just received terrible news and feels that life is now unbearable and no longer has meaning may be exhibiting such catastrophizing. Yes, things may be difficult and undesirable, but are they factually unbearable? The other side of this distortion is the process of reducing or minimizing the importance of some experience or event. This would be the case of the person who chooses to ignore some medical symptom and refuses to have it checked out, stating, "It's no big deal!"
Emotional reasoning	Emotional reasoning occurs when a person uses their emotions and feelings to draw conclusions about reality. This would be the case of a person who feels overwhelmed with a work assignment and uses this feeling to conclude that it is hopeless and that the job cannot be done.

(Continued)

TABLE 5.1 (Continued)

Shoulds and musts	With "should" and "must" beliefs, we take something that we wish, hope, or merely desire and turn it into a "have to," no longer a preference but a mandate. Individuals who engage in this form of information processing firmly believe that they and the world are obligated to be a certain way. When applied to oneself, "should-ing" often results in guilt and frustration. "I can't believe I got that question wrong; I should know better." When we employ shoulds and musts when viewing the actions of others, we often experience increased frustration and anger since it is likely they are not adhering to our rules. Comments such as, "They have no right saying that!" or, "How dare they act like that?" reflect an individual's self-created rules for the world, rules that they feel are being violated.

Testing and Reformulating

As the client identifies those thoughts, interpretive schemas, and core beliefs that are at the root of their dysfunctional feelings and actions, the focus of therapy will shift to efforts to facilitate change at all levels of cognition. Given the time constraints of brief CBT, the focus will most often center on automatic thoughts rather than core beliefs.

Cognitive behavioral therapists will help clients review their interpretation, their cognitions, in light of actual circumstances, identifying distortions as they occur. The goal is to assist clients in assessing the degree to which inferences and conclusions correspond to what other objective individuals may conclude. When this is not the case, reformulating those cognitions will then be the focus of the therapy. Cognitive behavioral therapists will model and directly engage the client in the process of disputing dysfunctional beliefs and restructuring cognitions so that they are more in line with reality and service of client functioning (see Case Illustration 5.2).

CASE ILLUSTRATION 5.2

Devastated

Therapist: So, Aisha, if I understand correctly, you really believe you are not loveable and that you will be alone all your life.

Aisha: But that's true.

Therapist: I know it feels true, but let me ask you a question: What is the evidence that it is true? Upon what are basing that belief?

Aisha: Let's start with the fact that I just got dumped by my boyfriend. We have dating for 2 months, and he just called and said that he was no longer interested.

(Continued)

> ### CASE ILLUSTRATION 5.2 (*Continued*)
>
> **Therapist:** You sound as if that was unexpected and really upsetting.
>
> **Aisha:** Upset? Try devastating!
>
> **Therapist:** I'm not sure I understand. The fact that this relationship of 2 months ended completely destroyed your whole life?
>
> **Aisha:** No, not him, actually we were having problems, but I mean if I can't keep a relationship with him, I won't be able to have a relationship with anyone.
>
> **Therapist:** Oh, so it wasn't the actual event that made you so sad; it's the belief that this one event is evidence that you will never find anyone or have a relationship with anyone. Is that it?
>
> **Aisha:** Yeah.
>
> **Therapist:** Wow, I get it, and it seems that if it were true that you will spend your entire life without a loved one or friends, and as such truly be all alone; I can see how that could be quite an issue. What I don't understand is how that conclusion is supported by this one event, the ending of one, less than satisfying relationship?
>
> **Aisha:** Okay, Okay. Maybe I'm overreacting. However, I don't know what to do.
>
> **Therapist:** Well, let's first look at the facts to see if you are overreacting or distorting the impact of this event, and then we can plan what to do.

Table 5.2 provides a sampling of interventions that can be employed in CBT to challenge and reframe several specific forms of cognitive distortion.

TABLE 5.2 INTERVENTION TARGETING A SAMPLING OF SPECIFIC DISTORTIONS

Cognitive distortion	Underlying fundamental beliefs	Targets and strategies for intervention
Catastrophizing	Unless things are the way I want them to be it is a disaster, an unbearable situation.	Begin to identify the real, the most probable, the worst-case scenario. What is the worst thing likely to happen? With this definition of the outcome, ways of reducing negative outcomes and/or developing a tolerance can be targeted.

(*Continued*)

TABLE 5.2 (*Continued*)

Cognitive distortion	Underlying fundamental beliefs	Targets and strategies for intervention
Selective abstraction	Only specific data are essential to perceive and retain that those things that do not fit my self-perception or view of the world are irrelevant and should ignore or modified.	Have clients engage in mini experiments in which they log all that happened so that the counselor can point out successes that have been discounted. Invite the client to imagine how they would respond to a friend who was selective in their processing of the data.
Should's and must's	An absolute sense of duty and right and wrong; the view that our way is the only way.	Invite the client to analyze the impact of replacing should's and must's with wishes, wants, and preferences. For example, what would happen if the client believed "I wish and truly want to get that promotion" rather than rigidly believing that "It is unfair, I *should* be promoted"?

Source: Parsons, R., & Neale-McFall, C. (2018, p. 164). Intentional counseling: Practice guided by theory. Cognella.

As is true for most brief therapies, brief CBT employs homework to extend the therapy outside the time constraints of an office visit (Beck et al., 1979). The homework will typically engage the client in identifying the interpretations they have assigned to events and experiences and efforts to dispute irrational beliefs, reformulating those to be more rational and functional (Ellis & Dryden, 1997). In addition, clients will often be encouraged to experiment with using their reformulated beliefs in a specific situation. The hope is that if clients enter situations acting as if the new belief is true, they will experience outcomes that further support the validity of this new way of viewing self and the world. For example, a client who holds unrealistic standards for herself may be encouraged to publicly share when she makes an error and experience the real (and less devastating) consequence of human error.

Time Limited

While the core concepts and strategies employed in brief CBT are the same as those present in the more traditional forms of CBT, the significant difference is that the former operates within a limited number of sessions. However, it is essential to note that the number of sessions is not fixed but rather will vary as a reflection of the client's uniqueness, client issues, and therapist.

TABLE 5.3 POTENTIAL SCHEDULE BRIEF CBT

	Session Content and Focus
Session 1	Orient the patient to CBT. Assess patient concerns. Initial case conceptualization. Set initial treatment plan/goals.
Session 2	Assess patient concerns and set initial goals (continued). or Begin intervention techniques. Maladaptive thoughts, behavioral activation, problem-solving, relaxation.
Session 3	Begin/continue intervention techniques.
Session 4	Continue intervention techniques. Reassess goals/treatment plan.
Session 5	Continue/refine intervention techniques.
Session 6	Continue intervention techniques.
Session 7	Continue intervention techniques. Discuss ending treatment and prepare for maintaining changes.
Session 8	End treatment and help patient to maintain changes.

Adapted from Cully, J. A., & Teten, A. L. (2008, p. 7). A therapist's guide to brief cognitive therapy. Department of Veterans Affairs South Central MIRECC. https://athealth.com/wp-content/uploads/2014/03/Guide_CBT_03-14.pdf

Cully and Teten (2008) offer a model 8-week session-by-session outline (Table 5.3). These authors note that it is essential to remain flexible and adaptive and that it is not expected that one rigidly adheres to the schedule as set out in Table 5.3.

One of the consequences of employing brief CBT is that therapists often limit work at identifying, challenging, and reformulating automatic thoughts. While it may be possible to challenge core beliefs in later sessions, it is more likely that such a process will require more than the eight sessions prescribed by Cully and Teten (2008).

Supportive Research

CBT is the psychological therapy with the most solid and broad evidence base for efficacy and effectiveness (Cully & Teten, 2008). Numerous meta-analytic studies (e.g., Cristea et al., 2015; Cuijpers et al., 2013; David et al., 2017; Hoffman et al., 2012; Roth & Fonagy, 2005) have found support for the efficacy of CBT across populations, settings, and presenting complaints.

While most of the research has focused on the more traditional forms of CBT, other research, such as that of Cape et al. (2010), Gavita et al. (2012), and Haughland et al. (2020), expand the support for CBT's effectiveness to brief, time-limited formats.

Suitability

Brief CBT has demonstrated effectiveness and suitability for many presenting concerns. In 1990, Safran and colleagues published their Suitability for Short-Term Cognitive Therapy Rating Scales (SRS). They reported the following 10 criteria to be associated with clients for whom short-term CBT was effective: (a) *accessibility of automatic thoughts*, or the capacity of patients to report on their thinking in problematic situations; (b) *awareness and differentiation of emotion*, or the capacity to label different emotional states in the past and present and to be able to work with them; (c) *acceptance of personal responsibility for change*, or the extent to which patients see their own role in recovery; (d) *compatibility with cognitive rationale*, or the extent to which the patient sees the value of key tasks in CBT, such as examining the link between thoughts, emotion, and behavior and doing homework assignments; (e) *alliance potential (in-session evidence)*, or the potential of the patient to form a therapeutic alliance based on in-session quality of the relationship between patient and interviewer; (f) *alliance potential (out-of-session evidence)*, or the potential for the therapeutic alliance based on the history of past meaningful relationships, including previous therapies; (g) *chronicity*, or the duration of the patient's problems; (h) *security operations*, or the intensity and manner of efforts to block exploration of anxiety-producing content, such as intellectualization or avoidance; (i) *focality*, or the capacity to remain focused and work on a problem in depth; and (j) *general optimism/pessimism regarding therapy*.

KEYSTONES

- CBT results from the integration of a behavioral orientation, one that focuses on classical conditioning and operant learning, social learning theory, and the influence of modeling, with cognitive theory and its focus on the role of thoughts and beliefs and attributions.
- The emergence of cognitive behavior therapy can be accredited to the 20th-century work of behaviorists such as Joseph Wolpe (1958) and cognitive therapists such as Albert Ellis (1957, 1958) and Aaron Beck (1970, 1975).
- CBT is brief by definition and origin, lasting from 12 to 20 sessions; brief CBT is shortened

- even more, extending just over four to eight sessions.
- The primary premise of brief CBT is that there is no direct link between life events and one's emotional reaction to those events. Instead, it is one's thoughts, beliefs, attitudes, and perceptual biases, the meaning that one assigns to an experience, that crafts the emotional response.
- CBT is problem-focused and action-oriented engaging strategies to assist clients in replacing dysfunctional thoughts and behaviors with new information-processing skills and coping behaviors.
- Assumptions and guiding principles of brief CBT include humans as meaning makers, cognitions as mediators of feelings and behaviors, cognitions that operate at various levels of awareness and can be functional or dysfunctional, and cognitions that are able to be changed but resistant to such change.
- CBT typically includes (a) assisting the client in understanding and embracing the reality of the connection between thoughts and feelings; (b) monitoring and recognizing specific forms of cognitive distortions and dysfunctional thinking; (c) testing the logic, validity, and adaptiveness of the identified cognitions; and (d) reformulating cognitions and underlying beliefs so that they result in a more functional, adaptive processing of life experiences.

ADDITIONAL RESOURCES

Bond, F. W., & Dryden, W. (2002). *Handbook of brief cognitive behavioral therapy*. Wiley.

DiGiuseppe, R. A., Doyle, K. A., Dryden, W., & Backx, W. (2013). *A practitioner's guide to rational-emotive behavior therapy*. Oxford University Press.

Greenberger, D., & Padesky, C. A. (2016). *Mind over mood: Change how you feel by changing the way you think* (2nd ed.). Guilford.

Parsons, R. (2019). *Cognitive therapy: Principles and practices applied in professional and personal life*. Cognella.

REFERENCES

Barlow, D. H. (1988). *Anxiety and its disorders: The nature and treatment of anxiety and panic*. Guilford.

Beck, A. T. (1970). *Depression: Causes and treatment*. University of Pennsylvania Press.

Beck, A. T. (1975). *Cognitive therapy and the emotional disorders*. International Universities Press.

Beck, A. T., Rush, A. J., Shaw, B. F., & Emery, G. (1979). *Cognitive therapy of depression*. Guilford.

Beck A. T., & Weishaar M. (1989). Cognitive therapy. In A. Freeman K. M. Simon L. E., Beutler, & H. Arkowitz (Eds.), *Comprehensive handbook of cognitive therapy* (pp. 21–36), Springer.

Beck, J. S. (2011). *Cognitive behavior therapy: Basics and beyond* (2nd ed.). Guilford.

Cape, J., Whittington, C., Buszewicz, M., Wallace, P., & Underwood, L. (2010). Brief psychological therapies for anxiety and depression in primary care: Meta-analysis and meta-regression. *BMC Medicine, 8*, 38. https://doi.org/10.1186/1741-7015-8-38

Clark, D. M (1986). A cognitive approach to panic. *Behaviour Research and Therapy, 24*(4), 461–470.

Cristea, I. A., Huibers, M. J., David, D., Hollon, S. D., Andersson, G., & Cuijpers, P. (2015). The effects of cognitive behavior therapy for adult depression on dysfunctional thinking: A meta-analysis. *Clinical Psychology Review, 42*, 62–71.

Cuijpers, P., Berking, M., Andersson, G., Quigley, L., Kleiboer, A., & Dobson, K. S. (2013). A meta-analysis of cognitive-behavioural therapy for adult depression, alone and in comparison with other treatments. *Canadian Journal of Psychiatry, 58*(7), 376–385.

Cully, J. A., & Teten, A. L. (2008). *A therapist's guide to brief cognitive therapy*. Department of Veterans Affairs, South Central MIRECC. https://athealth.com/wp-content/uploads/2014/03/Guide_CBT_03-14.pdf

David, D., Cotet, C., Matu, S., Mogoase, C., & Simona, S. (2017). 50 years of rational-emotive and cognitive-behavior therapy: A systematic review and meta-analysis. *Journal of Clinical Psychology, 74*(3), 303–318. https://doi.org/10.1002/jclp.22514

David, E., Lynn, S. J., & Ellis, A. (2010). *Rational and irrational beliefs: Research, theory and clinical practice*. Oxford University Press.

Ellis, A. (1957). Rational psychotherapy and individual psychology. *The Journal of Individual Psychology, 13*(1), 38–44.

Ellis, A. (1958). Rational psychotherapy. *Journal of General Psychology, 59*, 35–49.

Ellis, A. (1995). Changing rational-emotive therapy (RET) to rational emotive behavior therapy (REBT). *Journal of Rational-Emotive & Cognitive-Behavior Therapy, 13*(2), 85–89.

Ellis, A. (2002). *Overcoming resistance: A rational emotive behavior therapy integrated approach* (2nd ed.) Springer.

Ellis, A., & Dryden, S. W. (1997). *The practice of rational-emotive behavior therapy* (2nd ed.). Springer.

Folsom, T. D., Merz, A., Grant, J. E., Fatemi, N., Fatemi, S. A., & Fatemi, S. H. (2016). Profiles in history of neuroscience and psychiatry. In S. Fatemi & P. Clayton (Eds.), *The medical basis of psychiatry* (pp. 925–1007). Springer. https://doi.org/10.1007/978-1-4939-2528-5_42,

Freeman, A., Pretzer, J., Fleming, B., & Simon, K. M. (1990). Clinical assessment in cognitive therapy. In *Clinical applications of cognitive therapy* (pp. 27–47). Springer. https://doi.org/10.1007/978-1-4684-0007-6_2

Gaviţa, O. A., David, D., Bujoreanu, S., Tiba, A., & Ionuţiu, D. R. (2012). The efficacy of a short cognitive-behavioral parent program in the treatment of externalizing behavior disorders in Romanian foster care children:

Building parental emotion-regulation through unconditional self-and child-acceptance strategies. *Children and Youth Services Review, 34*(7), 1290–1297.

Haugland, B. S. M., Haaland, A. T., Valborg, B., Bjaastad, J. F., Hoffart, A., Rapee, R. M., Raknes, S., Himle, J. A., Husabø, E., & Wergeland, G. R. (2020). Effectiveness of brief and standard school-based cognitive-behavioral interventions for adolescents with anxiety: A randomized noninferiority study. *Journal of the American Academy of Child & Adolescent Psychiatry, 59*(4), 552–564. https://doi.org/10.1016/j.jaac.2019.12.003

Hoffman, S. G., Asnaani, A., Vonk, I. J. J., Sawyer, A. T., & Fang, A. (2012). The efficacy of cognitive behavioral therapy: A review of meta-analyses. *Cognitive Therapy and Research, 36*(5), 427–440. https://doi.org/10.1007/s10608-012-9476-1

Long, A. A. (2002). *Epictetus: A Stoic and Socratic guide to life.* Oxford University Press.

Maultsby, M. C., Jr. (1984). *Rational behavior therapy.* Prentice-Hall.

Oatley, K. (2004). *Emotions: A brief history.* Wiley.

Parsons, R. (2019). *Cognitive therapy: Principles and practices applied in professional and personal life.* Cognella.

Piaget, J. (1985). *The equilibration of cognitive structures: The central problem of intellectual development.* University of Chicago Press.

Rachman, S. (1997). The evolution of cognitive behaviour therapy. In D. Clark, C. G. Fairburn, & M. G. Gelder (Eds.), *Science and practice of cognitive behaviour therapy* (pp. 1–26). Oxford University Press.

Rokeach, M. (1968). A theory of organization and change within value-attitude systems. *Journal of Social Issues, 24*(1), 13–33.

Roth, A., & Fonagy, P. (2005). *What Works for Whom? A Critical Review of Psychotherapy Research (Second Edition).* Guillford Press.

Rush, A. J., Beck, A. T., Kovacs, M., & Hollon, S. D. (1977). Comparative efficacy of cognitive therapy and pharmacotherapy in the treatment of depressed outpatients. *Cognitive Therapy and Research, 1*, 17–38. https://doi.org/10.1007/BF01173502

Safran, J. D., Segal, Z. V., Shaw, B. F., & Vallis, T. M. (1990). Patient selection for short-term cognitive therapy. In J. D. Safran & Z. V. Segal (Eds.), *Interpersonal process in cognitive therapy* (pp. 226–247). Basic Books.

Vinograd, M., & Craske, M. G. (2020). History and theoretical underpinnings of exposure therapy. In T. S. Peris, E. A. Storch, & J. F. McGuire (Eds.), *Exposure therapy for children with anxiety and OCD* (pp. 3–20). Academic Press/Elsevier.

Wolpe, J. (1958). *Psychotherapy by reciprocal inhibition.* Stanford University Press.

Wolpe, J. (1976). *Themes and variations: A behavior therapy casebook.* Pergamon.

Wolpe, J. (1990). *The practice of behavior therapy* (4th ed.). Pergamon.

CHAPTER 6

Acceptance and Commitment Therapy

Why is it so hard to be human?

—Steven C. Hayes and Jason Lillis

In the introduction to their book, *Acceptance and Commitment Therapy*, Hayes and Lillis (2012) present a question that has energized the research and practice of acceptance and commitment therapy (ACT). While other therapies and therapists may have pondered a similar question, especially about a client within their care, ACT "has pursued a different possible answer: that a small set of normal and necessary psychological processes can give rise to human suffering or limit to human flourishing" (Haye & Lillis, 2021, p. 6).

ACT is a mindfulness-based behavioral approach, one that employs an eclectic mix of cognitive, experiential and value-guided behavioral interventions. ACT emphasizes active acceptance and mindfulness of one's experience as the foundation for taking actions guided by their values (Morris & Oliver, 2012).

ACT has been categorized as part of the "third wave" in the development of behavioral therapies, with the second wave being that of cognitive behavioral integration (Hayes, 2004). ACT approaches psychological problems in a dynamic context of social, verbal, emotional, and other direct sensory influences on behavior, with a particular emphasis on how suffering emerges predominantly within the uniquely human abilities in language and thought (Feliu-Soler et al., 2018).

As will be discussed, ACT is more than an adaptation of CBT; it presents as much more eclectic in approach and less traditionally Western in its perspective. The current chapter reviews the guiding principles and assumptions and the specific strategies and techniques employed by therapists embracing an acceptance and commitment model of therapy. Upon completion of this chapter, the reader will be able to do the following:

1. Describe how ACT differs from traditional cognitive therapy.
2. Explain what is meant by psychological flexibility and how it serves as a goal for those engaged in ACT.

3. Explain what is meant by each of the following and their role in ACT: comprehensive distancing, acceptance, diffusion, self as context, contact with the present moment, and values and commitment.

History and Contributors

The term *acceptance and commitment therapy* was not used until the early 1990s, first appearing in print in 1994 (Hayes & Wilson, 1994). Steve Hayes and his research associates are identified as giving form to ACT starting in the 1980s (Hayes & Lillis, 2012).

ACT can trace its roots to cognitive behavior therapy. However, it is neither a traditional behavioral nor cognitive model. ACT moved from what was felt to be a too constricted behavioral approach, one that focused on learning, experience, and behavior at the expense of value insights gleaned from humanistic and psychoanalytic approaches. ACT valued cognitive therapy's identification of the interaction of the cognitive, emotional, and behavioral domains. However, ACT emerged from a different set of assumptions and questioned a cognitive approach that emphasized an almost rigid stance that cognitions caused emotions and behavioral responses and, as such, should be the targets for change.

A New Look at "Distancing"

While on the surface appearing to be much in line with cognitive models, Hayes (1989) was finding that it was not the presence of particular cognitions that was problematic, but rather the function of these experiences (Morris & Oliver, 2012). One of the critical elements in cognitive therapy was the use of cognitive distancing, a metacognitive process of "view[ing] one's thoughts (or beliefs) as constructions of 'reality' rather than as reality itself" (Alford & Beck, 1997, p. 142). The intent was not only to observe one's thoughts unfold without compliance or attachment, taking what was helpful and leaving the rest to be shaped by experience, but to change those as needed (Hayes & Lillis, 2012).

ACT presented a new look a cognition, focusing on the context and function of psychological events, such as thoughts, sensations, or emotions, rather than primarily targeting the content, validity, intensity, or frequency of such events. The thesis was that many psychological problems were a result, not directly due to these psychological events, but rather an individual's attempt to control and eliminate them.

Comprehensive Distancing

The process of cognitive distancing was seen as valuable in the ACT model. However, the emphasis in ACT shifted away from changing the content of thought to increasing awareness of and relations to thoughts. It was felt that verbal disputation techniques might interfere with psychological distance (Robertson, 2013).

To distinguish this emphasis, the term *comprehensive distancing* was introduced. The position taken was that even distancing, if engaged in to control the problem, would become the source of continued emotional distress. As such, distancing should include detaching from such control (Hayes, 1987; Hayes & Melancon, 1989). Methods that emerged from this concept were employed to help clients create more distance from their thoughts, help them feel their emotions more deeply, and learn from them.

Renaming ACT

While the model that was unfolding had initially been linked to the label comprehensive distancing, it appeared that the possible connotation of promoting disassociation led to the use of other titles such as "contextual therapy" (Zettle & Rains, 1989). According to Zettle (2011), the first documented use of the term *acceptance and commitment therapy* was in a paper by Wilson, Khorakiwala, and Hayes (1991).

ACT gained significant attention upon Hayes et al. (1996) publication of a treatment manual. However, its acceptance within the scientific community began with a series of addresses presented by Steven Hayes, particularly one at the International Congress of Cognitive Therapy in Catania, Italy, in 2000 (Morris & Oliver, 2012) and with the publication of the first randomized controlled trial of ACT that demonstrated the effectiveness of this approach (Bond & Bunce, 2000). By 2011 ACT was listed by Division 12 (Society of Clinical Psychology) of the American Psychological Association and by the National Registry of Evidence-Based Programs and practices maintained by the U.S. Substance Abuse and Mental Health Services Administration as an evidence-based treatment.

Perspective

It is intuitively appealing to assume that all psychotherapy shares a desire to assist clients in ridding themselves of emotional distress and presenting complaints, concerns, and symptoms. Contrary to this perspective, therapists employing an acceptance and commitment model to guide their practice decisions do not prioritize symptom reduction as a goal to therapy.

The perspective taken is that pain, distress, and disappointment are inevitable. The goal is not to avoid these conditions but instead productively adapt to these challenges. Therapists employing ACT do not see presenting concerns or symptoms as pathological and thus needing to be removed. The ACT approach posits that psychological suffering is due to a lack of behavioral flexibility and effectiveness, which emerges from experiential avoidance, cognitive entanglement, difficulty with perspective taking, loss of contact with the present, and failure to take needed behavioral steps in accord with core values (Hayes et al., 2011).

The ACT therapist is interested in what the client wants their life to be about (values). They are interested in understanding what clients are currently doing and the environments in which they occur. The ACT therapist is particularly interested in understanding the purpose of actions, specifically if they are in service of escape or avoidance, rather than as an approach guided by values. The goal of ACT is to facilitate the client's increased engagement in meaningful life events, even while experiencing negative thoughts and emotions. This is accomplished by cultivating psychological flexibility.

Psychological flexibility is "the process of contacting the present moment fully as a conscious human being and persisting or changing behavior in the service of chose values" (Hayes & Lillis, 2012, p. 42). Psychological flexibility is achieved through a committed pursuit of value life areas and directions and resisting the desire to escape or avoid troubling experiences, emotions, and thoughts.

While having solid roots in behavioral and cognitive theory, ACT is a model that finds integration of that which is empirical and experiential, often presenting as more existential and humanistic than behavioral.

Assumptions and Principles Guiding Practice

ACT is effective even when administered in a time-limited context and via various delivery methods, including in 1-day workshops (Dindo, 2015), online and smartphone interventions (Bricker et al., 2013), and 20-minute sessions integrated into primary care visits (Robinson & Strosahl, 2009). Clinicians employing ACT adhere to the following assumptions and principles to guide their practice decisions.

Suffering as Normal

In contrast to most Western psychology, ACT does not assume that humans, by their very nature, are psychologically healthy and that psychological problems are reflections of unusual pathological processes. The ACT model assumes that emotional pain is normal for human beings (Morris & Oliver, 2012). ACT is not about getting rid of bad feelings or getting over old trauma. Instead, it is about creating a rich, full, and meaningful life (Strosahl et al., 1998).

Language: Roots of Psychological Suffering

While emotional and psychological distress is seen as a normal part of the human condition, ACT also assumes that our capacity for language, especially the private language of cognition, can amplify our pain and lead to suffering. Private language (i.e., cognitions) can create conditions in which the individual dwells on and re-experiences painful events from the past, create anxieties about imaged futures, and create rules that can be destructive and life constricting. ACT operates from the assumption that clinical problems are contextually determined, with a significant context being language (Hayes & Batten, 2000).

Experiential Avoidance

ACT posits that language, while certainly a resource that has benefited humans, can create psychological suffering by setting the stage for engaging in a process called experiential avoidance. The concept is that when confronted with something threatening, humans engage in problem solving, which often results in avoiding such dangerous experiences. While this may be valuable when applied to external, real-world threats, ACT holds that when applied to our interior world of thoughts, memories, feelings, and urges, efforts to avoid or escape these experiences can create additional suffering rather than reducing it. The example often employed is addiction, where the addictive behavior, which was often employed to avoid undesirable thoughts or feelings, now becomes a self-sustaining problem.

Functional Contextualism and Workability

ACT employs functional contextualism, which views human psychological problems due to psychological inflexibility fostered by cognitive fusion and experiential avoidance. ACT emphasizes attempting to understand how the individual's actions, thoughts, and feelings are "working" as they interact in and with historically and situationally defined contexts. This pragmatic stance of focusing on that which is or is not successful is vital in the ACT model. Therapists employing ACT attempt to help clients develop a greater awareness of their behaviors, noting whether those behaviors are working to effectively solve the problem and move them toward valued ends (Hayes et al., 1999).

Principles in Action

ACT views psychological challenges as the result of an individual's psychological inflexibility and their continuing use of unworkable solutions (Kashdan & Rottenberg, 2010). Therapists engaging in acceptance and commitment therapy use acceptance and mindfulness processes along with commitment and behavior change processes to produce greater psychological flexibility (Hayes et al., 2013). ACT helps clients experience a state of openness that allows them to be fully present in their experiences and make choices based on their values.

The Therapeutic Relationship

With a goal of increasing client psychological flexibility, the central focus of ACT, the therapist will establish a therapeutic relationship that "models, instigates, and reinforces client psychological flexibility" (Luoma et al., 2007, p. 223). As a reflection of the therapist's psychological flexibility, the therapist employing ACT places the client's values at the center of the therapy, making no preconceived rules or assumptions about what these values need to be or how acting in concert with them may look (Morris & Oliver, 2012). The perspective is that the therapist needs to help the client to flexibly work toward chosen values and not adhere to or follow imposed external rules.

The core processes of ACT (see Table 6.1) target fostering psychological flexibility. While each is a focal point for ACT, these processes are not addressed in a particular sequence. Instead, the specific focus for any session reflects the client's uniqueness, the therapist, and their relationship. The processes, each of which are achieved through the therapeutic use of specific methodology and strategies, are acceptance, diffusion, self as context, contact with the present moment, and values (Luoma et al., 2007).

TABLE 6.1 CENTRAL ACT PROCESSES

Process	Definition
Acceptance	The active and aware embrace of private events that are occasioned by our history, without unnecessary attempts to change their frequency or form, especially when doing so would cause psychological harm
Diffusion	The process of creating nonliteral contexts in which language can be seen as an active, ongoing relational process that is historical in nature and present in the current context
Self as context	A continuous and secure "I" from which events are experienced but is also distinct from those events
Contact present moment	Ongoing, nonjudgmental contact with psychological and environmental events as they occur
Values	Verbally constructed, global, desired, and chosen life directions
Committed action	Step-by-step process of acting to create a whole life, a life of integrity, true to one's deepest wishes and longings

Source: Morris, E., & Oliver, J. E. (2012, p. 76). Acceptance and commitment therapy. In W. Dryden (Ed.) Cognitive behaviour therapies (pp. 70–92). SAGE.

Acceptance

Acceptance refers to a process of letting go of unnecessary or unworkable struggles with unwanted psychological content such as distressing thoughts and emotions. For clients who have been engaged in experiential avoidance, attempts to control private experiences, such as unwanted thoughts and feelings, acceptance can be challenging. In the initial session, a therapist may invite the client to not only share the various strategies employed in an attempt to resolve their issue but follow up this discussion with a second question: "And so how has that worked for you?" (Hayes & Lillis, 2012, p. 25). Using paraphrasing and summarizing, the therapist helps clients realize that their strategies have not worked in the long term and, in fact, have often exacerbated the problem. The goal is not to create a sense of doom or hopelessness but to help clients allow for unpleasant feelings, sensations, memories, and other experiences. ACT assists clients to allow these private experiences to come and then go without attempting to control or escape them. While this may be contrary to the impulse to stop or avoid psychological pain and discomfort, acceptance does not mean resignation; it means allowing for the reality of distress and discomfort. ACT invites clients to experience these as temporary and transient experiences that dissipate on their own.

Therapists employing ACT will often call on metaphors as a technique for assisting clients to gain better insight into the unworkable nature of their efforts to exert control over their distress (see Table 6.2).

Many metaphors have been developed (e.g., Hayes & Lillis, 2012; Hayes et al., 1999; Stoddard & Afari, 2014). One such metaphor is the tug-of-war (Hayes & Lillis, 2012). The metaphor is used to highlight the counterproductive nature of such a battle for control. The metaphor invites the client to imagine that they are in a tug-of-war with a monster, which is made up of all their

TABLE 6.2 SAMPLE OF METAPHORS USED IN ACT

Drivers versus Passengers	The metaphor is used to help clients understand that when our negative emotions are in the driver's seat they can be destructive, taking us in directions we do not wish to go. While they may be unpleasant passengers, not allowing them to drive is key to reducing their impact on a person's life and choices. As such, the client needs to take up the driver's seat, even if and perhaps most notably when the negative emotionally object.
Beach ball underwater	Central to ACT is encouraging clients to resist attempting to stop or control difficult thoughts and feelings. The metaphor of trying to push a beach ball underwater helps the client understand how difficult and exhausting this can be and how ineffective it will be. Yes, there may be a momentary sense of relief, even satisfaction, as you submerge that ball (or, more accurately, the thoughts and feelings), but in short order, it (they) will reemerge.
Quicksand	Similar to the beach ball metaphor, the futility and dysfunctionality of attempting to control emotions can be illustrated with a metaphor of quicksand. The more one struggles to free themself, the more stuck they become in quicksand. While it may be counterintuitive, it is in relaxing and moving slowly and deliberately that one can free themselves from quicksand. The same is true for freeing oneself from difficult thoughts and feelings.
Finger trap	The futility of attempting to control emotions can also be illustrated with the Chinese finger trap game metaphor. The game involves placing one finger in a woven straw tube. If you attempt to escape by pulling your fingers away from the tube, the straw stretches and narrows and thus tightens on your fingers. The harder you pull, the narrower the tube and the more difficult it is to remove your fingers. Again, the solution is somewhat counterintuitive: Push your finger into the tube closer together and slide the tube off them with your thumb. The message is, the more you fight to control, the less control and the fewer options you have.

negative thoughts and things they have been attempting to avoid. As the metaphor goes, there is a bottomless ravine separating the client and the monster. The more the client tugs on the rope, the greater the monster tugs, and the result is that the client is being pulled closer and closer to the edge. The conclusion is that the best strategy is to surrender and drop the rope rather than continue this attempt to win.

Diffusion

Clients will often express negative thoughts about themselves, thoughts such as "I'm a loser," "I am a horrible person," or "I am totally incompetent." ACT posits that clients often make such thoughts central to their life, finding more supportive evidence throughout their days and spending more time emersed in that evaluation. When this occurs, the client typically takes the thought literally. When this happens, a client attaches to their beliefs to the degree that their actions are guided by the literal content of their thoughts rather than by direct experience. That is, because I think I am a loser, it must be true, regardless of the real-world evidence to the contrary. This, according to ACT, is a state of cognitive fusion and results in inflexibility (Bach & Moran, 2008).

With diffusion, clients are invited to notice the difference between their evaluation and judgment about a situation versus their actual experience. Therapists may use a statement such as "Notice when your mind says ..." as a way of defusing self from thought. Diffusion allows clients to perceive thoughts, images, memories, and other cognitions as simply neural processes instead of the threatening events, facts, and truths they appear to be. One often employed strategy is the thoughts on clouds exercise. In this exercise, the therapist will invite the client to relax, close their eyes, and begin to envision a beautiful, calming pastoral setting. The client will be invited to see themselves as lying down and looking at the sky and clouds moving above. As that image becomes clear, the therapist will ask the client to place a troublesome thought, belief, or memory on the cloud and watch it as it goes by. In processing the experience with the client, the therapist wants to discuss the impact of watching one's thoughts versus being caught up in them (Hayes & Lillis, 2012). Hayes and Lillis (2012) discuss five cognitive fusion processes and techniques designed to assist clients with diffusion. There are numerous strategies and techniques that can be employed to assist clients to defuse or unhook their minds (e.g., Evans, 2019). Exercise 6.1 invites the reader to engage in the process of cognitive diffusion.

ACT helps clients observe their thoughts in a detached way instead of getting involved in them. A technique as simple as inviting the client to repeat the thought over and over, helps to increase the client's awareness of their control of their thoughts. This insight allows for clients to see their thoughts as their creation, not their master.

Self as Context

Over one's lifetime, it is possible to develop a sense of self made up of memories, beliefs, and experiences. For example, the individual who perhaps has had a history of struggling in school or social relationships may conceive of themselves as "messed up." If such a sense of self takes

EXERCISE 6.1

Defusion

Directions:

Step 1: Remember a recent event where you engaged in a negative self-judgment and thoughts such as "I'm such a screw up" or "I'm so (something negative)." Try to reclaim the experience and the thought. Get in touch with how that thought affects you even at this moment.

Step 2: In an attempt to distance yourself and defuse, return to the negative judgmental thought about yourself, but this time start your reflection with an additional thought: "I am now re-creating the thought that I am ..." (finish with your negative judgment).

Reflection: Did the additional phrase provide distance from the original thought and, as such, reduce any negative feelings? If so, did defusing help not change the original thought, but rather the power or relationship that thought had to the here and now, transforming it from a reality to simply words and thoughts?

---

root, it can result in choices and behaviors that maintain a sense of consistency with that identity, behaviors that are destructive.

ACT assists clients to reframe this sense of self as a continuity of consciousness that is unchanging, ever present, and impervious to harm, not defined by such transient experiences. Yes, each individual has experienced and engaged in behaviors and made decisions that have worked and some that have not, but each of these events and experiences unfolded from a base of self and was not nor is not "the self." ACT encourages clients to use the observing part of their mind to notice the thoughts that come and go, accessing a transcendent sense of self. Thoughts such as "I am," rigidly defining the individual as an experience or a judgment, keep them stuck in unhelpful processes.

ACT helps individuals experience the reality that they are not their thoughts, feelings, images, memories, or roles, as these are all constantly changing and peripheral aspects of the individual's essence. One of the techniques used to illustrate this distinction is the use of the chessboard metaphor (Hayes et al., 1999). In this technique, the client is asked to think of their emotions or thoughts as pieces on a chessboard. In the metaphor, the client's positive thoughts and good experiences are in a battle against bad experiences. The client is invited to notice that the board remains consistent and stable, regardless of what takes place with the pieces. The message is that their self is the board; their experiences are the moving, transient pieces; and it is helpful to experience but not cling to neither the good or the bad, but the board.

Contact With Present Moment: Mindfulness

Clients often present as if stuck or at least preoccupied with thoughts about the past or future. ACT engages the client in the present moment. Therapists employing ACT as an operative model teach mindfulness or "present moment non-judgmental awareness" (Hayes & Lillis, 2012, p .96) to assist clients in becoming more fully aware of their here-and-now experiences, in terms of where they are and what they are doing and their thoughts and feelings. This is encouraged even when the experiences are difficult or even painful.

The rationale is that one cannot engage in diffusion or acceptance if unaware of what they are experiencing. The goal is to focus on and fully engage in the moment and what they are doing and experiencing at that moment. A key message communicated is that life in the present moment is already occurring and that problems do not need to be fixed before a valued life can be lived (Strosahl et al., 2004).

Such a focus on the moment can be encouraged in therapy at a point where a client becomes upset. Should the client begin to experience anxiety or anger, for example, in session the therapist might encourage the client to sit with the feeling, even investigate the specific sensations rather than attempt to control or escape them. Homework and mindfulness practice outside of the formal session may also be encouraged.

Values

Personal values are another central concept in ACT. ACT assists clients in clarifying the type of person they want to be by identifying that which is significant and meaningful to them and what they want to stand for in life. Inviting the client to consider their epithet or describe a series of testimonials they hope could be made on their 90th birthday will provide insight into that which is vital to the client, revealing core values.

The focus on values reflects the belief that one is most satisfied when acting in accordance with their values. Having clients identify these core values and assess the degree to which their choices and actions align with them is central to ACT.

Therapists employing ACT may engage the client in value clarification, attempting to help them elucidate what is important to them in their life. One of the tasks is to help clients distinguish values from goals. While an individual may identify having a good job or becoming financially secure as values, these are more likely goals that reflect underlying values. ACT therapists will help the client dig down to identify the value, which in this case may be "to be of value" or "to be secure." Rather than narrowly focusing on goals, identifying the underlying values opens multiple pathways to living a valued life. The therapist may ask clients questions that help them consider what is important to them and what actions they want to take to live this valued life.

Committed Action

With clarity about that which is personally valued, clients engaged in ACT will be supported in their efforts to follow through with decisions and actions that are in accordance with these values. Therapists will help clients set goals guided by values and then take effective action to achieve these goals. The therapist will also help the client embrace the reality that they may experience obstacles in moving forward, but these are natural and not to be avoided. Hayes et al. (1999) offer a metaphor, the swamp, to help in this situation:

> Suppose you are beginning a journey to a beautiful mountain you can see in the distance. No sooner do you start the hike that you walk right into a swamp that extends as far as you can see in all directions. You say to yourself, 'Gee, I didn't realize that I was going to have to go through a swamp. It's all smelly, and the mud is all mushy in my shoes. It's hard to lift my feet out of the muck and put them forward. I'm wet and tired. Why didn't anyone tell me about this swamp?'
>
> When that happens, you have a choice: abandon the journey or enter the swamp. We enter the swamp, not because we want to get muddy, but because it stands between us and where we are going. (p. 248)

The metaphor highlights the reality that, sometimes, action in line with values can introduce short-term pain and discomfort while providing long-term congruency with a life that is desired and has meaning (see Case Illustration 6.1).

CASE ILLUSTRATION 6.1

This Is Hard and Scary

The following exchange occurred at the fourth session between Dr. Z. and Eleanor. Eleanor originally came to therapy feeling anxiety as a result of now being an empty nester. Eleanor's youngest child (youngest of three), having graduated from law school, moved across the country to take a job with a prestigious law firm. With all her children now scattered throughout the United States, Eleanor was experiencing, by her definition, an "existential crisis." She did not know what to do or what value she had to offer, no longer being able to be the mother she has always been.

Eleanor: Dr. Z., you know it is funny that the way I have labeled myself as "mother" has blinded me to my abilities and the various ways I can continue to use those abilities in ways that I value.

Dr. Z.: Eleanor, it sounds like you have been doing quite a bit of work on clarifying your values and detaching the labels from you as a person. That is wonderful. Can you share what you may be seeing as your future?

Eleanor: Well, I did a little work (smiling) and went online to look into opportunities to volunteer in a hospital or preschool setting working with children who may need a little TLC and support. It was a bit discouraging at first.

(Continued)

CASE ILLUSTRATION 6.1 (*Continued*)

Dr. Z: Discouraging?

Eleanor: Well, most of the openings that I saw required you to have some formal training and at least an associate degree.

Dr. Z: Okay, so?

Eleanor: Well, I have not been in school for over 35 years.

Dr. Z: Okay, so?

Eleanor: The thought of going to school is terrifying. I mean, this will be hard.

Dr. Z: Let's stop for a second and consider what you are saying and perhaps thinking (pauses). Eleanor, can you share your thoughts or the images you have when you think about going back to school?

Eleanor: (sitting quietly at the moment) The first thing I think of is, "I am too old." (smiles) Then I think, "Wow, this will take a lot of time and energy."

Dr. Z: Okay. So you label yourself as "too old." Might I ask too old for what? Is there some age maximum for getting into our community college?

Eleanor: (smiling) No! It is just me being a little silly and inflexible. Okay, so I am 58 years old. That is a fact. Being too old is my judgment, an opinion—not a fact.

Dr. Z: That is right on. So, how might you test out that opinion?

Eleanor: (again, smiling) Give it a try?

Dr. Z: Again, right on.

Eleanor: But it is going to take time and effort. I just don't know.

Dr. Z: You don't know? What is it you don't know? Is it that you don't know if this is something you want? Or is this the way you want to use your time and effort?

Eleanor: Oh, I do want it. I'm excited about it. It is just going to require some adjustments in my life and my routines, and that may be hard.

Dr. Z: Remember the metaphor of the swamp? It looks like it applies here. I understand that there may be an opportunity cost to going to school. You will most likely have to make some adjustments to your life and your routines. So? I guess the decision to be made is, do you want to wade through that muck or abandon this phase of your journey? I guess the thing that you need to decide is which choice serves your life values and goals.

Eleanor: (broad smile) One small sloshing step at a time!

Dr. Z: Fantastic. Let's talk about what those steps may look like.

Supportive Research

The turn of the century introduced numerous studies supporting the effectiveness of ACT with varied populations and a wide range of presenting issues. For example, randomized controlled trials have demonstrated the effectiveness of ACT depression (Corrigan, 2001), substance abuse (Hayes et al., 2004), borderline personality disorder (Gratz & Gunderson, 2006) and psychosis (Bach & Hayes, 2002; Gaudiano & Herbert, 2006). Meta-analyses of outcome studies (e.g., Dimidjian, 2016; Öst, 2008; Powers et al., 2009) provide evidence that ACT is significantly better than waitlist controls or treatment as usual.

Suitability

With its focus on promoting psychological flexibility, ACT is felt suitable for addressing any domain of life with regard to unwanted internal experiences such as thoughts, feelings, and physical sensations. Supporters of this approach feel that ACT has broad applicability, going beyond any single mental or physical health condition, and thus offering a unified model of behavioral change suitable for a variety of clinical (e.g., depression, anxiety, OCD, substance disorders) and nonclinical issues (e.g., stress, life transitions, grief, relational issues).

KEYSTONES

- ACT is a mindfulness-based behavioral approach, one that employs an eclectic mix of cognitive, experiential, and value-guided behavioral interventions.
- Steve Hayes and his research associates are identified as giving form to ACT starting in the 1980s.
- ACT presented a new look at cognition, focusing on the context and function of psychological events, such as thoughts, sensations, or emotions, rather than primarily targeting the content, validity, intensity, or frequency of such events.
- The perspective taken is that pain, distress, and disappointment are inevitable. The goal is not to avoid these conditions but instead productively adapt to these challenges.
- ACT posits that psychological suffering is due to a lack of behavioral flexibility and effectiveness, which emerges from experiential avoidance, cognitive entanglement, difficulty with perspective taking, loss of contact with the present, and failure to take needed behavioral steps in accordance with core values.
- The goal of ACT is to facilitate the client's increased engagement in meaningful life events, even while experiencing negative thoughts and emotions. This is accomplished by cultivating psychological flexibility.
- The core processes of ACT, each of which are achieved through the therapeutic use of specific methodology and strategies, are acceptance, diffusion, self as context, contact with the present moment, and values.
- Supporters of this approach feel that ACT has broad applicability, going beyond any single mental or physical health condition, and thus offering a unified model of behavioral change

suitable for a variety of clinical (e.g., depression, anxiety, OCD, substance disorders) and nonclinical issues (e.g., stress, life transitions, grief, relational issues).
- Meta-analyses of outcome studies (e.g., Dimidjian, 2016; Öst, 2008; Powers et al., 2009) provide evidence that ACT is significantly better than waitlist controls or treatment as usual.

ADDITIONAL RESOURCES

Gordon, T., & Borushok, J. (2017). *The ACT approach*. PESI Publishing & Media.

Harris, R. (2019). *ATC made simple* (2nd ed.). New Harbinger.

Hayes. S. C., & Lillis, J. (2012). *Acceptance and commitment therapy*. American Psychological Association.

Luoma, J. B., Hayes, S. C., & Walser, R. D. (2007) *Learning ACT: An acceptance and commitment therapy skills-training manual for therapists*. New Harbinger.

Morris, E., & Oliver, J. E. (2012). Acceptance and commitment therapy. In W. Dryden (Ed.) *Cognitive behaviour therapies* (pp. 70–92). SAGE.

REFERENCES

Alford, B. A., & Beck, A. T. (1997). *The integrative power of cognitive therapy*. Guilford.

Bach, P., & Hayes, S. C. (2002). The use of acceptance and commitment therapy to prevent the rehospitalization of psychotic patients: A randomized controlled trial. *Journal of Consulting and Clinical Psychology, 70*, 1129–1139.

Bach, P. A. P., & Moran, D. J. (2008). *ACT in practice: Case conceptualization in acceptance and commitment therapy*. New Harbinger.

Bond, F. W., & Bunce, D. (2000). Mediators of change in emotion-focused and problem-focused worksite stress management interventions. *Journal of Occupational Health Psychology, 5*, 156–163.

Bricker, J., Wyszynski, C., Comstock, B., & Heffner, J. L. (2013). Pilot randomized controlled trial of web-based acceptance and commitment therapy for smoking cessation. *Nicotine & Tobacco Research, 15*(10), 1756–1764. https://doi.org/10.1093/ntr/ntt056

Corrigan, P. (2001). Getting ahead of the data: A threat to some behavior therapies. *The Behavior Therapist, 24*, 189–193.

Dimidjian, S., Arch, J. J., Schneider, R. L., Desormeau, P., Felder, J. N., & Segal, Z.V. (2016). Considering meta-analysis, meaning, and metaphor: A systematic review and critical examination of "third wave" cognitive and behavioral therapies. *Behavior Therapy, 47*, 886–905. https://doi.org/10.1016/j.beth.2016.07.002

Dindo, L. (2015). One-day acceptance and commitment training workshops in medical populations. *Current Opinion in Psychology, 2*, 38–42. https://doi.org/10.1016/j.copsyc.2015.01.018

Evans, J. (2019, May 3). *Ten diffusion tips for unhooking your mind.* Philosophy for Life. https://www.philosophyforlife.org/blog/ten-defusion-techniques-for-unhooking-your-mind

Feliu-Soler, A., Montesinos, F., Gutiérrez-Martínez, O., Scott, W., McCracken, L .M., & Luciano, J. V. (2018). Current status of acceptance and commitment therapy for chronic pain: a narrative review. *Journal of Pain Research, 11,* 2145–2159. https://doi.org/10.2147/JPR.S144631

Gaudiano, B., & Herbert, J. D. (2006). Acute treatment of inpatients with psychotic symptoms using acceptance and commitment therapy: Pilot results. *Behaviour Research and Therapy, 44,* 415–437.

Gratz, K. L., & Gunderson, J. G. (2006). Preliminary data on an acceptance-based emotion regulation group intervention for deliberate self-harm among women with borderline personality disorder. *Behavior Therapy, 37,* 25–35.

Hayes, S. C. (1989). *Rule-governed behavior: Cognition, contingencies and instructional control.* Plenum.

Hayes, S. C. (2004). Acceptance and commitment therapy, relational frame theory and the third wave of behavioral and cognitive therapies, *Behavior Therapy, 35*(4), 639–665.

Hayes, S. C., & Batten, S. (2000). A primer of acceptance and commitment therapy, *European Psychotherapy, 1,* 2–9.

Hayes. S. C., & Lillis, J. (2012). *Acceptance and commitment therapy.* American Psychological Association.

Hayes, S. C., Livein, M. E., Plumb-Vilardaga, J., Villatte, J. L., & Pistorello, J. (2013). Acceptance and commitment therapy and contextual behavioral science: Examining the progress of a distinctive model of behavioral and cognitive therapy. *Behavior Therapy, 44*(2), 180–198. https://doi.org/10.1016/j.beth.2009.08.002

Hayes, S. C., & Melancon, S. M. (1989). Comprehensive distancing, paradox, and the treatment of emotional avoidance. In M. Ascher. (Ed.), *Paradoxical procedures in psychotherapy* (pp. 184–218). Guilford.

Hayes, S. C., Strosahl, K. D., & Wilson, K. G. (1999). *Acceptance and commitment therapy. An experiential approach to behavior change.* Guilford.

Hayes, S. C., Strosahl, K. D., & Wilson, K. G. (2011). *Acceptance and commitment therapy: The process and practice of mindful change* (2nd ed.). Guilford.

Hayes, S. C., Villatte, M., Levin, M., & Hildebrandt, M. (2011). Open, aware, and active: Contextual approaches as an emerging trend in the behavioral and cognitive therapies. *Annual Review of Clinical Psychology, 7,* 141–168. https://doi.org/10.1146/annurev-clipsy-032210-104449

Hayes, S. C., & Wilson, K. G. (1994). Acceptance and commitment therapy: Altering the verbal support for experiential avoidance. *The Behavior Analyst, 17,* 289–303.

Hayes, S. C., Wilson, K. G., Gifford, E. V., Bissett, R., Piasecki, M., Batten, S. V., Byrd, M., & Gregg, J. (2004). A randomized controlled trial of twelve-step facilitation and acceptance and commitment therapy with polysubstance abusing methadone-maintained opiate addicts. *Behavior Therapy, 35,* 667–688.

Hayes, S. C., Wilson, K. G., Gifford, E. V., Follette, V. M., & Strosahl, K. (1996). Experiential avoidance and behavioral disorders: A functional dimensional approach to diagnosis and treatment. *Journal of Consulting and Clinical Psychology, 64*(6), 1152–1168.

Kashdan, T. B., & Rottenberg, J. (2010). Psychological flexibility as a fundamental aspect of health. *Clinical Psychology Review, 30*(7), 865–878. https://doi.org/10.1016/j.cpr.2010.03.001

Luoma, J. B., Hayes, S. C., & Walser, R. D. (2007) *Learning ACT: An acceptance and commitment therapy skills-training manual for therapists.* New Harbinger.

Morris, E., & Oliver, J. E. (2012). Acceptance and commitment therapy. In W. Dryden (Ed.) *Cognitive behaviour therapies* (pp. 70–92). SAGE.

Öst, L. (2008). Efficacy of the third wave of behavioral therapies: A systematic review and meta-analysis. *Behaviour Research and Therapy, 46,* 296–321.

Powers, M. B., Vörding, M., & Emmelkamp, P. M. G. (2009). Acceptance and commitment therapy: A meta-analytic review. *Psychotherapy and Psychosomatics, 8,* 73–80.

Robertson, D. (2013). *Cognitive distancing in Stoicism.* https://donaldrobertson.name/2013/01/18/cognitive-distancing-in-stoicism/

Robinson, P. J., & Strosahl, K. D. (2009). Behavioral health consultation and primary care: Lessons learned. *Journal of Clinical Psychology in Medical Settings, 16*(1), 58–71. https://doi:.org/10.1007/s10880-009-9145-z

Stoddard, J. A., & Afari, N. (2014). *The big book of ACT metaphors: A practitioner's guide to experiential exercises and metaphors in acceptance and commitment therapy.* New Harbinger.

Strosahl, K., Hayes, S. C., Wilson, K. G., & Gifford, E. V. (2004). An ACT primer: Core therapy processes, intervention strategies and therapist competencies. In S. C. Hayes & K. Strosahl (Eds.), *A practical guide to acceptance and commitment therapy* (pp. 31–58). Springer.

Strosahl, K. D., Hayes, S. C., Bergan, J., & Romano, P. (1998). Does field based training in behavior therapy improve clinical effectiveness? Evidence from the Acceptance and Commitment Therapy training project. *Behavior Therapy, 29,* 35–64.

Wilson, K. G., Khorakiwala, D., & Hayes, S. C. (1991, May). *Change in acceptance and commitment therapy* [Paper presentation]. Meeting of the Association for Behavior Analysis, Atlanta, GA.

Zettle, R. D. (2011). The evolution of a contextual approach to therapy: From comprehensive distancing to ACT. *International Journal of Behavioral Consultation and Therapy, 7*(1), 76–82. http://dx.doi.org/10.1037/h0100929

Zettle, R. D., & Rains, J. C. (1989). Group cognitive and contextual therapies in treatment of depression. *Journal of Clinical Psychology, 45,* 436–445.

CHAPTER 7

Dialectical Behavioral Therapy

Wisdom lies neither in fixity nor in change, but in the dialectic between the two.

—Octavio Paz

Clinicians are often presented with clients who are "stuck" in fixity, exhibiting intensely emotional and rigid reactions to everyday situations. This was the experience of Marsha Linehan (1993) as she worked with individuals diagnosed with borderline personality disorders and those who were multi-problematic and suicidal. It was her work attempting to assist in moving her clients to the dialectic between fixity (acceptance) and change that took form as dialectical behavioral therapy (DBT).

DBT is an adaptation of cognitive and behavioral therapies. DBT integrates cognitive behavioral strategies for reality testing and emotion regulation, emphasizing that life is not divided into opposing categories and thus assists clients in avoiding black-and-white thinking (Bass et al., 2014). Central to DBT is the engagement with clients to develop the ability to integrate what they perceive as opposing ideas, particularly the value of nonchange, and acceptance while embracing the desire to change. It is a process that allows clients to be more self-accepting and more adaptable in navigating life.

The current chapter reviews the history and evolution of DBT and its underlying assumptions, basic tenets, and therapeutic processes. Upon completion of this chapter, the reader will be able to do the following:

1. Describe what is meant by dialectics.
2. Describe the dialectics that are central to DBT.
3. Explain the five functions addressed in the standard, comprehensive program of DBT treatment.
4. Describe the stages of the standard, comprehensive program of DBT.

History and Contributors

Marsha Linehan specialized in treating women diagnosed with borderline personality disorders and who engaged in chronic suicidality and self-injury. These were clients who were typically thought of as difficult, if not impossible, to treat. According to Linehan and Wilks (2015), DBT was a trial-and-error clinical effort based on the application of behavioral principles (Bandura, 1969) and social learning theory (Staats & Staats, 1963) to suicidal behaviors (Linehan, 1981).

Linehan's efforts initially employed the CBT model. Her experience was less than successful. Linehan (1993) noted that the somewhat confrontational nature of CBT left her clients feeling misunderstood, often angry and disengaging from therapy. In response, Linehan (1993) moved to a more humanistic and acceptance-based mindfulness approach. This shift also proved ultimately ineffective.

Her experience with these different strategies ultimately led her to incorporate both models in an approach that reflected a movement between acceptance and change (Vaughn, 2021). According to Linehan and Wilks (2015), "Integrating Zen and contemplative practices into behavioral therapy also created challenges" (p. 99).

Linehan (1993) found a basis for her balanced approach in the dialectical philosophies of early Greeks (Pederson, 2015). From a dialectical perspective, it is assumed the following:

1. Everything, even that which seems opposite and opposing, shares a connection.
2. Change is constantly occurring.
3. Truth is found by integrating supposedly opposing ideas.

DBT came to rest on a foundation of dialectical philosophy, whereby therapists strive to continually balance and synthesize acceptance and change-oriented strategies (Chapman, 2006). It is the coming together, often with opposite perspectives on what is healthy and desirable, which through therapeutic dialogue can result in healthier ideas and more adaptable behavior. This integration and balancing of what may appear to be opposite perspectives and even approaches is the essence of DBT.

Linehan's (1993) use of DBT produced empirical support for its value in treating those diagnosed with borderline personality disorders. Her model became standardized and included weekly individual therapy sessions (approximately 1 hour), a weekly group skills training session (approximately 1.5–2.5 hours), and a therapist consultation team meeting (approximately 1–2 hours).

Perspective: Acceptance and Change

While DBT has roots in CBT, it is an eclectic approach that values and integrates much from the humanistic approaches to therapy (Marra, 2005). DBT combines CBT with the concepts of distress tolerance (learning to bear pain skillfully), radical acceptance (a Buddhist concept about being willing to participate with life as it is) and mindful awareness (Linehan, 2015).

This blending of action and change-oriented models with those supporting an acceptance orientation reflects the dialectical philosophical framework that makes DBT unique.

The dialectical framework that is the core of DBT presents reality as consisting of opposing, polar forces that are in tension. The dialectical philosophy posits that these opposing forces are each incomplete and that there is a constant push toward balancing and synthesizing these opposites. As applied to psychotherapy, the view taken was that therapies (e.g., psychodynamic, behavioral, cognitive) that focus on client change and change-oriented efforts were incomplete. Similarly, it was felt that theories that operated from an acceptance framework (e.g., humanistic, existential models) were also incomplete. From the perspective of DBT, what is needed is the balancing of models of change with models of acceptance.

The tension between validation/acceptance and change is, in essence, that which is dialectal (Linehan, 1993). This dialect results in the DBT therapists continually seeking to balance and synthesize acceptance and change-oriented strategies. The perspective guides the therapist to find the balance between acceptance-based validation of the client without demand or expectations to change while supporting and encouraging the needed change.

The therapist works to provide this balance of acceptance and validation within each session with problem-solving/behavior change strategies (Chapman, 2006). DBT therapists will employ acceptance-based strategies such as tolerating distress, radical acceptance, and mindfulness, and change-based strategies, including reframing cognitions, changing environments, and reinforcement contingencies and problem-solving activities. The flow from poles toward integration is evident in the strategies employed and the therapist's style. DBT therapists may move from being lively and energetic to slow and methodical and from reciprocal and validating to irreverent and off-beat (Chapman, 2006).

Assumptions and Principles Guiding Practice

DBT is based on several assumptions that give form to a view of pathology, its etiology and treatment (Linehan, 1993; Lynch et al., 2013; Marra, 2005).

Biosocial Theory

DBT posits that an individual's emotional sensitivity, that is, their experiencing of a low threshold for emotional stimuli, their intense response to environmental cues, and their slow return to a calm, emotional baseline, is the result of their sensitive temperament interacting with an invalidating social environment (Linehan, 1993). While emotional dysregulation is viewed as having roots in a biological disposition, it is believed to be the reciprocal interaction of biology, psychosocial factors and behaviors that maintain client difficulties and thus are the focus for intervention efforts (Marra, 2005).

For DBT, an invalidating environment is one in which an individual experiences criticism, a rejection of their expression of private experiences, an oversimplification of problem solving, and either the punishment or intermittent reinforcement of emotional displays. This biosocial interaction results in the individual's limited ability to label or express emotions and regulate emotions and emotional behaviors. As might be expected from a theory with a dialectical philosophy, just as a thesis of emotional dysregulation is seen as the outcome of such biosocial interactions, the antithesis of emotional overregulation, often taking form in inhibited emotional expression, excessive self-control, limited adaptive flexibility, and isolated and disconnected relationships, is also thought to be the result of biology, psychosocial factors, and behaviors. While initially applied to those diagnosed with borderline personality disorders (American Psychiatric Association, 2013), emotional sensitivity as a result of sensitive temperament interacting with invalidating social environment has been applied to those with other clinical issues, including depression, anxiety, and anger.

Validation and Acceptance

Being raised in an abusive or neglectful environment or one in which there is constant negative evaluation and judgment, or even simple dismissing and discounting of one's experiences, can result in an experience of invalidation that results in psychological difficulties and emotional problems. Anytime one's emotional experiences have been dismissed, judged, or minimized, invalidation occurs (Pederson, 2015). The experience of validation is believed to decrease the intensity of emotions, whereas invalidation intensifies emotional dysregulation (Van Dijk, 2012). Individuals experiencing such an invalidating environment often fail to understand and accept their experiences, emotions, and thoughts.

In contrast, the experience of validation is one in which there is the communication of nonjudgmental acknowledgment and acceptance of one's own or another's feelings, experiences, and thoughts (Pederson. 2015). Validation in DBT involves focusing on the current context of a client's problems, acknowledging that personal thoughts, emotions, and behaviors are acceptable in the client's current context, and communicating that understanding to the client (Linehan, 1993).

While validation is similar to empathy, it differs in that it involves more communication than empathy regarding what was heard and seen in the client's behavior and actions, searching for what is valid in their experiences, thoughts, and feelings and assessing the validity of their responses. In short, while empathy is fundamental to understanding, validation has to draw conclusions (Linehan, 1997).

In DBT, total acceptance is akin to unconditional positive regard and accepting the uniqueness of the individual found in humanistic therapies. For therapists engaged in DBT, the use of validation and acceptance becomes primary to their work and interventions.

Dialectics

Dialectics, as a philosophy, recognizes the inherent contradictions and tensions that arise within an individual, between individuals, and between individuals and their interaction with the world. Dialectics views these contradictions and opposing viewpoints as equally valued and necessary to better understand any situation. The perspective taken is that reality is not black or white, but rather black and white, with many shades of gray in between. Therapists employing DBT seek to help themselves and their clients move from thinking in polarities to finding synthesis and balance of opposites to achieve a new perspective.

Validation Change

As applied to the therapeutic relationship and dynamic, dialectics direct the therapist and client to remain responsive to what works at any moment, adapting as the context of treatment and the nature of the relationship evolve. The choices a client makes at any one point make sense given their frame of reference and thus deserve validation. Thus, the therapist will exhibit sensitivity to balancing validation of the client and client's experience and choices with the promotion of change.

Mindful Acceptance: Distraction

While valuing the here and now and promoting client mindfulness, DBT therapists understand the need to sometimes balance such awareness with the need to escape or minimize the intensity of a moment until such intensity can be productively embraced.

Doing One's Best: While Needing to Do Better

Dialectics take form in the therapist's belief that a client is doing the best they can, while at the same time believing that the client needs to and can do better (Lienhan, 1993).

How is failing at a test, destroying a relationship, or taking steps to hurt oneself evidence of doing one's best? Exercise 7.1 invites you to consider this dialectic as applied to your own life and circumstances.

This extends to an appreciation of that which appears maladaptive, maybe that which is most adaptive for this client at this time. "Dialectically, there is always function in dysfunction, something adaptive in what is maladaptive" (Pederson, 2015, p. 35). Thus, the individual engaged in the act of self-harm, such as cutting, or one involved with substance abuse, may be employing these behaviors, destructive as they may be, to find relief or some escape from their current painful experience.

Nurturance: Accountability

Therapists, with their acceptance of unconditional positive regard for the client, are inclined to nurture clients. While such nurturance is to be valued, DBT posits the need to balance this with holding clients accountable. Therapists engaged in DBT believe that over-nurturance can be harmful if it implies the client's impotence to employ their resources and the need to be therapist dependent. Calling for client accountability conveys respect for the client and their capabilities.

Freedom: Structure

For those presenting to therapy in a state of crisis, being overwhelmed with the demands of the moment, structure, and safety it provides will be essential. This is undoubtedly the case for a client presenting with suicidal ideation.

EXERCISE 7.1

Could Have Done Better

Directions: There has likely been a time in your life or a particular task you attempted in which the outcomes were not exactly what you had hoped them to be. It is also possible that in reflecting on this experience you were perhaps self-evaluative, even berating, in believing that you could have done better. One dialectic presented within DBT is that you and all others are doing the best you can while at the same time needing and being able to improve. How can that be?

1. Think about a time when, in your estimation, you failed, messed up, or did less than you could have done. Describe it in as much detail as possible.
2. Review the description of the situation, your thoughts, attitudes, and motivations at the time, and any physical and social factors operating at that point. As you review these elements, identify something, perhaps your motivation, physical state, or social setting, that would have to be different for you to have done better.
3. Consider the following: Did the elements listed as needing to be changed (see #2) change? No? Then it is clear, given that reality, you did the best you could and doing anything other than that would require you to have had a different reality.
4. While doing your best at the moment—the best given the reality—what might you do in a future circumstance that may allow for a different, more desirable outcome?

DBT values structure as providing clients with the space that allows for their freedom to choose. The more a client experiences underregulated emotions and behaviors, the more needed and valued structure is. Clients with overregulation of behaviors and emotions invite the therapist to encourage more spontaneity and less routine and structure.

Client–Therapist Relationship

DBT is seen as a collaborative process, one in which there is coequal participation and contribution of client and therapist. As such, therapists adjust their roles from consultant to the client to that of doer for the client. When engaged as a consultant, the therapist demonstrates a belief, trust in the client's autonomy, and the ability to be their own best advocate and agent of change. This is balanced with the realization that, at times, a task is more efficiently accomplished by the direct action of the therapist. This would certainly be the case when a therapist has to engage in actions that protect the client from harming themself or another. The synthesis that is sought is that which results in the therapist providing the minimal amount of direct intervention as called for at any one point in the therapeutic process. Table 7.1 lists assumptions regarding clients, therapists, and therapy employed in DBT.

TABLE 7.1 ASSUMPTIONS ABOUT CLIENT, THERAPIST, AND THERAPY

About Clients

- Clients in DBT want to improve but may need support and skills.
- Clients are doing their best at any one moment but need to be motivated to work hard to change.
- Clients are responsible for solving their problems, regardless of who or what conditions may have caused them.
- For the suicidal client, life is unbearable as currently being lived.
- Behaviors learned in therapy need to be generalized to the client's day-to-day living experiences.
- Clients cannot fail in DBT, but DBT can fail clients.

About Therapists

- Therapists employ foundational skills and dispositions, including empathy, genuineness, respect, and nonjudgmental validation.
- Therapists follow ethical and professional guidelines in conducting competent and effective therapy.
- Therapists respect the integrity and rights of the patient and recognize and acknowledge clients' strengths as reflective in their emphasizing consulting to the client versus directly intervening with and on the client's behalf.
- Therapists are available for weekly therapy sessions and phone consultations and provide needed therapy backup.
- Therapists, no matter how well trained, are fallible and need to practice skills; as such, therapists meet regularly to obtain consultation and support to be motivated and effective in their work.
- Therapists follow the five basic functions of comprehensive DBT, including motivating clients, teaching skills, generalizing skills to natural environments, motivating and improving their therapeutic skills, and structuring treatment environment (Linehan, 1993).

About Therapy

- The treatment relationship is nonjudgmental, genuine, and, one of coequals.
- In therapy, clients practice and are reinforced for behaviors that will serve them in their lives and not those that do not work in life.
- Therapy can only help clients change in ways that bring them closer to their own ultimate goals.

Source: Adapted from Linehan (2015); Pederson (2015); and Vaughn (2021).

Principles in Action

Central to DBT, and that which is truly unique to this theory, is the focus on being dialectical. Clients often present with dialectical conflicts such as wanting to change but being fearful and unwilling to change or believing that their life is out of their control while engaging in controlling behaviors. Throughout therapy, there is a balancing of validating the client and client's reality and the value and need to change (Moonshine & Schaefer, 2019). To accomplish this, DBT operates as a comprehensive model ultimately designed to empower clients to build a life worth living (Linehan, 2015).

DBT is more than a single treatment method involving a therapist and a client. Standard DBT is a comprehensive, multimodal program of treatment that consists of weekly individual therapy, weekly group skills training, 24/7 phone coaching availability, and a weekly therapist consultation team (Linehan, 1993). It should be noted that while this describes the "standard" DBT, Linehan (1993) recognized that not all clients need such a comprehensive system of service delivery and that adjustments should be made as needed.

DBT is highly organized and includes the following components: mindfulness, distress tolerance, emotion regulation, and interpersonal effectiveness learning and using skills in each area.

Targets of Therapy and Functions Served

The standard, comprehensive treatment program serves the following five functions (Chapman, 2006; Pederson, 2015).

Enhancing Capabilities

With the assumption that clients enter therapy to develop or improve life skills, DBT engages clients through didactic presentations, skill practice, and homework. Skill training targets functional deficits and the replacement of unhealthy behaviors with more functional and adaptive behaviors. The skills most often targeted include (a) emotion regulation skills, (b) mindfulness skills, (c) interpersonal effectiveness, and (d) distress tolerance skills (Lynch et al., 2003).

Generalizing Capabilities

The value of skill training is in its application outside of therapy. Helping clients generalize their treatment gains in the context of their lives is the second critical function of DBT. Therapists working from a DBT orientation will encourage client application of these skills in their day-to-day interactions and be available by phone between sessions to support the application of the newly learned skills at the point of crisis.

The therapist employing DBT does not assume that generalization will be automatic. The therapist will often engage the client in analyzing the conditions of specific settings and interactions in which dysfunctional behavior is elicited and reinforced. This functional analysis will allow the therapist and client to develop the approach needed to successfully apply the new, adaptive behaviors in those settings.

Improving Motivation and Reducing Dysfunctional Behaviors

The client's engagement throughout therapy is essential, and thus, improving and maintaining client motivation becomes a central feature of DBT. Therapists will employ validation, coaching, reinforcement of effort, and even cheerleading to increase and maintain client motivation (Pederson, 2015).

Throughout individual therapy sessions, the therapist will have clients complete a self-monitoring form (i.e., diary card) to track specific treatment targets (e.g., actions of self-harm) (see Case Illustration 7.1). Factors that may be recorded on a diary card include emotions felt, actions taken or skills used, triggers for certain urges or responses, medications or substances used, and self-care behaviors employed.

The self-report diary card serves to focus therapy and prioritize issues to be addressed. Behaviors that threaten the client's life have primacy, followed by behaviors that interfere with therapy (e.g., resistance and noncollaboration), and finally, those that are impeding the client's quality of life.

CASE ILLUSTRATION 7.1

Sample Diary Card

The following provides a sample of the types of elements that may be included in a client's diary card assignment. Diary cards should be tailored to the individual client, reflecting treatment goals and progress as well as challenges and setbacks.

Directions: To assist us in monitoring your progress and setting goals and priorities for our sessions, please fill out your diary card daily. It is helpful to fill it out at the same time each day.

1. Using the scale we developed (0 = no experience or symptoms, 10 = worse I have encountered), rate your experience with the following:
   Anxiety _____ Depression _____ Anger _____
2. Again, using a 0 to 10 scale, rate the urge level you have felt in the last 24 hours to do the following:
   Self-injure _____ Engage in treatment-interfering behaviors _____ Suicide ideation _____
3. Have you (yes/no) taken steps to plan to engage in the actions listed in #2? If yes, please provide details.
4. Using a scale of 0 to 10, rate your urge to use drugs or alcohol over the past 24 hours.
   Drugs (include over-the-counter) _____ Alcohol _____
5. Have you (yes/no) taken steps to plan or engage in drug or alcohol use? If yes, please provide details.
6. Have you taken specific steps toward self-care? If yes, please describe the steps taken.
7. Are there other issues you have experienced this past 24 hours that concern you? If so, please describe.

With goals set, the therapist and client review antecedent conditions and consequences that may have elicited and reinforced these dysfunctional behaviors. Strategies for problem solving and application of adaptive functional behaviors will be reviewed, and clients will be encouraged, via commitment strategies, to apply these behavioral change methods (Linehan, 1993).

Enhancing and Maintaining Therapist Capabilities and Motivation

Given the collaborative nature of DBT, a function somewhat unique to this approach is efforts to maintain the motivation and skills of the therapists engaging with DBT, especially when treating clients with borderline personality disorders. Standard BT includes a once-a-week, therapist consultation team meeting. The role of the team is to support the therapists in maintaining a compassionate, nonjudgmental perspective on the client and developing skills and approaches that will facilitate effective treatment and reduce the potential of therapist burnout.

Structuring the Environment

While treatment is collaborative, the therapist retains the primary responsibility for structuring the therapy in a manner that effectively promotes progress. The goal of this structuring, which is tailored to each client and the specific needs manifested, is to reinforce effective behavior while reducing maladaptive behaviors.

Within the context of the therapy, structuring refers to the establishment of rules, roles, and tasks to be employed. This structuring is viewed as one of the most critical goals in DBT, given the need to create a safe environment to engage in the therapeutic process (Pederson, 2015).

When structuring therapy, therapists attempt to balance structure and client autonomy and freedom. In general, the degree of therapist-imposed structure is responsive to each client's needed level of care, as reflected by safety-related concerns and clinical history.

Structuring the environment refers to the nature of the therapeutic interaction and the client's environment outside the confines of therapy. For example, when working with a client struggling with substance abuse, DBT therapists may engage the client in strategies to avoid social contact with others heavily involved in drugs and alcohol. At other times, for example, when the client is in crisis and their life is in danger, the therapist will be more active in the decisions on restructuring the environment to ensure client safety.

Stages in a Comprehensive Program

DBT employs a set of priorities based on the concept of level of disorder, which includes imminent life-threatening risk, severity, pervasiveness, and complexity of the disorder and disability (Linehan & Wilks, 2015). Targets for each client are or can be arranged in a set of recommended stages.

It is important to note that DBT was developed for individuals entering stage 1 of treatment (Linehan & Wilks, 2015). Clients presenting with non-life-threatening behaviors may experience a modification in this programming of stages.

Pretreatment

While the term *pretreatment* may be misleading in the sense that one fails to see the therapeutic value of these sessions, the term is meant to highlight a preliminary stage of gaining complete client understanding of DBT, the roles of client and therapist, and the establishment of therapeutic goals and a therapeutic alliance. In a standard approach, the first three to four sessions are devoted to these ends.

Stage 1: Stability

The initial stage of DBT, one usually taking 6 or more months, focuses on assisting the client in eliminating any life-threatening behaviors (e.g., suicide attempts, homicidal behaviors), as well as those that are most significantly impacting the quality of their life (e.g., rage, substance abuse). The therapist will also address therapy-interfering behaviors during this initial stage, such as failing to complete homework and missing or coming late to sessions.

The focus of these early sessions is also on increasing behavioral skills that help the client manage emotions and develop and maintain healthy relationships. In general, the task is to assist the client in adjusting their behaviors in such a way as to increase their experience of a life worth living.

Stage 2: Quiet Desperation

Clients at stage 2 will experience that "action is controlled, but emotional suffering is not (Linehan & Wilks, 2015, p. 100). Therefore, the goal at stage 2 is to assist the client in experiencing a full range of emotions. The goal during this stage is to continue building the skills established in stage 1 while targeting symptoms of anxiety, depression, and posttraumatic stress.

The extent of engagement in stage 2 is a function of the degree to which the client has experienced trauma and stress. If PTSD is not an issue for a client, the focus in stage 2 turns to engaging clients in mindfulness practices as well as exposure experience in order to assist them in developing "a qualitatively different relationship to emotions" (Pederson, 2015, p. 85).

Stage 3: Problem in Living

Respecting each client's uniqueness and experience, the third stage of DBT targets the specific behaviors the client wishes to change. Often these take the form of addressing typical life problems and adjustment demands and affirming and strategizing toward the achievement of life goals.

Stage 4: A Sense of Completeness

In stage 4 of treatment, the focus is expanded beyond survival and self-protection to developing the capacity for experiencing freedom, joy, and a greater sense of peace. At some level, the goals at stage 4 are more existential and spiritual, assisting clients in their personal growth.

Engaging Acceptance and Change Skills

Throughout the various stages of DBT, therapists will engage the client in skills targeting change and those fostering acceptance. Acceptance strategies focus on increasing client awareness of reality, without bias and judgment and without attempting to control it. Linehan (1993) designed four primary skill modules: mindfulness, distress tolerance, emotional regulation, and effectiveness. These modules were developed in response to the initial work with those who were highly suicidal. New skills have been developed in response to research and clinical needs. Each module provides psychoeducation and experiential practice to assist the client in developing competencies with the skills. Skills training is didactically focused, including modeling, instructions, stories, behavioral rehearsal, feedback and coaching, and homework assignments.

Mindfulness

As a practice of observing and experiencing without judgment, mindfulness facilitates the client's awareness while reducing the use of self-criticism or emotional responding. Mindfulness can be engaged using various strategies, such as deep breathing and meditation. The goal, regardless of method, is to experience the moment without the influence of the past or future and without judgment. This skill is helpful in the promotion of acceptance.

Distress Tolerance

One skill often engaged when pain or suffering cannot be changed is that of radical acceptance. Such reality acceptance has been shown to be effective for survivors of Nazi concentrate camps (Frankl, 1985). Clients are also taught to tolerate mild or moderate stress and unpleasant experience and prevent such experiences from eliciting unproductive thoughts and dysfunctional behaviors (Linehan, 1993).

Emotion Regulation

Assisting clients to manage their emotional reactions better is also a strategy employed in DBT. Clients developing emotion regulation skills will be taught how to identify and describe emotions, change emotional responses, reduce vulnerability to negative emotions, and manage difficult emotions (Linehan & Wilks, 2015). In addition to developing skills to control negative emotional experiences, clients are taught the value of self-care and the skills needed to increase positive emotions.

Various techniques, including cognitive reappraisal and reframing, are employed to help clients regulate and reduce the intensity of their emotions at the moment. The goal is to help the client proactively create emotional stability.

Interpersonal Effectiveness

Mindfulness, emotional regulation, and distress tolerance will help clients establish and maintain emotional stability, balance. However, clients with histories and experiences of invalidation may need to develop effective interpersonal behaviors.

Clients engaged in DBT often present with interpersonal problems and conflicts, quite often involving uncontrolled anger. Interpersonal effectiveness skills assist the client in learning to navigate relationships with self and others. Clients learn how to advocate for their wants and needs while respecting others. Clients are taught to manage interpersonal conflict, develop new friendships or end destructive ones, and reinforce the environment effectively (Linehan & Wilks, 2015).

Supportive Research

Meta-analytic studies (e.g., Cook & Gorraiz, 2016; Panos et al., 2014) have demonstrated the effectiveness of DBT in treating depression, life-threatening suicidal and parasuicidal acts, and emotion dysregulation. Research supports the effectiveness of DBT with clients presenting with borderline personality disorders (e.g., May et al., 2016) and those with suicidal ideation (Ward-Ciesielski, 2013). DBT has also been adapted and successfully employed with a broad variety of presenting concerns, including eating disorders (Blood et al., 2020; Erb et al., 2013; Safer & Joyce, 2011), depression (Lynch et al., 2007), and substance abuse and alcohol dependence (Maffei et al. 2018; Schuman et al., 2014). Additionally, research has supported its effectiveness as a short-term treatment and outpatient treatment of a diagnostically diverse client population, reducing psychological distress, functional impairment, and symptoms (Warlick et al., 2021; Wieczorek et al., 2021).

Suitability

The patient populations for which DBT has the most empirical support include parasuicidal women with borderline personality disorder. However, there have been promising findings for patients with borderline personality disorder and substance use disorders, persons who meet the criteria for binge-eating disorder, and depressed elderly patients (Chapman, 2006). Additionally, some research has examined DBT-oriented treatments for other clinical problems such as depression and anxiety (Marra, 2004).

DBT, while having modules that address stress and trauma, is not a standalone treatment for trauma and may not be the first treatment of choice for those clients combating the effects of trauma. The engagement with mindfulness and dialectics may present a challenge to those with intellectual disabilities or uncontrolled schizophrenia. However, the modular nature of DBT does invite adjustment and adaptation in ways that may make it useful for these populations (Lew et al., 2006).

KEYSTONES

- DBT came to rest on a foundation of dialectical philosophy, whereby therapists strive to balance and synthesize acceptance and change-oriented strategies continually.
- The dialectics of DBT include validation of change, mindful acceptance, doing one's best while needing to do better, nurturance and accountability, and freedom and structure.

- DBT is more than a single treatment method. It is a comprehensive, multimodal program of treatment that consists of weekly individual therapy, weekly group skills training, 24/7 phone coaching availability, and a weekly therapist consultation team.
- The standard, comprehensive treatment program serves five functions: enhancing capabilities, generalizing capabilities, improving motivation and reducing dysfunctional behaviors, enhancing and maintaining therapist capabilities and motivation, and structuring the environment.
- The stages of DBT reflect a set of priorities based on the concept of level of disorder, which includes imminent life-threatening risk, severity, pervasiveness, and the complexity of the disorder and disability.
- DBT therapists will employ acceptance-based strategies such as tolerating distress, radical acceptance and mindfulness, and change-based strategies, including reframing cognitions, changing environments and reinforcement contingencies, and problem-solving activities.
- Research continues to support the effectiveness of DBT with clients presenting with borderline personality disorders, as well as with those experiencing suicidal ideation, eating disorders, depression, and substance abuse and alcohol dependence.

ADDITIONAL RESOURCES

Linehan, M. M. (2015). *DBT skills training manual* (2nd ed.). Guilford.

Marra, T. (2005). *Dialectical behavior therapy in private practice: A practical and comprehensive guide.* New Harbinger.

McKay, M. Wood, J. C., & Brantley, J. (2019). *The dialectical behavior therapy skills workbook: Practical DBT exercises for learning mindfulness, interpersonal effectiveness, emotion regulation and distress tolerance.* New Harbinger.

Pederson, L., & Pederson, C. S. (2020). *The expanded dialectical behavioral therapy skills training manual: DBT for self-help and individual and group treatment settings* (2nd ed.). PSI Publishing and Media.

REFERENCES

American Psychiatric Association. (2013). *Diagnostic and statistical manual of mental disorders* (5th ed.). Author.

Bandura, A. (1969). Social-learning theory of identificatory processes. In D. A. Goslin (Ed.), *Handbook of socialization theory and research* (pp. 213–262). Rand McNally & Company.

Bass, C., van Nevel, J., & Swart, J. (2014). A comparison between dialectical behavior therapy, mode deactivation therapy, cognitive behavioral therapy, and acceptance and commitment therapy in the treatment of adolescents. *International Journal of Behavioral Consultation and Therapy, 9*(2), 4–8. https://doi.org/10.1037/h0100991

Blood, L., Adams, G., Turner, H., & Waller, G. (2020). Group dialectical behavioral therapy for binge-eating disorder: Outcomes from a community case series. *International Journal of Eating Disorders, 53*(11), 1863–1867. https://doi.org/10.1002/eat.23377

Chapman A. L. (2006). Dialectical behavior therapy: Current indications and unique elements. *Psychiatry, 3*(9), 62–68.

Cook, N. E., & Gorraiz, M. (2016). Dialectical behavior therapy for nonsuicidal self-injury and depression among adolescents: Preliminary meta-analytic evidence. *Child and Adolescent Mental Health, 21*(2), 81–89. https://doi.org/10.1111/camh.12112

Erb, S., Farmer, A., & Mehlenbeck, R. (2013). A condensed dialectical behavior therapy skills group for binge eating disorder: Overcoming winter challenges. *Journal of Cognitive Psychotherapy, 27*(4), 338–358.

Frankl, V. E. (1985). *Man's search for meaning*. Simon and Schuster.

Lew, M., Matta, C., Tripp-Tebo, C., & Watts D. (2006). Dialectical behavior therapy (DBT) for individuals with intellectual disabilities: A program description. *Mental Health Aspects of Developmental Disabilities, 1*, 1–12.

Linehan, M. M. (1981). A social-behavioral analysis of suicide and parasuicide: Implications for clinical assessment and treatment. In H. Glazer & J. F. Clarkin (Eds.), *Depression, behavioral and directive intervention strategies* (pp. 229–294). Garland.

Linehan, M. M. (1993). *Cognitive-behavioral treatment of borderline personality disorder*. Guilford.

Linehan, M. M. (1997). Validation and psychotherapy. In A. C. Bohart & L. S. Greenberg (Eds.), *Empathy reconsidered: New directions in psychotherapy* (pp. 353–392). American Psychological Association. https://doi.org/10.1037/10226-016

Linehan, M. M. (2015). *DBT skills training manual* (2nd ed.). Guilford Press.

Linehan, M. M., & Wilks, C. R. (2015). The course and evolution of dialectical behavior therapy. *American Journal of Psychotherapy (Association for the Advancement of Psychotherapy), 69*(2), 97–110. https://doi.org/10.1176/appi.psychotherapy.2015.69.2.97

Lynch, T. R., Cheavens, J. S., Cukrowicz, K. C., Thorp, S. R., Bronner, L., & Beyer, J. (2007). Treatment of older adults with co-morbid personality disorder and depression: A dialectical behavior therapy approach. *International Journal of Geriatric Psychiatry, 22*(2), 131–143.

Lynch, T. R., Gray, K. L. H., Hempel, R. J., Titley, M., & Chen, E. Y. (2013). Radically open dialectical behavior therapy for adult anorexia nervosa: Feasibility and outcomes from an inpatient program. *BMC Psychiatry, 13*, 293. https://doi.org/10.1186/1471-244X-13-293

Lynch, T. R., Morse, J. Q., Mendelson, T., & Robins, C. J. (2003). Dialectical behavior therapy for depressed older adults: A randomized pilot study. *The American Journal of Geriatric Psychiatry: Official Journal of the American Association for Geriatric Psychiatry, 11*(1), 33–45.

Maffei, C., Cavicchioli, M., Movalli, M., Cavallaro, R., & Fossati, A. (2018). Dialectical behavior therapy skills training in alcohol dependence treatment: Findings based on an open trial. *Substance Use & Misuse, 53*(14), 2368–2385. https://doi.org/10.1080/10826084.2018.1480035

Marra, T. (2004). *Depressed and anxious: The dialectical behavior therapy workbook for overcoming depression and anxiety.* New Harbinger.

Marra, T. (2005). *Dialectical behavior therapy in private practice: A practical and comprehensive guide.* New Harbinger.

May, J. M., Richardi, T. M., & Barth, K. S. (2016). Dialectical behavior therapy as treatment for borderline personality disorder. *The Mental Health Clinician, 6*(2), 62–67. https://doi.org/10.9740/mhc.2016.03.62

Moonshine, C., & Schaefer, S. (2019). *Dialectical behavior therapy* (Vol. 1, 2nd ed.). PESI Publishing & Media.

Panos, P. T., Jackson, J. W., Hasan, O., & Panos, A. (2014). Meta-analysis and systematic review assessing the efficacy of dialectical behavior therapy (DBT). *Research on Social Work Practice, 24*(2), 213–223. https://doi.org/10.1177/1049731513503047

Pederson, L. (2015). *Dialectical behavior therapy: A contemporary guide for practitioners.* Wiley.

Safer, D. L., & Joyce, E. E. (2011). Does rapid response to two group psychotherapies for binge eating disorder predict abstinence? *Behaviour Research and Therapy, 49*(5), 339–345.

Schuman, D., Slone, N., Reese, R., & Duncan, B. (2014). Using client feedback to improve outcomes in group psychotherapy with soldiers referred for substance abuse treatment. *Psychotherapy Research, 25*(4), 396–407. https://doi.org/10.1080/10503307.2014.900875

Staats, A. W., & Staats, C. K. (1963). *Complex human behavior.* Holt, Rinehart & Win.

Van Dijk, S. (2012). *DBT made simple.* New Harbinger Press.

Vaughn, S. (2021). *History of DBT: Origins and foundations.* Psychoterapy Academy. https://psychotherapy-academy.org/dbt/history-of-dialectical-behavioral-therapy-a-very-brief-introduction/

Ward-Ciesielski, E. F. (2013). An open pilot feasibility study of a brief dialectical behavior therapy skills-based intervention for suicidal individuals. *Suicide and Life-Threatening Behavior, 43*(3), 324–335.

Warlick, C. A., Poquiz, J., Huffman, J. M., DeLong, L., Moffitt-Carney, K., Leonard, J., Schellenger, B., & Nelson, J. (2021). Effectiveness of a brief dialectical behavior therapy intensive-outpatient community health program. *Psychotherapy.* https://doi.org/10.1037/pst0000388

Wieczorek, M., Kacen, T., King, B., & Wilhelm, K. (2021). The effectiveness of a short-term DBT skills group in a "real-world" clinical setting. *Australasian Psychiatry, 29*(6), 600–603. https://doi.org/10.1177/10398562211038907

CHAPTER 8

Emotion-Focused Therapy

I feel, therefore I am.

—L.S. Greenberg

I feel therefore I am (Greenberg, 2017, p. 5) is a succinct reflection of the focus taken by those practicing emotion-focused therapy (EFT). EFT is an approach to therapy that, while valuing the role that cognitions and behaviors play in the human experience, posits that there has been an overemphasis on these domains of the human condition at the expense of valuing the role played by emotions. The EFT model prioritizes emotion and emotional regulation as the key organizing agents in individual experience and relationship interactions. A significant premise guiding intervention in EFT is that transformation is possible only when individuals accept themselves as they are.

EFT is based on humanistic-experiential and attachment theory and family systems theory. While EFT initially emerged as a relationship and marriage counseling model, it has since evolved to become a widely used approach for interpersonal and individual therapy. It is designed to help clients become aware and make productive use of their emotions. The overriding goals of EFT are strengthening the self, regulating affect, and creating new meaning (Greenberg, 2017).

The current chapter reviews the history and evolution of EFT, its perspective and guiding assumptions and fundamental principles applied in therapy. Upon completion of this chapter, the readers will be able to do the following:

1. Describe the basic principles of EFT.
2. Explain the stages of therapy as articulated in EFT.
3. Describe the techniques that are fundamental to EFT.

History and Contributors

Leslie Greenberg became interested in emotion theory (Arnold, 1960) and researched the role of emotion in human functioning. His view was that emotional responses promoted the personal significance of events for clients and thus should be the focus of therapeutic intervention (Rice & Greenberg, 1984). Throughout the 1980s and 90s, Greenberg and associates Laura Rice and Robert Elliott identified and articulated the basic principles of a process-oriented, experiential approach that focused on emotion scheme change (Greenberg et al., 1993). The approach, which was initially called *process experiential psychotherapy* (Greenberg et al., 1993), presented a significant counterpoint to those theories emphasizing cognitions and behaviors. The name was thought to be the best descriptor of the therapy, fitting with a humanistic framework while capturing it as both process-oriented and experiential (Goldman, 2019).

While the roots of EFT can be found in other humanistic-existential theories, its uniqueness rests in the centrality of importance given to the role emotions play in the therapeutic process of change. EFT proposes that emotional change is central to enduring change as a theory of human functioning and therapeutic practice.

To highlight the central role played by emotions in all human functioning, the name of their approach changed from process experiential therapy to *emotion-focused therapy*. The new title, which was introduced in the 2004 book *Learning Emotion-Focused Therapy: The Process-Experiential Approach to Change* (Elliot et al., 2004), was felt to be an integrative title referring to all treatments that emphasized emotions as the focus of intervention. In this work, the authors laid out the theory, principles, and approach of EFT.

The fundamental principles of this overarching emotion-focused approach were presented in the book *Emotion-Focused Therapy: Coaching Clients to Work through Their Feelings* (Greenberg, 2015). Since these early days of its formulation, various iterations and adaptations of the basic theory have emerged and found application with groups, families, couples, and individuals. According to Greenberg (2017), the term emotion-focused therapy will "be used in the future, in its integrative sense, to characterize all therapies that are emotion-focused be hey psychodynamic, cognitive-behavioral, systemic or humanistic" (p. 148).

Perspective: I Feel, Therefore, I Am

As might be apparent, given the title of the theory, EFT takes the perspective that emotions are central to one's identity, guiding individual choices and decisions. EFT views our emotional systems as essential to survival and adaptation, playing a vital role in goal-directed behavior (Greenberg, 2017).

EFT posits that emotions such as anger, fear, and sadness are foundational to an individual's successful navigation of their environment. Whereas a therapist operating from a cognitive orientation might suggest that as one thinks one feels and acts, the therapist with an emotion-focused orientation would hold that as one feels one thinks and acts.

Emotional change is seen as the key to enduring cognitive and behavioral change from this perspective.

A fundamental tenet underlying EFT is that the organism possesses an innate tendency toward maintenance, growth, and mastery. The growth tendency is embedded in the adaptive emotion system, or what EFT refers to as emotion schemes (Greenberg et al., 1993). Emotion schemes are the internal emotion memory structures that have synthesized affective, motivation, cognitive, and behavioral elements into an internal organization, schemes throughout one's life.

EFT holds that our primary mode of processing information and responding reflects our emotion schemes. Further, those embracing EFT as a therapy model see emotions as basically adaptive. In contrast, emotion schemes can be maladaptive and problematic due to past traumas, skill deficits, or emotion avoidance.

Maladaptive emotion schemes, lack of emotional awareness or avoidance of emotions and emotional experience, and conflict between two emotionally based parts of the self serve as the basis for pathology (Greenberg & Watson, 2006). EFT's perspective is that in assisting individuals to experience, reown, regulate, use, and transform their emotions, as needed, a therapist can help clients function more effectively (Greenberg, 2017).

Assumptions and Principles Guiding Practice

EFT has taken the subjectivity and phenomenological perspective of humanistic theories and connected this perspective to a constructivist epistemology that sees people as self-organizing systems (Greenberg & Van Balen, 1998). With this as a general foundation, EFT operates from the following assumptions and guiding principles.

Dialectical-Constructivist View

EFT operates from the assumption that individuals are constantly making sense out of their emotions (Greenberg & Pascual-Leone, 2001). The perspective is that personal meaning emerges by the self-organization and explication of an individual's emotional experience. It is further believed that optimal adaptation involves the integration of emotion and reason. This process occurs by the ongoing circular process of symbolizing bodily felt sensations in awareness and then articulating them in language, thus constructing a new experience. The process is viewed as circular in that attending to, and discovering preconceptual elements of an experience, influences the process of meaning construction while the process of meaning construction influences what is experienced (Greenberg, 2004). If, for example, I notice that my heart rate is accelerating, respiration is becoming more shallow and rapid, and my muscles are starting to tremble, and I label these sensations an anxiety response, that label, if within a personal history of panic attacks, may serve as the source of additional body reactions, which increase the belief that this an anxiety attack. What started as body sensations, which may have been stimulated due to a number of conditions, including too much caffeine or even positive excitement, once labeled as anxiety preliminary to panic, circles back to increase the original sensations.

Emotions Central to Thought and Action

A central premise of EFT is that emotion is foundational in the construction of the self and is a crucial determinant of self-organization. At the most basic level of functioning, emotions are an adaptive form of information processing and action readiness that orients people to their environment and, when adaptive, promotes their well-being (Greenberg & Paivio, 1997).

EFT operates from the perspective that emotion not only governs our views of self and others but also strongly influences interactions and behaviors as well as our thoughts. When people feel angry, they think angry thoughts and act angrily (Whelton & Greenberg, 2005). EFT assumes that accessing emotion provides access to an individual's network of thoughts, feelings, beliefs, desires, and bodily experiences.

Client Experiences: Guiding Practice Decisions

EFT is a humanistic, marker-driven, evidence-based approach emphasizing moment-to-moment tracking of client emotional experiencing. Rather than working from a diagnosis or template reflecting enduring personalities, therapists working from an EFT orientation attend to their clients' experiences and ways of engaging at the moment, identifying markers, such as clients statements and behaviors, that indicate current emotional concerns and core pain. The operating principle is that the client's expression of pain and emergent markers provide a guiding framework for intervention more than does a diagnosis (Greenberg, 2004).

Process Versus Content

Whereas other brief therapies may have detailed schedules and targets for each session, the EFT therapist assumes the role of a process expert, allowing the process and not predetermined schedules to direct the unfolding of the therapy (Goldman & Greenberg, 2015). EFT therapists see themselves as process experts who are carefully attuned to their clients' moment-by-moment experience, listening for that which is most poignant or that which calls for further exploration and using this process awareness to guide therapy decisions (Greenberg, 2017).

Therapeutic Relationship as Vital to Outcomes

Given that emotion-focused therapists see the therapeutic process as a discovery-oriented one (Greenberg et al., 1993), the establishment of a trusting, safe therapeutic relationship in which the client is comfortable to disclose becomes vital to therapeutic outcomes (Elliott et al., 2004). As experts in their own experience, clients will act as a compass guiding the therapist and therapy to the core issues to be addressed (Elliott et al., 2004). It is up to the therapist to establish the conditions of a therapeutic relationship that provides for client disclosure and therapist understanding of what is being shared.

Principles in Action

The overriding goal of EFT is to help clients develop emotional competence as reflected in their ability to access their emotional experience, regulate and transform maladaptive emotions, and develop positive identity narratives (Greenberg, 2015). To achieve this goal, the therapist follows two major treatment principles: (a) the provision of a therapeutic relationship and (b) the facilitation of therapeutic work (Greenberg et al., 1993).

The Therapeutic Relationship

In EFT, the therapeutic relationship is seen as not only essential to the work of exploration and the creation of new meaning but is, in and of itself, curative (Greenberg, 2017). Central to EFT is the creation of an I–thou therapy relationship based on principles of presence, empathy, acceptance, and congruence (Geller & Greenberg, 2012). The therapist's style in this relationship combines "following" with "guiding" (Greenberg, 2017).

Three principles guide the therapeutic relationship in EFT: presence and empathic attunement, communication of Rogerian core conditions (Rogers, 1957), and the creation of a working alliance.

Empathic Attunement

Empathic attunement is the ability to join with the client in their lived experience and thus understand how the client experiences the world. Empathic attunement requires the therapist to let go of preconceived notions of the client. The therapist actively enters the client's lived experience, attending to the content of that being shared and the impact as experienced by the client. Empathic attunement is considered a core competency for successful EFT intervention (Johnson, 2009).

Core Conditions

In addition to empathic attunement, therapists with an EFT orientation must employ the core conditions essential to developing a therapeutic encounter. EFT therapists can convey genuineness, nonjudgmental acceptance, and an unconditional valuing of their clients. These conditions make it possible to create a therapeutic bond, reflecting an I–thou therapy relationship (Geller & Greenberg, 2012).

Working Alliance

The relationship is one marked by the collaboration of client and therapist in establishing therapeutic goals and tasks. In EFT, goals are often identified and agreed on by having the client identify the enduring pain they have been experiencing and choose to resolve that pain rather than set goals for behavioral change (Greenberg, 2017). The therapist's style in this relationship combines with guiding (Greenberg, 2017).

The Therapeutic Work

A fundamental tenet of EFT is that clients must experience emotion to be informed and moved by it and make it accessible to change (Greenberg, 2015). EFT believes that clients do not change their emotions simply by talking about them or even understanding them. Experience is essential. As a result, the therapy often takes the form of a bottoms-up process. Therapists, in session, will guide clients to attend to felt senses and emotions while developing more adaptive responses. The bottom-up element of the process consists of clients learning to observe and follow the unattended to or avoided sensorimotor reactions that are activated in the present. EFT therapists invite clients to engage in specific experiences designed to assist them in accessing their emotions. In EFT, there is no direct attempt to change or fix the client; instead, the assumption is that with experience and acceptance, change may follow.

EFT therapy is guided by three principles: experiential processing, task completion and focus, and self-development.

Experiential Processing

Experiential processing reflects the value placed on assisting the client in increasing awareness of their emotion schemes, reactions to emotions, and emotion regulation. The therapist will coach the client in new ways of processing experiential information. The therapist may invite the client to actively search for internal experiences to identify and name the experience, reflecting on it to make sense of it and create new meaning in a process of self-reflection.

Task Completion and Focus

EFT therapists help clients identify key treatment foci and help them work on these over several sessions. This requires the development of clear treatment goals and the tracking of clients' current tasks within each session.

Self-Development

EFT therapists value client freedom and the ability for self-determination. As such, a guiding principle of EFT is an emphasis placed on the client's responsibility and opportunity for generating their emotional experiences. The therapist helps clients explore growth possibilities in these experiences.

Therapeutic Tasks Responding to Markers

A hallmark of EFT is the use of specific therapeutic tasks offered in response to in-session verbal and nonverbal markers provided by the client. Therapists attend to the clients' language and behaviors as they indicate problematic cognitive-affective processes (see Case Illustration 8.1).

In Case Illustration 8.1, the client is presenting with one of the significant markers, self-interruptive split. In this case, one part of himself is interrupting and constricting his ability for

CASE ILLUSTRATION 8.1

Not Going to Cry

Therapist: Elliot, could you tell me what it is that you are doing with your mouth and lips right now?

Elliot: Wow, I didn't realize it, but I am biting my lip.

Therapist: Can we stop for a moment? It might be helpful if you could close your eyes and share what sensations you may be experiencing at the moment.

Elliot: My body feels really tense, I have a lump in my throat, I feel really sad, and I can hear myself saying, "Stop, get control, choke it down, you're not going to cry."

---

emotional expression, crying. As we continue the case, the therapist (see Case Illustration 8.2) introduces a two-chair enactment exercise to help the client make the interrupting part explicit. By experiencing himself as the agent shutting down the emotional expression, he can react to and challenge the interruptive part of the self. Resolution involves the expression of the blocked experience (Greenberg, 2017).

CASE ILLUSTRATION 8.2

Two-Chair Enactment

Therapist: Elliot, I would like you to try something. You have shared your awareness of how you have been holding back from crying and even what seems to be a mandate to push those feelings down, to deny them and escape them.

Elliot: (nods)

Therapist: I would like you to imagine that those words, that directive or mandate to stop yourself from crying, were actually over there in that chair speaking to you. How do they sound? What are the words? How is the tone?

Elliot: (very loudly) "You're such a wuss. Men don't cry. What the hell are you, a little girl? Hey little girl, are going to cry? Cry baby, Cry. You should be ashamed of yourself."

Therapist: Now I want to repeat these words; tell me what you are sensing, what you feel when you hear them.

(Therapist repeats the words in a similar tone.)

(Continued)

CASE ILLUSTRATION 8.2 (*Continued*)

Elliot: It's strange; on one hand, I feel like crying more, yet I can feel how anxious I'm getting. I can feel myself swallowing and trying to distract myself from the sad feelings.

Therapist: I will say the words again, but this time, I would like you to talk back to them; argue with me as I say the words.

(The process continues.)

Elliot: (Begins to experience anger and challenges the words) "This is stupid, crying is part of feeling, part of being human. Males who are healthy, secure cry when they are hurt or upset or sad."

Therapist: Great job. As you are debating or refuting those words, what is going inside? What are you feeling? What are your sensations? Your thoughts?

Elliot: I started to get angry, and my thoughts were, "Hell yeah, I have a right to cry," and then it seemed silly to me, silly that I was working so hard to simply allow myself to feel. I heard myself saying, "Actually, it is okay to cry when it is what your feeling."

Markers often reflect the client's expression of self-criticism, evidence of unresolved feelings and trauma, and in-session efforts to avoid awareness or expression of feelings (Greenberg, 2015). Greenberg et al. (1993) identified six main markers and suggested interventions (see Table 8.1).

TABLE 8.1 MARKERS AND INTERVENTIONS

Marker	Intervention
Problematic reactions: The client will express confusion about emotional or behavioral responses to a situation.	The therapist will guide the client through a reexperiencing of the situation and the reaction to facilitate awareness of the connection of the situation, thoughts, and emotional reaction.
Unclear felt sense: Clients are unclear about their current experience or feelings.	The therapist will assist the client in focusing, helping them attend and placing words to their bodily felt sense.
Conflict splits: One aspect of the client's self opposes another.	A therapist might employ two-chair work to help the client put these parts into live contact with each other to foster integration.

(*Continued*)

TABLE 8.1 (Continued)

Marker	Intervention
Self-interruptive splits: Clients constrict or interrupt their emotional experience or expression of emotion.	A therapist might use two-chair enactment, where the client is helped to make the interrupting part explicit.
Unfinished business: This reflects unresolved feelings the clients hold toward a significant other.	Empty-chair dialogue can engage the client in their interval view of this significant other and experience their emotional reactions to this other.
Vulnerability: The client is giving evidence of feeling ashamed, insecure, vulnerable.	The therapist will convey empathic attunement and validate and normalize the client's experience.

As presented in Case Illustration 8.2, EFT therapists respond to these markers by offering the intervention to raise client awareness of their emotions and emotional responses. Throughout therapy, the therapist helps clients experience and explore feelings related to their difficulties, goals, and tasks. Tasks involve immediate within-session goals such as resolving the conflict, the creation of new meaning, or the expression of blocked experience. Exercise 8.1 invites you to reflect on these core markers as you may have experienced them in your own life.

EXERCISE 8.1

Markers

Directions: As noted in Table 8.1, client verbal and nonverbal behaviors often indicate areas of their emotional life that are causing distress. The exercise invites you to reflect on each of the following markers, an attempt to identify those that perhaps you have experienced, the context(s) in which you may have experienced, and the emotions that they reflect.

Marker	Context	Emotion(s)
(Example) Problematic reaction	When I am in a situation where people are expressing sadness, I become sarcastic and dismissive.	Anxiety
Problematic reactions: The client will express confusion about emotional or behavioral responses to a situation.		

(Continued)

Chapter 8 **Emotion-Focused Therapy** | 129

EXERCISE 8.1 (Continued)

Marker	Context	Emotion(s)
Unclear felt sense: Clients are unclear about their current experience or feelings.		
Conflict splits: One aspect of the client's self opposes another.		
Self-interruptive splits: Clients constrict or interrupt their emotional experience or expression of emotion.		
Unfinished business: This reflects unresolved feelings the clients hold toward a significant other.		
Vulnerability: The client is giving evidence of feeling ashamed, insecure, vulnerable.		

Phases of Treatment

EFT progresses through three significant phases (Greenberg & Watson, 2006). These phases include bonding and awareness, evoking and exploring, and concluding therapy with transformation and the construction of new emotions reflecting a new client narrative (see Table 8.2).

Bonding and Awareness

The therapist engaged in EFT begins by exploring current problems' history, key aspects, and focal issues. During the initial interactions, the therapist will pay special attention to the client's emotional processing style and their capacity for emotion regulation. The therapist works with clients to help the client approach, tolerate, regulate, and accept their emotions.

Evoking and Exploring

As treatment progresses, attention will turn to the exploration of painful material. This material provides insight into the client's emotion schemes, which are the focus of therapy and objects of transformation. It is crucial for the therapist to "facilitate optimal emotional arousal, but not so much that it is dysregulating or disorienting" (Greenberg, 2017, p. 87).

TABLE 8.2 PHASES AND STEPS EMPLOYED

Phase	Steps
Phase 1: Bonding and awareness	Attending to, empathizing with, and validating the client's feelings and current sense of self Providing a rationale for working with emotions Promoting awareness of internal experience Establishing a collaborative focus
Phase 2: Evolving and exploring	Establishing support for emotional experience Evoking and arousing problematic feelings Undoing interruption of emotions Developing the client's access to primary emotions or core maladaptive schemes
Phase 3: Transformation	Generating new emotional responses to transform core maladaptive schemes Promoting reflection to make sense of experience Validating new feelings and supporting an emerging sense of self

The therapist listens for markers that indicate that they can introduce therapeutic tasks. Through these tasks, the client and the therapist understand the key thematic issues related to the client's underlying emotion schemes. This understanding and the resulting new meaning acquired are tied back to the difficulties that brought the client to therapy.

Transformation

As previously noted, EFT is not intended to change or fix the client directly. EFT assumes that with experience and acceptance clients will increase their emotional competence, as reflected in their ability to access emotional experience, regulate and transform maladaptive emotions, and develop positive identity narratives.

Transformation of maladaptive emotions and distressing feelings begins with the client attending to the feeling and then exploring the cognitive-affective sequences that generate these feelings (Greenberg, 2017). EFT suggests that a maladaptive emotional state can be transformed by undoing it with another, more adaptive emotion. EFT posits that with such awareness clients will move to the expression of adaptive grief or hurt and empower anger or self-soothing, and these are believed to facilitate a sense of self-acceptance and agency. (Greenberg & Watson, 2006). It is the belief that the co-activation of the more adaptive emotion along with or in response to the maladaptive emotion helps transform the maladaptive emotion (Greenberg & Paivio, 1997). "Transformation occurs when these maladaptive states are differentiated into adaptive needs, which act to refute the core negative evaluations about the self embedded in their core maladaptive schemes" (Greenberg, 2017, p. 86). Transformation requires the client to feel their emotions, understand the scheme underlying them, and rather than attempting to change these painful emotions accept them. Thus, a client with a history of childhood abuse and the maladaptive scheme "I am rejectable and unlovable" will experience the need to be respected and loved. The client will accept the reality of their experience while accepting and valuing themselves. The impact of these two opposing experiences takes shape in adaptive anger at the abuser or sadness. As a result, the client will have a new experience and a more positive evaluation of self, perhaps as an assertive, worthwhile and lovable individual.

Therapy involves changing both emotional experience and the narratives in which they are embedded (Angus & Greenberg, 2011). In order to change, clients need to activate new adaptive experiences in therapy, develop new narratives that assimilate experience into existing cognitive structures, and generate new ones.

Supportive Research

EFT has been developed and applied to work with various populations and clinical disorders (Wiebe & Johnson, 2016). EFT has extensive support for its effectiveness in couples therapy (e.g., Johnson et al., 1999; Najafi et al., 2015; Wiebe & Johnson, 2016). The International Centre for Excellence in Emotionally Focused Therapy (ICEEFT, n.d.), founded by Sue Johnson, provides an extensive database supporting the efficacy of EFT, especially in the form of couples therapy.

While its effectiveness has been most empirically studied and validated with couples and marital therapy, EFT has support for its effectiveness in treating anxiety and depression (Denton et al., 2012; Dessaulles et al., 2003; Ellison et al., 2009; Robinson et al., 2014), trauma (Paivio & Pascjal-Leone, 2010), social anxiety (Elliott & Shahar, 2017), generalized anxiety (Watson & Greenberg, 2017), and eating disorders (Robinson et al., 2015; Wunk et al., 2015).

Suitability

EFT is being used increasingly by couples and individual therapists. It is being integrated into other therapeutic approaches, including psychodynamic and cognitive models (Greenberg, 2013). As noted within the chapter, EFT requires clients to have the ability to access, tolerate, and express a range of emotions, including difficult or painful feelings. Therefore, the suitability for any one client may be a function of the degree to which that client can and is willing to access and experience painful feelings.

An additional point to consider is that the overall goal of EFT is to assist clients in improving overall functioning. Clients seeking treatment with the goal of specific symptom reduction may be less suitable for EFT.

KEYSTONES

- While the roots of EFT can be found in other humanistic-existential theories, its uniqueness rests in the centrality of importance given to the role emotions play in the therapeutic process of change.
- A fundamental tenet underlying EFT is that the organism possesses an innate tendency toward maintenance, growth, and mastery. The growth tendency is seen as being embedded in the adaptive emotion system, or what EFT refers to as emotion schemes.
- Emotion schemes are the internal emotion memory structures that have synthesized affective, motivation, cognitive, and behavioral elements into an internal organization, schemes throughout one's life.
- Maladaptive emotion schemes, lack of emotional awareness or avoidance of emotions and emotional experience, and conflict between two emotionally based parts of the self serve as the basis for pathology.
- The overriding goal of EFT is to help clients develop emotional competence as reflected in their ability to access their emotional experience, regulate and transform maladaptive emotions, and develop positive identity narratives.
- EFT believes that clients do not change their emotions simply by talking about them or even understanding them. Experience is essential. EFT therapy is guided by three principles: experiential processing, task completion and focus and, self-development.
- A hallmark of EFT is the use of specific therapeutic tasks offered in response to in-session verbal and nonverbal markers provided by the client.
- EFT progresses through three major phases: bonding and awareness, evoking and exploring, and concluding therapy with transformation and the construction of new emotions reflecting a new client narrative.

ADDITIONAL RESOURCES

Greenberg, L. S., & Goldman, R. N. (Eds.). (2019). *Clinical handbook of emotion-focused therapy.* American Psychological Association. https://doi.org/10.1037/0000112-000

Greenman, P. S., Johnson, S. M., & Wiebe, S. (2019). Emotionally focused therapy for couples: At the heart of science and practice. In B. H. Fiese, M. Celano, K. Deater-Deckard, E. N. Jouriles, & M. A. Whisman (Eds.), *APA handbook of contemporary family psychology: Family therapy and training* (Vol. 3, pp. 291–305). American Psychological Association. https://doi.org/10.1037/0000101-018

Johnson, S. M. (2019). *Attachment theory in practice: Emotionally focused therapy (EFT) with individuals, couples, and families.* Guilford. https://doi.org/10.4324/9781351168366

Johnson, S. M. (2019). *The practice of emotionally focused couple therapy: Creating connection* (3rd ed.). Routledge.

REFERENCES

Angus, L. E., & Greenberg, L. S. (2011). *Working with narrative in emotion-focused therapy: Changing stories, healing lives.* American Psychological Association.

Arnold, M. B. (1960). *Emotion and personality.* Columbia University Press.

Denton, W. H., Wittenborn, A. K., & Golden, R. N. (2012). Augmenting antidepressant medication treatment of depressed women with emotionally focused therapy for couples: A randomized pilot study. *Journal of Marital and Family Therapy, 38,* 23–38.

Dessaulles, A., Johnson, S. M., & Denton, W. H. (2003). Emotion-focused therapy for couples in the treatment of depression: A pilot study. *The American Journal of Family Therapy, 31,* 345–353.

Elliott, R., & Shahar, B. (2017). Emotion-focused therapy for social anxiety (EFT-SA). *Person-Centered & Experiential Psychotherapies, 16*(2), 1–19. https://doi.org/10.1080/14779757.2017.1330701

Elliott, R., Watson, J., Goldman, R., & Greenberg, L. S. (2004). *Learning emotion-focused therapy: The process-experiential approach to change.* American Psychological Association.

Ellison, J. A., Greenberg, L. S., Goldman, R. N., & Angus, L. (2009). Maintenance of gains following experiential therapies for depression. *Journal of Consulting and Clinical Psychology, 77*(1), 103–112. https://doi.org/10.1037/a0014653

Geller, S. M., & Greenberg, L. S. (2012). *Therapeutic presence: A mindful approach to effective therapy.* American Psychological Association.

Goldman, R. N. (2017). Case formulation in emotion-focused therapy. *Person-Centered and Experiential Psychotherapies, 16*(2), 88–105. https://doi.org/10.1080/14779757.2017.1330705

Goldman, R. N. (2019). History and overview of emotion-focused therapy. In L. S. Greenberg & R. N. Goldman, (Eds.), *Clinical handbook of emotion-focused therapy* (pp. 3–35). American Psychological Association.

Goldman, R. N., & Greenberg, L. S. (2015). *Case formulation in emotion-focused therapy: Co-constructing clinical maps for change.* American Psychological Association.

Greenberg, L. S. (2004). Emotion-focused therapy. *Clinical Psychology and. Psychotherapy., 11,* 3–16.

Greenberg, L. S. (2015). *Emotion-focused therapy: Coaching clients to work through their feelings.* American Psychological Association.

Greenberg, L. S. (2017). *Emotion-focused therapy, revised edition.* American Psychological Association. http://dx.doi.org/10.1037/15971-001

Greenberg, L. S. & Paivio, S. C. (1997). *Working with emotions in psychotherapy. The practicing professional.* Guilford.

Greenberg, L. S., & Pascual-Leone, J. (2001). A dialectical constructivist view of the creation of personal meaning. *Journal of Constructivist Psychology, 14*, 165–186.

Greenberg, L. S., Rice, L. N., & Elliott, R. (1993). *Facilitating emotional change: The moment-by-moment process.* Guilford.

Greenberg, L. S., & Van Balen, R. (1998). The theory of experience-centered therapies. In L. S. Greenberg, J. C. Watson, & G. Lietaer (Eds.), *Handbook of experiential psychotherapy* (pp. 28–57). Guilford.

Greenberg, L. S., & Watson, J. C. (2006). *Emotion-focused therapy for depression.* American Psychological Association. http//dx.doi.org/ 10.1037/11286-000

International Centre for Excellence in Emotionally Focused Therapy. (n.d.). *EFT research.* https://iceeft.com/eft-research-3/

Johnson, S. M. (2009). Attachment theory and emotionally focused therapy for individuals and couples. In J. H. Obegi & E. Berant (Eds.), *Attachment theory and research in clinical work with adults* (pp. 410–433). Guilford.

Johnson, S. M., Hunsley, J., Greenberg, L., & Schindler, D. (1999). Emotionally focused couples therapy: Status and challenges. *Clinical Psychology: Science and Practice, 6*, 67–79.

Najafi, M., Soleimani, A., Ahmadi, K., Javidi, N., & Hoseini Kamkar, E. (2015). The study of the effectiveness of couple emotionally focused therapy (EFT) on increasing marital adjustment and improving the physical and psychological health of the infertile couples. *Iran Journal of Obstetrics, Gynecology, & Infertility, 17*(133), 8–21.

Paivio, S. C. (2013). Essential processes in emotion-focused therapy. *Psychotherapy, 50*(3), 341–345. https://doi.org/10.1037/a0032810

Paivio, S. C., & Pascual-Leone, A. (2010). *Emotion-focused therapy for complex trauma: An integrative approach.* American Psychological Association.

Rice, L. M., & Greenberg, L. S. (Eds.) (1984). *Patterns of change: An intensive analysis of psychotherapeutic process.* Guilford.

Robinson, A. L., Dolhanty, J., & Greenberg, L. (2015). Emotion-focused family therapy for eating disorders in children and adolescents. *Clinical Psychology & Psychotherapy, 22*(1), 75–82. https://doi.org/10.1002/cpp.1861

Robinson, A. L., McCague, E. A., & Whissell, C. (2014). "That chair work thing was great: A pilot study of group-based emotion-focused therapy for anxiety and depression. *Person-Centered & Experiential Psychotherapies, 11*(4), 267–277. https://doi.org/10.1080/14779757.2014.910131

Rogers, C. (1957). The necessary and sufficient conditions of therapeutic personality change. *Journal of Consulting Psychology, 21*(2), 95–103.

Watson, J. C., & Greenberg, L. S. (2017). *Emotion-focused therapy for generalized anxiety.* American Psychological Association. https://doi.org/10.1037/0000018-000

Whelton, W. I., & Greenberg, L. S. (2005). Emotion in self-criticism. *Personality and Individual Differences, 59,* 339–345.

Wiebe, S. A., & Johnson, S. M. (2016). A review of the research in emotionally focused therapy for couples. *Family Process, 55,* 390–407. https://doi.org/10.1111/famp.212229

Wunk, S., Greenberg, L., & Dolhanty, J. (2015). Emotion-focused group therapy for women with symptoms of bulimia nervosa. *Eating Disorders Journal of Treatment and Prevention, 23,* 253–261. http://dx.doi.org/10.1080/10640266.2014.9644612

CHAPTER 9

Interpersonal Psychotherapy

Our study is total common sense and it works.

—Myrna M. Weissman

Interpersonal psychotherapy (ITP; Weissman et al., 2017) is a brief form of therapy that targets the intersection of interpersonal dysfunction with psychiatric symptoms. As noted by Myrna Weissman, one of the originators of ITP, it is common sense, and it does work.

IPT is based on the principle that relationships and life events impact mood and that the reverse is also true (Markowitz et al., 1998). IPT operates from the perspective that psychiatric disorders occur in an interpersonal context. This context needs to be addressed if the resolution of client problems and distress is achieved. With an emphasis on relationships, interactions, and attachment issues, ITP centers on helping clients resolve interpersonal problems, managing relationships, and experiencing symptomatic recovery (van Hees et al., 2013).

The current chapter reviews the history and evolution of IPT, its central tenets and concepts, and the structure and strategies employed by therapists employing ITP. Upon completion of this chapter, the reader will be able to do the following:

1. Explain how the medical model takes form in the application of IPT.
2. Describe the phases of IPT and the primary goal in each.
3. Describe the four problem areas or focal points for IPT.

History and Contributors

The roots of interpersonal psychotherapy (IPT) can be found in the initial research of Gerald Klerman, Eugen Paykel, and Myrna Weissman, who in the 1970s investigated the efficacy of tricyclic antidepressant medications. At the time, it was known that many clients treated with tricyclic antidepressants would often relapse into depression. The focus of this early research centered on the role, if any, that psychotherapy may play in relapse prevention.

Developing a new theoretical approach to psychotherapy was not the intent of these researchers. However, to study the potential impact of psychotherapy, the nature and specific protocol of psychotherapy to be used in the study had to be standardized.

The design of the study, conducted at the Depression Research Unit in Connecticut, required that the psychotherapy employed be time-limited and high-impact (Weissman, 2020). The initial research showed that medication prevented relapse, and this "high-contact" psychotherapy improved social functioning (Weissman et al., 1976). With evidence of efficacy, the high contact form of psychotherapy being employed was more fully defined and described as interpersonal psychotherapy (Weissman, 2006). A manual describing the theoretical orientation of the interpersonal approach and the strategies that could be used outside of this research were developed in the early 1980s (Klerman et al., 1984) and later revised in 2007 (Weissman et al., 2007) and again in 2017 (Weissman et al., 2017).

Interest in IPT began to grow with the development of two studies in the late 1980s and early 1990s, the NIMH TCRP (Elkin et al., 1989) on training and use of IPT and the Pittsburg study "Maintenance Therapies in Recurrent Depression" (MTRD; Frank et al., 1990). In 2004, the International Society of Interpersonal Psychotherapists (ISIPT) held its first meeting and established itself as the center of communication for those interested in IPT. Since its introduction, IPT has had extensive research on its application, not only with depression but, in modified form, with other psychological disorders.

Perspective

Operating from the position that there is a relationship between the experience of depression and the individual's social and interpersonal relationships, the team turned to the work of Harry Stack Sullivan (1953), Adolf Meyer (1908), and John Bowlby (1969) to formulate the therapeutic approach to be used. These individuals highlighted the role that interpersonal life experiences played in developing and treating psychopathology.

Meyer (1957) emphasized the role of one's psychosocial environment in creating mental illness. Meyer's position was that mental illness was "an attempt by the individual to adapt to the changing environment" (Klerman et al., 1984, p. 42). In addition to the influence of Meyer, ITP embraced the perspective that clients must develop and maintain social support networks that can be of service at times of distress. This perspective reflected findings on attachment (Bowlby, 1969) and the emphasis given by Sullivan (1947) on the role interpersonal relationships play in the development of one's personality.

With these as the framework for IPT, the theory focused on and emphasized the client's relationship difficulties, attachment schema (Bartholomew & Horowitz, 1991), and maladaptive metacommunication patterns (Kiesler & Watkins, 1989). The overriding goal was to help clients improve interpersonal and intrapersonal communications skills within their relationships and social network to improve the quality of their relationships and the social support they provided (Ravitz & Watson, 2014; Weissman et al., 2007).

Assumptions and Principles Guiding Practice

Central to IPT is the assumed link between interpersonal dysfunction and psychopathology. In addition to this central assumption, IPT holds to several fundamental principles and concepts that guide practice.

A Medical Model

Given that the creation of IPT took place in a medical setting, with a number of the participants coming from a medical background, it is not surprising that the theory embraces a medical model of disease. IPT uses the medical model as a conceptual framework for clients' mood symptoms. In initiating IPT, the therapist conducts a psychiatric history and diagnosis. Therapists employing IPT identify the illness and then separate that illness from the client's innate personality.

The approach identifies the client's difficulties as stemming from a form of mental sickness in combination with a particular interpersonal context. The principle is to approach the client as having a medical illness, not one with a personality flaw or defect. It is felt that this framework reduces the client's self-criticism or guilt.

Clients are not seen as having some psychological, emotional, or moral fault but rather are the victims of an illness. The focus of treatment is not on their sense of self or character but the disease they are encountering (Markowitz et al., 1998). This perspective allows for the employment of adjunctive medical and pharmacological interventions as part of the treatment protocol (Frank & Levinson, 2011).

Goals

IPT operates with the dual aims of resolving an interpersonal issue and relieving the disorder's symptoms (Markowitz & Weissman, 2004). The primary assumption is that the focus of therapy needs to be on the client's current symptoms and interpersonal experiences, not personality change (Frank & Levinson, 2011). Given these overriding goals, the client needs to understand the connection of interpersonal difficulties with the presenting symptoms.

In the short term, the goal of IPT is to quickly ease symptoms and help clients adjust to their immediate social situation (Weissman et al., 2000). As such, an IPT therapist may help clients build the necessary communication skills to assert themselves in a specific context or with a specific individual who presents as a challenge. In the long term, however, the goal is to help clients better manage relationships without the regular assistance of a therapist, thereby helping them avoid the onset of mood-related symptoms stemming from their interpersonal interactions (Rafaeli & Markowitz, 2011).

Here and Now

IPT focuses treatment around interpersonal events in the client's current life. For this reason, IPT is often referred to as having a here-and-now focus (Markowitz et al., 1998). Rather than delving into a client's early childhood or developmental history, IPT focuses the therapeutic interaction around recent interpersonal experiences and uses that as the context for discussing the client's mood and behaviors. This here-and-now focus helps the client and the therapist better understand the client's view of self and others (Weissman et al., 2000).

Time Limited With Phases

Interpersonal psychotherapy is a short-term, focused therapy (Frank & Levinson, 2011). IPT is presented across 12–16 weeks in three phases (Markowtiz & Weismann, 2004). The time-limited nature of IPT encourages clients and therapists to stay focused on tasks. While seeking to understand the client" interpersonal history, the focus centers on the present concerns. Table 9.1 provides a summary description of the goals for each of these phases. The specifics of the tasks of each phase are discussed in more detail in the following sections.

Collaborative

Even though the IPT is presented as a process that progresses through stages or phases (see Table 9.1), the therapeutic relationship remains flexible, collaborative, and responsive to individual variation. The client and therapist are expected to work together—collaboratively—toward reducing symptoms and improving the client's well-being (Weissman et al., 2000).

Therapist Active

The therapist employing IPT is openly supportive and acts as an ally who brings an optimistic outlook to the interaction. IPT therapists serve as advocates for their clients (Weissman et al., 2017). The therapist takes an active, positive, cheerleading role with the client, especially when

TABLE 9.1 OVERVIEW: IPT PHASES AND GOALS

Phase	Weeks in Treatment	General Goals
Beginning phase	Weeks 1–4	As an assessment phase, the client's interpersonal style will be identified and the target diagnosis placed within an interpersonal context.
Middle phase	Weeks 5–12	Client and therapist work on identifying target and area of concern. Therapist provides practical tools for improving social interactions and reducing symptoms.
Termination	Weeks 13–16	The therapist provides strategies for the client to manage their interpersonal relationships following termination of the therapy. Sometimes there are monthly follow-ups.

clients present with feelings of helplessness (Markowitz & Weissman, 2004). While collaborating with clients around content and focus of sessions, the therapist takes active responsibility for structuring sessions and maintaining the goal focus of sessions.

Therapists engaged in IPT, while being supportive and encouraging, do not necessarily offer the level of unconditional positive regard found in other therapies (Frank & Spanier, 1995). They actively reframe the presenting problems as the result of mental illness or issues in the outside world and not a reflection of the client as being damaged or at fault. At the same time, the message conveyed is that it is up to the client to do what is needed to address that which is causing distress.

Principles in Action

The specific elements included in IPT are (a) using the medical model to define the onset of symptoms, diagnose the condition and give the client the "sick role"; (b) eliciting an interpersonal inventory; (c) setting time limits for therapy; and (d) presenting a formulation linking the interpersonal problem area (e.g., grief, role dispute, role transition, or interpersonal deficit) to the diagnosis (Weissman et al., 2017). Developed as an acute treatment (12–16 weeks), IPT has three phases: a beginning (one–three sessions), middle (10–14 sessions), and end (three sessions), each with specific tasks.

IPT was initially developed as an approach for treating major depression. While it has subsequently been adapted for use with other disorders, the description presented of its principles in action reflects the original depression-focused therapy. Table 9.4 outlines the phases, tasks, goals, and sample strategies of IPT as applied to major depression.

Beginning (One to Three Sessions)

The initial phase of IPT requires the therapist to identify the target diagnosis and the interpersonal context in which it presents. The therapist will review the client's symptoms and help the client understand how these will be treated with IPT.

Throughout this phase, while identifying and naming symptoms, the therapist will also normalize them as part of the disease (e.g., depression) or as a limitation or consequence of a disease. Thus, the fact that a depressed individual is experiencing difficulty making social commitments or appointments will be framed as a normal or expected consequence of the disease of depression. Clients will be helped to accept these realities without guilt or blame (see Case Illustration 9.1).

Clients are given the "sick role," a temporary status recognizing that their illness keeps them from functioning at total capacity (Weissman et al., 2000). For some, the idea of being identified as being "sick" may be received as insult or perhaps as permission to abdicate responsibility (see Exercise 9.1). While noting that it is not the client's fault that they cannot do certain things because of their illness, the therapist employing IPT will help the client understand that it remains their responsibility to do what is necessary to get better.

CASE ILLUSTRATION 9.1

Introducing the Sick Role

The client is a 49-year-old woman who has been diagnosed with major depressive disorder. The exchange occurred during the first session of IPT.

Client: I'm such a horrible person—a burden to my family, such a disappointment, a complete failure as wife and mother.

Therapist: I can hear in your voice how upset you feel. I'm not sure what you mean when you say you are a burden to your family. Is that what they say?

Client: Oh, no. They are wonderful. They tell me that they love me and that they are concerned about me. They are so wonderful; they deserve better than me.

Therapist: If they are being supportive and expressing their love and concern, what is it that you see that makes you feel like a burden, a disappointment, a failure in the role of mother and wife?

Client: I haven't cleaned the house in weeks, barely can make an edible meal, and my husband and I have not been intimate for the longest time.

Therapist: Oh. So, the fact that you have had difficulty with making dinner or doing house cleaning and that it has been hard for you to be interested and available to your husband, these are the things that you see as evidence that you are a horrible person?

Client: (crying) Sure, don't you?

Therapist: I'm wondering. Would you feel the same way about your husband if he contracted a major illness, one that kept him in bed? I mean, would he be horrible for not going to work, or doing the yard work, or being able or interested in sharing intimate moments with you?

Client: No. He would be sick. That's not his fault.

Therapist: Exactly, that would not be his fault, and in fact he would be acting precisely as he should act, as a person who is ill—and so are you. You have a disease and illness. That is what depression is. The fact that you find little energy to do the things you used to do makes total sense. This is what you are expected to experience. The things that you are beating yourself up about are the result of being ill and are not your fault.

EXERCISE 9.1

Sick?

Directions: Being assigned a sick role is intended to reduce a client's tendency to be self-downing about their emotional state. It is not meant to be an excuse for nonaction or not taking responsibility. Consider each of the following experiences as they may apply to you.

As you reflect on each these situations, consider the following: Does the concept of "sick" apply? Does responsibility and reasonable action still come to play? Does the assignment of a sick role reduce the self-blame or embarrassment?

1. You have contracted COVID-19 and are so weak that you can't get out of bed to attend class. This means you will miss delivering your part of your group's presentation.
2. On your way to class, you had a car accident, and while not physically hurt, you are experiencing an anxiety attack and are unable to attend class.
3. You celebrated your birthday last night and are feeling the effects of too much alcohol. As a result, you call of out of work.
4. You just experienced the death of your dog whom you have had for over 12 years. You are finding it impossible to study for your exam that will be administered tomorrow.

During this initial phase of treatment, therapists will have clients complete an interpersonal inventory. The inventory will provide data on the nature of their interactions with significant others, the nature of satisfying and unsatisfying relationships, and the changes the client may desire in their relationships. The data collected from this interpersonal inventory will help both the client and the therapist identify current social conflicts and stressors that contribute to the onset and maintenance of the disease. These interpersonal conflicts and stressors then become targets for intervention. As a final element to this initial phase of IPT, the therapist and client will identify a focal area for treatment. The problem areas addressed by IPT therapists fall into four groups (see Table 9.2).

Middle Phase (10–14 Sessions)

The middle phase of IPT is where strategies will be employed to address the agreed-on problem area (see Table 9.2). With a primary problem identified, the client and therapist work collaboratively to improve the current interpersonal problem (Klerman et al., 1984; see Case Illustration 9.2).

In this phase, the client and therapist work on the client's ability to assert his needs and wishes in interpersonal encounters. Client emotions, for example anger, will be normalized as an interpersonal signal, one that calls for an adaptive response, and they will be encouraged to take appropriate social risks.

TABLE 9.2 IPT PROBLEM AREAS

Problem Area	Life Situation	Goals of Therapy	Sample Strategies
Grief	• Complicated bereavement following the death of a significant other or close relative	• Facilitate mourning • Re-establish interest and relationships	• Psychoeducation about grief/depression • Facilitate client experience of feelings and catharsis • Identify new activities/relationships
Role dispute	• Struggle, disagreement with spouse, lovers, child, other family member, friend, or coworker	• Help client identify disagreement • Help client choose a plan of action • Help client modify communications and expectations	• Help clients identify their feelings about the relationship, as well as what they want • Assist client with expressing/asserting personal wants • Role-play, negotiating
Role transition	• Life change: graduation, a new job, leaving one's family, divorce, going away to school, a move, a new home, retirement, medical illness, immigration	• Give up the old role • Mourn the loss • Explore new opportunities • Develop new social support and attachments • Recognize the positive aspects of the new role	• Cost-benefit analyses of old role • Clarification of needs, wants • Skills (social and work) training
Interpersonal deficits	• No acute life events; paucity of attachments, loneliness, social isolation, boredom	• Assist client to tolerate social anxiety • Increase client's self-confidence • Strengthen current relationships and develop new ones	• Review past relationships, identifying patterns of strengths and difficulties • Help reframe encounters as learning opportunities • Set small social engagement goals • Role-play

Adapted from Myrna M. Weissman, John C. Markowitz, and Gerald L. Klerman, "Table 4.2: IPT Problems Area," *The Guide to Interpersonal Psychotherapy*, p. 36. Copyright © 2017 by Oxford University Press.

CASE ILLUSTRATION 9.2

Transitioning Is Difficult

The client is a 68-year-old male who presented as depressed and anxious. Following the intake history and interpersonal inventory, the client and therapist identified the precipitants of his depression and anxiety as his recent retirement as the president and CEO of the company he created and has now passed over to his son. The therapist invited the client to conceptualize the focus of treatment to be on role transition, or more accurately a transition from several roles (e.g., president, CEO, father, family provider). While the retirement appeared to be the primary precipitant, the client's constant checking up with his son, who was making changes to the company, and the fact that his wife decided to engage in volunteer work 3 days a week, which took her out of the house and his company, contributed to the worsening of his anxiety and depression.

After the initial phase of therapy, the client and therapist set the following as goals for therapy:

1. The facilitation of the client's grieving of his loss of position and the termination of what he saw as his role in developing and nurturing his baby (i.e., the business)
2. The cost-benefits analysis of his current role as retired
3. Identifying alternative approaches to satisfying his wants and needs, including those that involved his wife and their relationship

---

During this phase, the therapist continues to support a therapeutic alliance and maintain a focus on the agreed-on goals. ITP therapists will call on various techniques and strategies to assist the client in understanding their experience and helping them develop alternative ways of responding to those situations associated with these distressing experiences. Therapists will employ techniques such as focusing on affect, communication analysis, decision analysis, psychoeducation, and role-play to assist the client in developing the interpersonal skills required to navigate their symptoms and improve their interpersonal functioning (see Table 9.3). Clients will often role-play with the therapist in preparation for applying new interpersonal skills outside the therapist's office (Markowitz & Weissman, 2004).

Treatment centers on the client's real-life outside environment, not the therapy itself. Therapists typically introduce IPT sessions with questions such as "How have things been since we last met?" (Markowitz & Weissman, 2017, p. 40). In sessions, therapists and clients review the past week's events. Clients are reinforced for successful and healthy engagement of interpersonal skills and assisted in analyzing and adjusting when things were less than successful.

TABLE 9.3 **TREATMENT ELEMENTS AND STRATEGIES**

Linking distress to context	As previously noted, ITP emphasizes a here-an-now perspective, one that focuses on the client's present experience instead of a deep dive into their past. Therapists will often begin the session by simply asking, "How has the previous week been?" Regardless of the response, the therapist will link current distress or improvements to the events that have transpired. This helps continue addressing the presenting concerns and problems within the social context.
Encouragement of affect	Therapists employing ITP will encourage client expression of affect. The goal is to help the client identify feelings about a person or a situation, make decisions on managing these emotions more effectively, and implement changes based on these emotions (Weissman et al., 2007).
Communication analysis	Since communication skills are central to interpersonal functioning, ITP therapists will often elicit from a client a specific conversation that may have gone awry. The therapist will listen for communication patterns that may contribute to the client's difficulty and work with the client on brainstorming ways to express their intentions more effectively.
Psychoeducation	Clients are taught about the condition or disease they are encountering in an attempt to normalize their experience and to continue to connect the onset and maintenance of the experience to social context and interpersonal difficulties.
Decision analysis	With detailed information about problematic situations, the therapist and client will explore options in an attempt to identify alternatives within that situation. These alternatives will be assessed, and decisions on how to proceed will follow (Weissman et al., 2020). The therapist will be active in this process and may suggest options not initially identified by the client (Klerman et al., 1984). While such an intervention can be helpful, a therapist working from an IPT model seeks to help the client independently generate and select options to employ.
Role-plays	Role-play is often used to assist the client to more clearly understand feelings in a situation and practice new communicational styles and relationship skills (Weissman et al., 2007). Role-play, in the confines of the therapist's office, can provide an opportunity to move from talking about the desire to change to engaging in change strategies.

Final Phase: Termination

As is true of all brief therapies, IPT is not an open-ended treatment. The time-limited nature of IPT is discussed during the initial sessions with the client. As termination approaches, therapists will review the client's accomplishments and invite open discussion about termination.

Termination of therapy is, in itself, a role transition and may be difficult for clients. The move toward termination is also evidence of the client's capabilities. The therapist will review the progress made, credit the client's hard work, and address additional issues. When necessary, the therapist and the client will plan for additional and or ancillary treatment or strategies for maintaining the progress achieved.

TABLE 9.4 OUTLINE OF IPT STAGES AND TASKS

Therapist's Role

Be the patient's advocate (not neutral).
Be active, not passive.
The therapeutic relationship is not interpreted as transference.
The therapeutic relationship is not a friendship.

Initial Sessions

1. Diagnose the depression and its interpersonal context.
2. Explain depression as a medical illness and present the various treatment options.
3. Evaluate need for medication.
4. Elicit interpersonal inventory to assess potential social support and problem areas.
5. Formulation: Relate depression to interpersonal context (derived from interpersonal inventory).
6. Explain IPT concepts and contract.
7. Define the framework and structure of treatment and set a time limit.
8. Give the patient the sick role.

Intermediate Sessions

	Greif/Complicated Bereavement	Role Disputes	Role Transitions	Interpersonal Deficits
Goals	1. Facilitate the mourning process. 2. Help the patient reestablish interests and relationships.	1. Identify the dispute. 2. Explore options and choose a plan of action. 3. Modify expectations or faulty communications to bring about a satisfactory resolution.	1. Facilitate mourning and acceptance of the loss of the old role. 2. Help the patient regard the new role in a more positive light. 3. Help the patient restore self-esteem.	1. Reduce the patient's social isolation. 2. Encourage the patient to form new relationships.

(Continued)

TABLE 9.4 (*Continued*)

	Greif/Complicated Bereavement	Role Disputes	Role Transitions	Interpersonal Deficits
Strategies	Review depressive symptoms/syndrome. Relate symptom onset to the death of the significant other. Reconstruct the patient's relationship with the deceased.	Review depressive symptoms/syndrome. Relate the symptom onset to an overt or covert dispute with significant other with whom the patient is currently involved.	Review depressive symptoms/syndrome. Relate depressive symptoms to difficulty in coping with recent life change. Review positive and negative aspects of old and new roles.	Review depressive symptoms/syndrome. Relate depressive symptoms to problems of social isolation or lack of fulfillment.
Strategies	Describe the sequence and consequences of events just prior to, during, and after the death.	Determine the stage of dispute: 1. Renegotiation (calm the participants to facilitate resolution) 2. Impasse (increase disharmony in order to reopen negotiation) 3. Dissolution (assist mourning) Understand how nonreciprocal role expectations relate to the dispute: *What are the issues in the dispute?* *What are the differences in expectations and values?* *What are the options?* *What is the likelihood of finding alternatives?*	Explore the patient's feelings about what is lost. Explore the patient's feelings about the change itself. Explore opportunities in the new role. Realistically evaluate what is lost. Encourage appropriate release of affect. Encourage development of social support system and of new skills called for in new role.	Review past significant relationships, including their negative and positive aspects. Explore repetitive patterns in relationships. Discuss the patient's positive and negative feelings about the therapist and encourage the patient to seek parallels in other relationships.

(*Continued*)

TABLE 9.4 *(Continued)*

	Greif/Complicated Bereavement	Role Disputes	Role Transitions	Interpersonal Deficits
		What resources are available to bring about change in the relationship? Are there parallels in other relationships? What is the patient gaining? What unspoken assumptions lie behind the patient's behavior? How is the dispute being perpetuated?		

Termination Phase

1. Explicitly discuss termination.
2. Acknowledge that termination is a time of (healthy) sadness—a role transition.
3. Move toward the patient's recognition of independent competence.
4. Deal with nonresponse:
   - Minimize the patient's self-blame by blaming the treatment.
   - Emphasize alternative treatment options.
5. Assess the need for a continuation/maintenance treatment.
   - Renegotiate the treatment contract.

Source: Myrna M. Weissman, John C. Markowitz, and Gerald L. Klerman, "Table 2.1: IPT Outline," The Guide to Interpersonal Psychotherapy, pp. 16-18. Copyright © 2017 by Oxford University Press. Reprinted with permission.

Supportive Research

IPT is recognized by the American Psychological Association (APA) and the National Institutes of Health (NIH) as an effective mode of treatment for mental health issues (Weissman & Markowitz, 2017). The utility of IPT for treating major depressive disorders has been supported by studies of the National Institute of Mental Health (NIMH) and Treatment of Depression Collaborative Research Program (Elkin et al., 1989). IPT has been reported as effective as a maintenance treatment for those experiencing recurrent depression (Frank et al., 1990).

IPT has been adapted as an effective treatment for bipolar disorders (Frank, 2005), social phobia (Lipsitz et al., 2008), panic symptoms (Cyranowski et al., 2004), posttraumatic disorders (Krupnick et al., 2016), and eating disorders (Cuijpers et al., 2016; Murphy et al., 2012). Research continues to test the efficacy of IPT, and data reflecting this research can be found at the International Society of Interpersonal Psychotherapy website (https://www.interpersonalpsychotherapy.org/).

Suitability

The research pointing to the efficacy of IPT would suggest that it is a suitable approach for clients presenting with a mood disorder. Research (e.g., Frank et al., 2011) suggests that the use of medication or medication combined with IPT is more effective than IPT alone when treating those with more significant depression severity and suicidal ideation. Caution appears appropriate when considering the employment of IPT with depressed clients who present with comorbid conditions, especially substance abuse (Weissman et al., 2007). IPT also appears less suitable for clients presenting with avoidant or borderline personality traits or disorders, who are self-critical perfectionists, who experience attachment difficulties, or who have a history of trauma (Ravitz et al., 2011).

KEYSTONES

- The roots of IPT can be found in the initial research of Gerald Klerman, Eugen Paykel, and Myrna Weissman.
- As a theory, ITP focuses and emphasizes the client's relationship difficulties, attachment schema, and maladaptive metacommunication patterns.
- The overriding goal of IPT is to help clients improve interpersonal and intrapersonal communications skills within their relationship and social network in order to improve the quality of their relationships and the social support they provided.
- IPT uses the medical model as a conceptual framework for clients' mood symptoms, with therapists separating the client from clients' innate personalities.
- The primary assumption is that the focus of therapy needs to be on the client's current symptoms and interpersonal experiences, not personality change.
- The specific elements included in IPT are (a) using the medical model to define the onset of symptoms, diagnose the condition, and give the client the sick role; (b) eliciting an interpersonal inventory; (c) setting time limits for therapy; and (d) presenting a formulation linking interpersonal problem area (e.g., grief, role dispute, role transition, or interpersonal deficit) to the diagnosis.
- IPT progresses through three phases: beginning (one to three sessions); middle, where strategies will be employed to address the agreed-on problem area; and termination, where the therapist will review the progress made, credit the hard work of the client, and address additional issues.
- IPT has supportive evidence for effectiveness in treating major depressive disorders and with adaptation treating bipolar disorders, social phobia, panic symptoms, posttraumatic disorders, and eating disorders.

ADDITIONAL RESOURCES

Frank, E., & Levenson, J. C. (2011). *Interpersonal psychotherapy*. American Psychological Association.

Markowitz, J. C. (2021). *In the aftermath of the pandemic: Interpersonal psychotherapy for anxiety, depression and PTSD*. Oxford University Press.

Tasca, G. A., Mikail, S. F., & Hewitt, P. L. (2020). *Group psychodynamic-interpersonal psychotherapy*. American Psychological Association.

Weissman, M. M., Markowitz, J. M., & Klerman, G. L. (2017). *Comprehensive guide to interpersonal psychotherapy: Updated and expanded version*. Oxford University Press.

REFERENCES

Bartholomew, K., & Horowitz, L. (1991). Attachment styles among young adults: A test of a four-category model. *Journal of Personality and Social Psychology, 61*(2), 226–244.

Bowlby, J. (1969). *Attachment*. Basic Books.

Cuijpers, P., Donker, T., Weissman, M. M., Ravitz, P., & Cristea, I. A. (2016). Interpersonal psychotherapy for mental health problems: A comprehensive meta-analysis. *American Journal of Psychiatry, 173*, 680–687.

Cyranowski, J. M., Frank, E., Winter, E., Rucci, P., Novick, D, Pikonis, P., Houck, P., Maccarelli, L., & Kupfer, D. J. (2004). Personality pathology and outcome in recurrently depressed women over 2 years of maintenance interpersonal psychotherapy. *Psychological Medicine, 34*, 659–669.

Elkin, I., Shea, M. T., Watkins, J. T., Imber, S. D., Sotskyh, S. M., Collins, J. F., Glass, D. R., Pilkonis, P. A., Leber, W. R., & Doherty J. P. (1989). National Institute of Mental Health treatment of depression collaborative research program: General effectiveness of treatments. *Archives of General Psychiatry, 1989, 46*(11), 971–982.

Frank, E. (2005). *Treating bipolar disorder: A clinician's guide to interpersonal and social rhythm therapy*. Guilford.

Frank, E., Cassano, G., Rucci, P., Thompson, W. K., Kraemer, H. C., Fagiolini, A., Maggi, L., Kupfer, D. J., Shear, M. K., Houck, P. R., Calugi, S., Grochcinski, V. J., Scocco, P., Buttenfield, J., & Forgione, R. M. (2011). Predictors and moderators of time to remission of major depression with interpersonal psychotherapy and SSRI pharmacotherapy. *Psychological Medicine, 41*, 151–162.

Frank, E., Kupfer, D. J., Perel, J. M., Cornes, C., Jarrett, D. B., Malligner, A. G., Thase, M. E., McEachran, A. B., & Grochocinski, V. J. (1990). Three-year outcomes for maintenance therapies in recurrent depression. *Archives of General Psychiatry, 1990, 47*, 1093–1099.

Frank, E., & Levenson, J. C. (2011). *Interpersonal psychotherapy*. American Psychological Association.

Frank, E., & Spanier, C. A. (1995). Interpersonal psychotherapy for depression: Overview, clinical efficacy and future directions. *Clinical Psychology: Science and Practice, 2*, 349–369.

Klerman, G. L., & Weissman, M. M. (Eds.) (1993). *New application of interpersonal psychotherapy*. American Psychiatric Press.

Kiesler, D., & Watkins, L. M. (1989). Interpersonal complementarity and the therapeutic alliance: A study of relationship in psychotherapy. *Psychotherapy, 26*(2), 183–94.

Klerman, G L., Weissman, M. M., Rounsaville, B. J., & Chevron, E. (1984). *Interpersonal psychotherapy of depression*. Basic Books.

Krupnick, J. L., Melnikoff, E., & Reinhard, M. (2016). A pilot study of interpersonal psychotherapy for PTSD in women veterans. *Psychiatry, 79*, 56–69.

Lipsitz, J. D., Gur, M., Vermes, D., Petkova, E., Cheng, J., Miller, N., Laino, J., Liebowitz, M., & Fyer, A. J. (2008). A randomized trial of interpersonal therapy versus supportive therapy for social anxiety disorder. *Depression and Anxiety, 25*(6), 542–553. https://doi.org/10.1002/da.20364

Markowitz, J. C., Svartberg, M., & Swartz, H. A. (1998). Is IPT time-limited psychodynamic psychotherapy?. *The Journal of Psychotherapy Practice and Research, 7*(3), 185–195.

Markowitz, J. C., & Weissman, M. M. (2004). Interpersonal psychotherapy: Principles and applications. *World Psychiatry: Official Journal of the World Psychiatric Association (WPA), 3*(3), 136–139.

Meyer, M. (1908). What do histories of cases of insanity teach us concerning preventive mental hygiene during the years of school life? *Psychological Clinic, 2*(4), 89–101.

Rafaeli, A. K., & Markowitz, J. C. (2011). Interpersonal psychotherapy (IPT) for PTSD: A case study. *American Journal of Psychotherapy, 65*(3), 205–223.

Ravitz, P., McBride, C., & Maunder, R. (2011). Failures in interpersonal psychotherapy (IPT): Factors related to treatment resistance. *Journal of Clinical Psychology, 67*(11), 1129–1139. https://doi.org/10.1002/jclp.20850

Ravitz, P., & Watson, P. (2014). Interpersonal psychotherapy: Healing with a relational focus. *Focus, 12*, 275–284.

Sullivan, H. S. (1947). *Conceptions of modern psychiatry*. William A. White Psychiatric Foundation.

Sullivan, H. S. (1953). *The interpersonal theory of psychiatry*. Norton.

van Hees, M. L., Rotter, T., Ellermann, T., & Evers, S. M. (2013). The effectiveness of individual interpersonal psychotherapy as a treatment for major depressive disorder in adult outclients: A systematic review. *BMC Psychiatry, 13*, 22. https://doi.org/10.1186/1471-244X-13-22

Weissman, M. M. (2006). A brief history of interpersonal psychotherapy. *Psychiatric Annals, 36*(8), 553–567. https://doi.rog/10.3928/00485713-20060801-03

Weissman, M. M. (2020). Interpersonal psychotherapy: History and future. *American Journal of Psychotherapy, 73*(1), 3–7. https://doi.org/10.1176/appi.psychotherapy.20190032

Weissman, M. M., Kasl, S. V., & Klerman, G. L. (1976). Follow-up of depressed women after maintenance treatment. *American Journal of Psychiatry, 133*(7), 757–760.

Weissman, M. M., Markowitz, J. M., & Klerman, G. L. (2000). *Comprehensive guide to interpersonal psychotherapy*. Basic Books.

Weissman, M. M., Markowtiz, J. M., & Klerman, G. L. (2007). Clinician's quick guide to interpersonal psychotherapy. Oxford University Press.

Weissman, M. M., Markowitz, J. M., & Klerman, G. L. (2017). *Comprehensive guide to interpersonal psychotherapy: Updated and expanded version*. Oxford University Press.

CHAPTER 10

Single-Session Therapys

Single-session therapy:
When the First Session may be the Last

—Michael F. Hoyt
https://www.brieftherapyconference.com/download/
handouts/HOYT.pdf

Despite traditional theoretical biases or even the secular belief that more is always better, evidence shows that there is no established direct correlation between the severity and duration of a problem and the duration of effective treatment (Hoyt et al., 1992, 2018; Talmon, 1990). Treatment success is not equated with the length or quantity of therapy. Rather, a successful outcome is associated with the quality of therapy (Hoyt & Talmon, 2018; Slive & Bobele, 2012).

In single-session therapy (SST), therapists seek to make the most of their meeting with clients, approaching their work as if it could be the only session. SST operates under the assumption that ongoing sessions, while an option, may not be necessary (Cannistrà & Piccirilli, 2018; Slive & Bobele, 2012; Young, 2018).

The current chapter reviews the unique mind-set that defines SST, its basic tenets, and a model illustrating its application. Upon completion of this chapter, the reader will be able to do the following:

1. Describe what is meant by mind-set defining the perspective of SST.
2. Explain how the findings on session attendance and outcome laid the foundation for SST.
3. Explain what is meant by service at point of need versus service at point of availability.
4. Describe the phases of SST and the primary targets to be addressed at each phase.

History and Contributors

Single-session therapy is not new to the 21st century. Freud and Breuer (1893), Gustav Halher in 1910 (Kuehn, 1965) and Alfred Adler (1930/2013) in his child guidance clinics of the 1920s all provided evidence of single-session treatment. More recently, Albert Ellis (Ellis & Jofee, 2002) and Milton Erickson (O'Hanlon & Hexum, 1990) have demonstrated the effectiveness of single-session treatment. However, as presented within this chapter, single-session therapy, as a unique mind-set and intentional approach to therapy, has its roots in the work of Moshe Talmon (1990, 1993).

Talmon and his colleagues working at the Kaiser Permanente Medical Center in California discovered that the modal number of sessions for clients was one session. The group also found that 78% of the clients, who terminated after one session, did so because they achieved what they wanted to achieve in the initial session (Talmon, 2008). Thus, termination was not evidence of therapeutic failure. Instead, termination after one session reflected the client's positive experience and their belief that the change experienced with one session was sufficient. While it was not Talmon's initial intent to develop a model of psychotherapy, his experience and research soon gave form to a model of single-session psychotherapy.

It should be noted that all within the professional community did not immediately embrace the idea that a single session can be "therapy." The College of Registered Psychotherapists of Ontario, for example, removed SST as a qualifying experience for those seeking to acquire a certificate of registration and thus be allowed to use the title "psychotherapist." Their actions were challenged in court and, given the research that supported the establishment of a therapeutic relationship in a single session, the court decision was overturned (Young & Jebree, 2019). This was a significant factor in establishing SST as a legitimate form of psychotherapy.

Since Talmon's work in the early 1990s, interest in employing and researching single-session treatment expanded worldwide (Slive et al., 2008; Taylor et al., 2010). Community-based organizations, including walk-in clinics, became more widespread, and in an effort to improve service delivery, many adopted SST as their modality of choice (Slive & Bobele, 2012). Others practitioner-researchers, such as Jeff Young (2012, 2014), Michael Hoyt (1992, 2014, 2018), and Windy Dryden (2018, 2019), have, through their research and writings, further popularized this approach. This popularity and legitimacy were further enhanced by the development of the International Conference on Single Session Therapy, which was first held in Melbourne, Australia, in 2012. The findings from the conference were presented in the publication *Capturing the Moment: Single Session Therapy and Walk-In Services* (Hoyt & Talmon, 2014). At the most recent conference, 2019, entitled "Single Session Thinking: Going Global One Step at a Time," SST was reported as a model of service being employed in the United States, Canada, Australia, UK, Israel, Mexico, Sweden, China, Cambodia, Turkey, Italy, and New Zealand.

Perspective: Mind-Set Not Mode

Despite common beliefs and traditional biases, there is no established direct correlation between the severity and duration of a problem and the duration of effective treatment (Hoyt et al., 1992, 2018; Talmon, 1990). Current research does not support the view that success should be equated with the length of therapy. Quality, not quantity, needs to be the focus (Hoyt et al., 2018; Slive & Bobele, 2012). This is undoubtedly a key position for those engaging in SST a position.

Unlike the other models and theories presented within this text, SST is not a new approach; instead, it is a new way of thinking about therapy (Young, 2018). There is no single unifying theory for SST. SST is meant to be a flexible and creative approach, where many different techniques and methods can be applied (Campbell, 2012; Hoyt et al., 2018; Talmon, 2012; Young et al., 2008). SST therapists may employ narrative or crisis-oriented theories, brief solution-focused therapy, postmodern, social constructivist, or systemic approaches. Regardless of the specific methods and techniques employed, single-session work is always meant to be pragmatic, strength based, and focused on clients' presenting concerns (Slive & Bobele, 2012).

What identifies a single-session therapist is not the specific techniques employed but rather the fact that practice decisions are informed by a single-session mind-set (Hoyt et al., 2020). When applied to SST, the mind-set shared across approaches is the expectation that some beneficial change, be that in thinking, feeling, or behaving, is possible as a result of SST.

Whereas much of the initial session in traditional therapy is devoted to history, assessment, and formal case formulation, SST is organized to engage in efforts at problem resolution, intervention, and change, right at the start of therapy. The goal for SST is for the client to leave a single session with a plan to resolve their problem, knowing that they can come back for further work as desired (Campbell, 2012).

Assumptions and Principles Guiding Practice

As a mind-set and mode of service delivery, SST does not operate in a single, set manner, nor follow a specific philosophy or set of assumptions about the human condition. SST does, however, embody a constructive, strength-based orientation and a collaborative yet directive mode of practice.

The Power of the One

SST challenges the basic notion of more being better. As previously noted, the modal number of sessions per treatment across therapy approaches is one (Hoyt et al., 2018). Therapists have not been typically apprised of this factor, and most conventional theories imply that more is better. The research does not support this belief (e.g., Lambert, 2013). SST operates from the assumption that a lot can be done in one session when a client and therapist work collaboratively (Dryden, 2022). Table 10.1 presents four conditions that result in rapid change (Dryden, 2019).

TABLE 10.1 CONDITIONS PROMOTING RAPID CHANGE

Knowledge	Knowing what to do is one element that can contribute to rapid change. When engaged in techniques and strategies such as those employed in CBT, knowledge, especially as applied to cognitive processes, is vital. Other approaches that may be employed in SST, such as modified Rogerian or Ericksonian approaches, may not rely too heavily on client understanding and knowledge.
Commitment	Clients need to have a good and committed reason to change. Having a goal that is valued and is somewhat time-bound (e.g., an approaching deadline) can facilitate rapid change.
Accepting costs	Clients need to be aware of and accept the cost (personal, interpersonal, and pragmatic) that may be involved with achieving goals. By definition, change will incur some form of cost, often in the form of client discomfort. For change to occur, these costs need to be understood and accepted.
Taking action	Perhaps the most apparent condition promoting rapid change is that involving client action. Being prepared to take action is supported by the previous three conditions. However, with the foundation laid, it is now up to the client to engage their resources and motivation to take the action necessary to move from what is to what is desired.

Not a Quick Fix, Nor Truncated Conventional Therapy

While focused on providing efficient service, SST is neither a quick fix nor superficial in its approach. SST attempts to find durable solutions to the problems presented, or, as needed, a meaningful path that will result in the resolution of the presenting concerns. The approach is not one of providing traditional therapy in a truncated or condensed format. SST is an approach that has its process and focus (Hoyt et al., 2018; Talmon, 1990).

Providing Help at Point of Need

SST operates from the principle of providing client help at the point of need. This principle suggests that SST is best done in the context where clients can be seen immediately and not placed on waiting lists. With an emphasis on meeting the need, therapists employing SST engage in therapy right from the outset of the relationship. Table 10.2 contrasts the assumptions of SST and its emphasis on providing help at the point of need with approaches that provide help at the point of availability.

TABLE 10.2 PROVIDING HELP AT POINT OF NEED OR AVAILABILITY

Providing Help at Point of Need	Providing Help at Point of Availability
• Better to provide some help rather than waiting to provide the best possible help	• Better to wait for the opportunity to provide the best possible help
• Immediate help is more critical than assessment	• Assessment is a necessary precondition
• Engage immediately in therapy	• Engage in case formulation following case history
• Offer therapy and watch how clients respond	• Offer therapy as a reflection of full assessment and case formulation
• Therapy length is best determined by the client	• Therapy length is best determined by the therapist
• Client not returning for an additional session may reflect client satisfaction	• Client not returning for additional sessions reflects bad outcome and client "dropout"

Constructive and Strength-Based

SST therapists assume that people, given support, can quickly help themselves. Therapists engaged in SST "use their expertise primarily to help clients better use their own expertise" (Hoyt et al., 2018, p. 15). SST views what the client brings to the therapy as the most significant resources available to achieve the desired goals. The SST therapist helps the client identify internal strengths and feel empowered to employ them.

Collaborative

SST is a process that fuses or integrates the strengths of the client with those of the therapist. SST therapists resist being seen or presenting as the "experts" but approach therapy viewing both participants (i.e., therapist and client) as having strengths and resources. The goal is to be sure that clients do not abdicate their strength and responsibility, surrendering to what they believe is the wisdom and insight of the therapist as an expert. SST is guided by the assumption that a collaborative approach will be most effective (Dryden, 2020).

Mind-Set

As previously noted, SST is not a new approach; rather, it is a new way of thinking about therapy (Young, 2018). There is no single unifying theory for SST. What binds therapists who employ SST is their acceptance of the following perspectives and mind-sets:

- In all therapy, there is a reality, that ultimately it is the client, not the therapist, who decides the number of sessions in which they will engage (Hoyt et al., 2020).
- One session has been shown to be effective and satisfying for any client, who thus feels no need nor interest in extending sessions (Hoyt & Talmon, 2014).
- Therapy begins with the initial contact.
- Clients bring strengths, resources, and competency to therapy.
- There is value in drawing on the client's resources and those within their environment to develop solutions that can be integrated into their lives (Dryden, 2020).

Principles in Action

Therapists employing SST will create an optimal environment for therapeutic change to occur (Young et al., 2017). This environment starts with creating a therapeutic alliance, one that is collaborative and committed to remaining focused on finding solutions and engaging client competency.

The specific therapeutic approach used in SST may vary and could include various methods and techniques such as those adopted from a solution-focused approach, CBT, and motivational interviewing (Hoyt et al., 2018; Young et al., 2008). As previously noted, it is not the nature of the strategy or technique but the orientation, perspective, or mind-set with which it is employed.

SST therapists approach their work using an "as-if" principle (Dryden, 2019). SST therapists approach the session as if it may be the one and only. With this mind-set, an SST therapist might start at the end by asking the client what they hope to achieve within this time together. Focusing on the end, that is, identifying what is hoped to be achieved from the beginning, rather than engaging in a lengthy discussion of psychological history or gathering diagnostic assessment data, allows the client and therapist to focus on the now and what needs to be done to make that now more in line with what is desired (see Case Illustration 10.1).

With an expectation that some form of beneficial change is possible, therapists and clients pursue an understanding of the strengths and competencies the client brings to the process of problem solving. The discussions will focus on discovering specific knowledge, skills, values, motivations, and commitments that can be expanded on and utilized to achieve the identified goals.

Working Alliance: A Collaboration

A significant focus is on the creation and maintenance of a working alliance (Bordin, 1979). To develop such an alliance, SST therapists are empathic, respectful, genuine, and valuing of

CASE ILLUSTRATION 10.1

Targeting the Now

Therapist: Good morning, Ellen; please have a seat. When we spoke on the phone, I explained that we would spend approximately 50 minutes together, and if I understood what you shared, it is your experience with panic attacks that had you contact the office. I hope that we can understand a little about what you are experiencing and what you would like to achieve and find the steps needed to help you move closer to your goals.

(After an explanation of confidentiality rules and answering client questions, the therapist moves into the "work" of therapy.)

Therapist: Ellen, I can hear the frustration and concern in your voice about this new round of panic attacks that you have been experiencing. If I understand you correctly, you went through a similar experience 5 years ago, when you started college. You may want to review that experience, but for now, I am wondering, assuming that our time together today is productive, what do you see might be the outcome of our meeting?

Ellen: I am not sure what you mean by outcome.

Therapist: Well, I mean, what would you like to experience or see change following our session today that would indicate that our work today was successful?

Ellen: (smiling) I guess I would like to know that I am not crazy. It would also be great if you could help me get rid of these panic attacks, or at least understand them better and maybe have some things I can do to reduce their frequency or duration.

Therapist: (writing) These are excellent goals and appear reasonable and doable, so let's begin.

(The therapist starts by sharing information about the nature of anxiety and the physiology of panic attacks. This education is used to verify that the therapist understands the client's experience and that it is not a reflection of being crazy. The information also sets the stage for the introduction of intervention strategies targeting cognitive reframing and relaxation.)

their clients. These conditions have been identified as therapeutic core conditions and facts contributing to developing a working alliance (Rogers, 1957).

While the SST therapist values the strengths and resources the client brings to the interaction, they also value their knowledge and skills. It is by integrating these resources of client and therapist that collaboration is enacted. While not assuming the role of experts, SST therapists will often share from their experience, but when they do, it will be with a tentative tone and offered as something to consider versus something that must be followed.

Maintaining Focus

The SST therapist will take the primary responsibility for keeping therapy and therapeutic interactions on target. While SST therapists can call on techniques and strategies from various sources, the principle of engaging the client will direct the SST therapist to help clients identify their strengths and develop the confidence and competence to employ them in making changes following the sessions.

SST therapists will often assist clients in seeing how they have been successful in dealing with other issues or problems, or even the resources they have tapped, in order to assist others as a way of helping them identify those resources that have an application to the current situation. Similar to solution-focused therapists (see Chapter 3), SST therapists may employ strategies such as finding exceptions to assist clients in identifying strengths and resources previously engaged that may be useful in the current situation.

Finding a Path to Follow

When identifying possible solutions or paths to achieving a client's goal, the SST therapist helps clients identify that which is most meaningful to them. The solution, once selected, may often be practiced within the session.

Given the limited nature of the contact, the SST therapist will not only help the client identify the next steps to be taken, but provide them with resources that will help in the process.

Phases of SST

Hoyt (2000) identified six phases of SST: decision, preparation, beginning, middle, ending, and follow-through/follow-up.

Decision

The decision phase reflects the initial contact of the client and therapist. The focus during this early connection is for the therapist to explain the nature of SST, the possible benefits and risks, and what is to be expected of the client and therapist. The focus of this contact is to help both the client and therapist assess whether SST is the most effective way to proceed.

Preparation

SST therapists approach this initial contact not only as a point of induction but as the first opportunity to foster change. Thus, for clients who share their desire to come to a session, the SST therapist might invite the client to gather data prior to the formal meeting. This is a way to bridge the connection of initial contact to actual therapy. It highlights the nature of SST as active, directive, and change oriented.

In addition to having clients consider what they wish to achieve in therapy, the therapist may ask the client to identify previous strategies they have employed to address the issue, information that they will be asked to share in the face-to-face meeting. Clients may also be asked to observe conditions existing when the problem occurs or varies in intensity.

SST therapists might ask the client to identify exceptions where the problem did not occur, even when it could have been expected, or when a previously unsuccessful strategy seemed to work. These data will be used to better understand the nature of the problem and tap client resources for resolving the problem.

Beginning

As the session begins, the focus is on identifying the nature of the client's problem and the goals they want to achieve in the session. In this process, therapists will identify the problem and assess its main features. Given the focused nature of this time-limited approach, SST therapists will help clients wade through several concerns to identify the one to be addressed in this therapeutic interaction. The SST therapist will attempt to assess the main features or factors involved with the problem identified. The therapist will identify factors or elements that create or maintain the problem. For example, some SST therapists may be interested in the contextual elements that appear to support the problem, while others may focus on the client's behavioral patterns or cognitive processing.

Once the therapists gain better insight into the nature of the problem to be addressed, the therapy will shift to negotiating a realistic and meaningful goal. In the case where the therapists, during the preparation phase, may have invited the client to consider goals and experiences, these data will now be reviewed and discussed. SST therapists will facilitate the client's articulation of the goal, helping them distinguish strategies from goals, and shape their goals into those that are specific, achievable, and measurable.

Middle

The therapist helps the client maintain focus on the task at hand throughout the session. The actions taken by the therapist, such as interrupting the client during off-task or irrelevant communication or directing clients to answer vital questions, require sensitivity and tact. Maintaining the working alliance and the collaborative involvement of clients becomes a focal point throughout this middle phase of therapy (Dryden, 2019).

With goals identified, the "work" of the therapy turns to how best to facilitate client change (Dryden, 2019). SST therapists, especially those taking a more active-directive approach, will introduce insights and skills from their experience (Hoyt et al., 2018). Some SST therapists with a constructive position will focus more on helping clients connect with their inner strengths, competencies, and external resources (Dryden, 2019). With a constructive orientation, SST therapists may draw on the client's past successes or identify strategies they may have used in helping others (see Case Illustration 10.2). In either case, SST therapists will engage the creative, configuring client resources to address the problem and facilitate progress toward the identified goal.

CASE ILLUSTRATION 10.2

A Constructive Approach: Working With Client Strengths

Therapist: Actually, I am kind of surprised that the strategies you previously used, especially your overpreparing and rehearsing your speech and practicing in front of your mom, did not help reduce the anxiety that you felt when presenting to the class. Do you have any ideas about why they were not as helpful as you wished?

Client: One of the problems is that my mom is over-the-top praising, and I know she would never be critical. However, when I see my classmates, I immediately think that they are judging me.

Therapist: Was there any benefit to practicing in front of your mom?

Client: Oh, yeah. It helped get my timing down and generally made me feel like I knew the material.

Therapist: That is great. Feeling confident that you know the material will undoubtedly reduce one source of anxiety. Do you have any ideas about what might help introduce a little anticipation that your practice audience is being judgmental, like you feel your classmates maybe are?

Client: (smiling) I could ask my brother to join my mom. He would definitely be judging me (laughs).

Therapist: So you feel like if your brother was sitting with your mom as your audience, that he may be critical?

Client: I know he would be—in a good way.

Therapist: A good way?

Client: Even though he would make faces and say things, I would not take it personally.

Therapist: Wow, that is something. So if you know your classmates were judging the speech and having ideas on how it could be better, and you were not taking it personally, then that would be less anxiety provoking?

Client: I think so.

Therapist: And even if some of the classmates were judging you, making fun of you, if you could approach them the same way you approach your brother, then even that would be less anxiety provoking?

Client: Yeah, but how do that?

Therapist: Great question, let us talk about what you do when your brother makes fun of you to make it so that you don't take it personally.

Solutions may take various forms, including behavioral adjustment, cognitive reframing, and/or adjustment in social and environmental surroundings. Thus, in the Case Illustration 10.2, the therapist may encourage the continuation of overpreparing, adjust the practice session to include the presence of a somewhat critical brother, and help the client identify the cognitive frame or self-talk she employs to dismiss the personal criticism from her brother. The solutions, when feasible, will be practiced within the session. This will allow the client to test the degree to which the solution feels right and is thus motivated to implement it. It will also provide the client and the therapist with information regarding any possible adjustments that need to be made.

Ending

The therapist encourages the client to summarize what they have learned or taken from the session and how they intend to take this forward. The client and therapist may consider the possibility of experiencing minor or more enduring setbacks and decide how best to address these. Discussion and agreement around future sessions or referral will also take place at this session's ending.

In addition to summarizing the progress made and planning on future directions, the SST therapist will help the client anticipate and prepare for relapse (Dryden, 2019). In doing relapse prevention work, the therapist might have the client identify early warning signs that the problem is returning and identify strategies that can be implemented, including reconnecting with therapy, should these signs appear (Hoyt & Rosenbaum, 2018).

Follow-Through/Follow-Up

With follow-through, additional sessions will be scheduled. If an additional session is scheduled, it should be close to the one that ended and focus on analyzing the implantation of the solution previously selected. The goal is to assess if an adjustment needs to be made to the original plan or if an alternative solution is desirable. With follow-up, the focus is on gathering client feedback on their view of the session and data reflecting an update as to progress.

Clinical Guidelines

Therapists employing SST approach each interaction creatively and flexibly. However, Hoyt and Miller (2000) offered several clinical guidelines to facilitate the process and outcome of SST.

Prepare clients. It is essential to seed change by engaging the client, pre-session, and encouraging the client to identify goals and even begin to collect valuable data reflecting competencies and past successes.

Develop a working alliance. SST is a collaborative process, and, as such, therapists need to facilitate the development of a working alliance. Client and therapist cocreate obtainable goals, and therapists obtain client cooperation and engagement.

Set a workable schedule. It is important in SST to create a workable timeline to allow for the completion of the process and the engagement of an intervention. This may require scheduling sessions longer than the traditional 50 minutes.

Consider reframing. While being empathic and entering the client's experience and worldview, the SST therapist should be sensitive to opportunities to offer a new perspective or reframe the possibilities that exist and may have been missed by the client.

Engage client strengths. The SST therapist should engage the client's strengths and resources in developing interventions or solutions.

Practice solutions. It is helpful for clients to rehearse the strategies identified for implementation in problem solving.

Provide a summary at termination. SST therapists should provide a summary of the session to highlight the client's progress and mastery and check for the client's understanding of and comfort with the identified solution strategy.

Keep the door open. While SST is, by definition, a single session, there are circumstances in which a new connection or even a referral would be beneficial. It is important to frame the possibility of returning to therapy as evidence of change and not depiction of failure.

In addition to these general guidelines, Paul and van Ommeren (2013) have outlined some do's and don'ts that therapists should consider when engaging in SST. While specifically directed to those operating within a crisis, the directives have value to all therapists employing SST (see Table 10.3).

TABLE 10.3 DO'S AND DON'TS IN SST

Do's		
	Team	• Work as a team (when possible); this ensures accountability • Engage supervision and therapeutic support
	Approach	• Build rapport quickly • Maintain a mind-set that this is the only session • Understand/believe a signal session can create change • Be inquisitive • Be actively present to the client • Work collaboratively • Employ various evidence-based strategies • Be sure approach and strategies are sensitive to context and culture • Keep client focused on what is happening at the moment
	Service provision	• Allow couples, small groups, individuals to participate together in session • Foster relationship of client to service versus relationship only with a therapist • Provide service accessible when needed

(Continued)

TABLE 10.3 *(Continued)*

	Intervention: General	• Explain the nature of the service and approach • Explore client's motivation and expectations • Explore what they have tried • Identify strengths and resources • Identify the most salient issue or the thing that will bring the most desired change • Normalize experience • Provide psychoeducation • Explore the level of risk (as necessary) • Refer as needed • Assure clients they can come back
Don'ts	Training	• Do not provide SST without sufficient training in counseling • Do not provide SST without knowledge of culture and context
	Therapeutic approach	• Do not operate as the expert advice giver • Do not think SST is suitable for all clients
	Intervention	• Do not spend time on irrelevant topics • Do not communicate the message that one session is or should be sufficient versus allowing the door to be open to additional assistance

Supportive Research

Evidence for the efficacy of a single therapeutic encounter on a variety of mental health problems was first systematically provided by Talmon (1990). In an extensive evaluation study of multiple walk-in therapy clinics in Ontario in 2014 (Hoyt et al., 2018; Young & Bhanot-Malhotra, 2014), there was substantial evidence for the effectiveness of SST. Research shows that a significant number of clients report improvements in their psychological functioning due to attending a single session (Ewen et al., 2018). Hoyt and Talmon (2014) provided an extensive annotated bibliography that offers many examples of research on SST. The research cited supports SST effectiveness in reducing alcohol and drug abuse, as well as reducing self-harm (cutting and overdoses), and assisting those with PTSD (Ollendick et al., 2009). An extensive review of the available research on the effectiveness of SST is presented by Hoyt et al. (2018).

Suitability

The traditional approach to identifying criteria for including or excluding clients from a treatment modality is contrary to the philosophy of SST (Dryden, 2020). SST shifts focus from assessing clients and defining suitability to structuring sessions to maximize therapeutic benefit. With SST, the client decides to come, as is the case of a walk-in clinic. SST is open to all (Dryden, 2020).

KEYSTONES

- Despite traditional theoretical biases, evidence shows no established direct correlation between the severity and duration of a problem and the duration of effective treatment.
- SST operates under the assumption that ongoing sessions, while an option, may not be necessary.
- As a unique mind-set and intentional approach to therapy, SST has its roots in the work of Moshe Talmon (1990, 1993) and his colleagues at the Kaiser Permanente Medical Center.
- SST is not a new approach; rather, it is a new way of thinking about therapy.
- Single-session work is always meant to be pragmatic, strength-based, and focused on clients' presenting concerns.
- SST embodies a constructive, strength-based orientation and a collaborative yet directive mode of practice.
- Therapists employing SST will focus on creating an optimal environment for therapeutic change to occur, starting with creating a collaborative alliance that is committed to remaining focused on finding solutions and engaging client competency.
- Hoyt (2000) identified six phases of SST: decision, preparation, beginning, middle, ending, and follow-through/follow-up.
- Guidelines for therapists engaging in SST include preparing clients, developing a working alliance, working with client strengths, practicing solutions, and keeping the door open.

ADDITIONAL RESOURCES

Dryden, W. (2019). *Single-session therapy: Distinctive features*. Routledge.

Dryden, W. (2022). *Single-session therapy: Responses to frequently asked questions*. Routledge.

Hoyt, M. F., Bobele, M., Slive, A., Young, J., & Talmon, M. (Eds.). (2018). *Single-session therapy by walk-in or appointment: Administrative, clinical, and supervisory aspects of one-at-a-time services*. Routledge.

REFERENCES

Adler, A. (2013). *Guiding the child*. Routledge. (Original work published 1930)

Bordin, E. S. (1979). The generalizability of the psychoanalytic concept of the working alliance. *Psychotherapy: Theory, Research and Practice, 16*, 252–260.

Campbell, A. (2012). Single-session approaches to therapy: Time to review. *Australian and New Zealand Journal of Family Therapy, 33*, 15–26.

Cannistrà, F., & Piccirilli, F. (2018). *Manuale italiano di terapia a seduta singola*. Firenze.

Dryden, W. (2018). *Single session integrated CBT (SSI-CBT)*. Taylor & Francis.

Dryden, W. (2019). *Single-session therapy: Distinctive features*. Routledge.

Dryden, W. (2020). Single-session one-at-a-time therapy: A personal approach. *Australian & New Zealand Journal of Family Therapy, 41*(3), 283–301.

Dryden, W. (2022). *Single-session therapy: Responses to frequently asked questions*. Routledge.

Ellis, A., & Joffe, D. (2002). A study of volunteer clients who experienced live sessions of rational emotive behavior therapy in front of a public audience. *Journal of Rational-Emotive & Cognitive-Behavior Therapy, 20*, 151–158.

Ewen, V., Mushquash, A. R., Mushquash, C. J., Bailey, S. K., Haggarty, J. M., & Stones, M. J. (2018). Single-session therapy in outpatient mental health services: Examining the effect on mental health symptoms and functioning. *Social Work in Mental Health, 16*(5), 573–589. https://doi.org/10.1080/15332985.2018.1456503

Freud, S., & Breuer, J. (1895). *Studien über hysterie*. Deuticke.

Hoyt, M. F. (Ed.). (2000). *Some stories are better than others: Doing what works in brief therapy and managed care*. Brunner/Mazel.

Hoyt, M. F., Bobele, M., Slive, A., Young, J., & Talmon, M. (Eds.). (2018). *Single-session therapy by walk-in or appointment: Administrative, clinical, and supervisory aspects of one-at-a-time services*. Routledge.

Hoyt, M. F., & Miller, S. (2000). Stage-appropriate change-oriented brief strategies. In M. F. Hoyt (Ed.), *Some stories are better than others: Doing what works in brief therapy and managed care* (pp. 207–236). Brunner/Mazel.

Hoyt, M. F., & Rosenbaum, R. (2018). Some ways to end an SST. In M. F. Hoyt, M. Bobele, A. Slive, J. Young, & M. Talmon (Eds.), *Single-session therapy by walk-in or appointment: Administrative, clinical, and supervisory aspects of one-at-a-time services* (pp. 318–323). Routledge.

Hoyt, M. F., Rosenbaum, R., & Talmon, M. (1992). Planned single-session psychotherapy. In S. H. Budman, M. F. Hoyt, & S. Friedman (Eds.), *The first session in brief therapy* (pp. 59–86).

Hoyt, M. F., & Talmon, M. (Eds.). (2014). *Capturing the moment: Single session therapy and walk-in services*. Crown.

Hoyt, M. F., Young, J., & Rycroft, P. (2020). Single session thinking 2020. *Australian & New Zealand Journal of Family Therapy, 41*(3), 218–230.

Kuehn, J. L. (1965). Encounter at Leyden: Gustav Mahler consults Sigmund Freud. *Psychoanalytic Review, 52*, 345–364.

Lambert, M. J. (2013). Introduction and historical overview. In M. J. Lambert (Ed.), *Bergin and Garfield's handbook of psychotherapy and behavior change* (pp. 3–20). Wiley.

O'Hanlon, W. H., & Hexum, A. L. (1990). *An uncommon casebook: The complete clinical work of Milton H. Erickson.* Norton.

Ollendick, T. H., Ost, L. G., Reuterskiöld, L., Costa, N., Cederlund, R., Sirbu, C., Davis, T. E., 3rd, & Jarrett, M. A. (2009). One-session treatment of specific phobias in youth: a randomized clinical trial in the United States and Sweden. *Journal of consulting and clinical psychology, 77*(3), 504–516. https://doi.org/10.1037/a0015158

Paul, K. E., & van Ommeren, M. (2013). A primer on single session therapy and its potential application in humanitarian situations, *Intervention, 11*(1), 8–23.

Rogers, C. R. (1957). The necessary and sufficient conditions of therapeutic personality change. *Journal of Consulting Psychology, 21*, 95–103.

Slive, A., & Bobele, M. (2012). Walk-in counselling services: Making the most of one hour. *Australian and New Zealand Journal of Family Therapy, 33*, 27–38.

Slive, A., McElheran, N., & Lawson, A. (2008). How brief does it get? Walk-in single session therapy. *Journal of Systematic Therapies, 27*, 5–22.

Stulz, N., Lutz, W., Kopta, S. M., Minami, T., & Saunders, S. M. (2013). Dose-effect relationship in routine outpatient psychotherapy: Does treatment duration matter? *Journal of Counseling Psychology, 60*(4), 593–600. https://doi.org/10.1037/a0033589

Talmon, M. (1990). *Single session therapy: Maximizing the effect of the first (and often only) therapeutic encounter.* Jossey-Bass.

Talmon, M. (1993). *Single-session solutions: A guide to practical, effective, and affordable therapy.* Addison-Wesley.

Talmon, M. (2008). "Once upon a therapy." In J. Young (Interviewer), *The development of single session therapy: Jeff Young interviews Moshe Talmon (Israel) and Robert Rosenbaum (USA)* [DVD]. Melbourne, Victoria: Bouverie Centre.

Talmon, M. (2012). When less is more: Lessons from 25 years of attempting to maximize the effect of each (and often only) therapeutic encounter. *Australian and New Zealand Journal of Family Therapy, 33*, 6–14.

Talmon, M. (2018). The eternal now: On becoming and being a single-session therapist. In M. F. Hoyt, M. Bobele, A. Slive, J. Young, J., & M. Talmon, (Eds.), *Single-session therapy by walk-in or appointment: Administrative, clinical, and supervisory aspects of one-at-a-time services* (pp. 149–154). Routledge.

Taylor, L., Wright, P., & Cole, C. (2010). Introducing brief therapy into a community mental health service. *Journal of Systemic Therapies, 29*(2), 15–25. https://doi.org/10.1521/jsyt.2010.29.2.15

Young, J. (2018). Single-session therapy: The misunderstood gift that keeps on giving. In M. F. Hoyt, M. Bobele, A. Slive, J. Young, & M. Talmon (Eds.), *Single-session therapy by walk-in or appointment: Administrative, clinical, and supervisory aspects of one-at-a-time services* (pp. 40–58). Routledge.

Young, K., & Bhanot-Malhotra, S. (2014). *Getting services right: An Ontario multi-agency evaluation study*. www.excellenceforchildandyouth.com

Young, K., Dick, M., Herring, K., & Lee, J. (2008). From waiting lists to walk-in: Stories from a walk-in therapy clinic. *Journal of Systemic Therapies, 27*(1), 67–83.

Young, K., Hibel, J., Tartar, J., & Fernandez, M. (2017). Single session therapy and neuroscience: Scaffolding and social engagement. In M. Beaudoin & J. Duvall (Eds.), *Collaborative therapy and interpersonal neurobiology: Evolving practices in action* (pp. 103–115). Routledge.

Young, K., & Jebreen, J. (2019). Recognizing single-session therapy as psychotherapy. *Journal of Systemic Therapies, 38*(4), 31–44.

Young, J., & Rycroft, P. (2012). Single session therapy: What's in a name? *Australian and New Zealand Journal of Family Therapy, 33*(1), 3–5.

Young, J., Rycroft, P., & Weir, S. (2014). Implementing single-session therapy: Practical wisdoms from down under. In M. F. Hoyt & M. Talmon (Eds.), *Capturing the moment: Single session-therapy and walk-in services* (pp. 121–140). Crown.

Index

A

acceptance and commitment therapy (ACT), 89–101
    acceptance, 94–96
    assumptions, 92–93
    case study, 99–100
    committed action, 98–100
    comprehensive distancing, 90–91
    diffusion, 96, 97
    distancing, 90
    experiential avoidance, 92–93
    functional contextualism, 93
    history and contributors, 90–91
    language in psychological suffering, 92
    mindfulness, 98
    perspective, 91–92
    principles guiding practice, 92–93
    principles in action, 93–100
    renaming of, 91
    self as context, 96–97
    suffering as normal, 92
    suitability, 101
    supportive research, 101
    therapeutic relationship, 93
    values, 98
    workability, 93
Acceptance and Commitment Therapy (Hayes and Lillis), 89
Adler, A., 6, 155
Alexander, F.,
    on time-limited dynamic psychotherapy, 53–54
    Psychoanalytic Therapy: Principles and Applications, 54
American Psychological Association (APA), 149
assimilation, 76
assumptions
    acceptance and commitment therapy (ACT), 92–93
    brief cognitive behavior therapy, 72–77
    dialectical behavioral therapy (DBT), 107–111
    emotion-focused therapy (EFT), 123–124
    interpersonal psychotherapy (ITP), 139–141
    single-session therapy (SST), 156–159
    solution-focused brief therapy, 35–37
    time-limited dynamic psychotherapy, 56–59
Aurelius, M., 69

B

Bale, L. S., 8
Barber, J. P., 65
Barlow, D., 71
Bateson, G., 7–8
Bauer, G. P., 53
Beck, A., 70–71, 85
Beck, J., 69
behavioral therapy, 11, 70. *See also* specific types
Berg, I. K., 33–34, 40–41, 42
Binder, J. L., 55
biosocial theory, 107–108
bonding and awareness in emotion-focused therapy (EFT), 130
Bowlby, J., 55, 138
Breuer, J., 155
brief cognitive behavior therapy, 69–85
    assumptions, 72–77
    behavioral therapy, 70
    case study, 81–82
    cognitions as functional and dysfunctional, 76–77
    cognitions as mediator, 73
    cognitions at varying levels of awareness, 73–75
    cognitions, modification of, 76–77
    cognitive change, 77

cognitive distortions, 79–81
cognitive therapy, 71
connecting thoughts and feelings, 77–79
history and contributors, 69–71
humans are meaning makers, 73
perspective, 72
principles guiding practice, 72–77
principles in action, 77–84
schemata as resistant to change, 76
suitability, 85
supportive research, 84–85
testing and reformulating, 81–83
time limited, 83–84
brief dynamic therapy, 54
brief theory, 3–12
   case study, 5, 22, 24
   client's stage of change, 28
   collaborative working alliance, 23
   common core, 17–18
   emergence of, 11–13
   engaging client systems, 25–26
   evolution of, 6–11
   flexibility of techniques, 25
   here-and-now focus, 20
   history and future of, 13
   multiple presentations, 17–18
   nonpathologizing, 18–20
   outcome focused, 23–24
   severity and complexity, 27
   shared technical characteristics, 18–21
   suitability, 27–28
   therapeutic alliance, 27
   therapists, 23
   therapy outside of office, 25–26
   time-limited, 21
   values and principles, 18
   valuing client strengths, 21–25
Brief Therapy Center, 9, 13, 34
Brief Therapy Family Center (BTFC), 34
Brief Therapy: Focused Problem Resolution (Weakland), 10
Budman, S. H., 18

C

Cape, J., 85
Capturing the Moment: Single Session Therapy and Walk-In Services (Hoyt and Talmon), 155
case study(ies)
   acceptance and commitment therapy (ACT), 99–100
   brief cognitive behavior therapy, 81–82
   brief theory, 5
   dialectical behavioral therapy (DBT), 113
   emotion-focused therapy (EFT), 127–128
   interpersonal psychotherapy (ITP), 142, 145
   single-session therapy (SST), 163
   solution-focused brief therapy, 38, 47
   time-limited dynamic psychotherapy (TLDP), 61
Change: Principles of Problem Formation and Problem Resolution (Watzlawick), 10
Clark, D., 71
client's stage of change, 28
cognitions
   as functional and dysfunctional, 76–77
   as mediator, 73
   at varying levels of awareness, 73–75
collaborative/collaboration, 40–42
   interpersonal psychotherapy (ITP), 140
   single-session therapy (SST), 158–161
   working alliance, 23
complainants, 40–41
coping questions, 46
Cully, J. A., 83
customer, 41–42
cyclical maladaptive pattern (CMP), 59–62

D

Davidowitz, D., 3
de Shazer, S., 33–34
Derks, J., 34
dialectical behavioral therapy (DBT), 105–117
   acceptance, 106–108, 115–117
   assumptions, 107–111
   biosocial theory, 107–108
   case study, 113
   change, 106–107
   change skills, 115–117
   comprehensive program, 114–115
   dialectics, 108–110
   functions served, 112–114
   history and contributors, 106
   perspectives, 106–107
   principles guiding practice, 107–111
   principles in action, 112–117
   suitability, 117
   supportive research, 117
   targets of therapy, 112–114
   validation, 108
dialectical-constructivist view, 123–124
dialectics, 108–110

diffusion in ACT, 96, 97
distancing in ACT, 90
distraction in dialectical behavioral therapy (DBT), 109
distress tolerance, 116
Dryden, W., 155
dysfunctional behaviors in DBT, 113–114

E

Ellis, A., 70–71, 85, 155
emotion-focused therapy (EFT), 121–132
    assumptions, 123–124
    case study, 127–128
    client experiences, 124
    dialectical-constructivist view, 123–124
    emotions in thought and action, 124
    history and contributors, 122
    markers and interventions, 128–129
    perspectives, 122–123
    phases of treatment, 130–132
    principles guiding practice, 123–124
    principles in action, 125–132
    process *versus* content, 124
    suitability, 132
    supportive research, 132
    therapeutic relationship, 124–125
    therapeutic tasks, 126–129
    therapeutic work, 126
emotion regulation in DBT, 116
emotions in EFT, 124
empathic attunement, 125
environmental structuring, 114
Epictetus, 69
Erickson, M. H., 7, 33, 155
experiential-affective theory, 56
experiential avoidance, 92–93
experiential learning in TLDP, 62–63
experiential processing in EFT, 126

F

Family Therapy Institute, 9
fast-forward questions, 43–44
Ferenczi, S., 6–7, 53
finding exceptions, 46–47
finding solutions, 45–48
Fisch, R., 9
freedom in DBT, 109–110

French, T. M., 53–54
    Psychoanalytic Therapy: Principles and Applications, 54
Freud, S., 6, 53, 155
functional contextualism in ACT, 93
functions served in DBT, 112–114

G

Garfield, S. L., 27
Gavita, O. A., 85
general paresis, 4
Gingerich, W., 34
goals
    interpersonal psychotherapy (ITP), 139–140
    setting, 42–44
Greenberg, L. S., 64
Gurman, A. S., 18

H

Haley, J., 8–9
Halher, G., 155
Haugland, B. S. M., 85
Hayes, S. C., 90, 91, 96, 99
    Acceptance and Commitment Therapy, 89
Hilsenroth, M. J., 65
Hopwood, L., 34
Hoyt, M., 161, 164, 166
    Capturing the Moment: Single Session Therapy and Walk-In Services, 155

I

identifying resources, 46
International Society of Interpersonal Psychotherapists (ISIPT), 138
interpersonal effectiveness in DBT, 116–117
interpersonal psychotherapy (ITP), 137–150
    assumptions, 139–141
    case study, 142, 145
    collaborative, 140
    goals, 139–140
    history and contributors, 137–138
    medical model, 139
    perspectives, 138
    principles guiding practice, 139–141
    principles in action, 141–150
    sessions, 144–146

stages and tasks, 147–149
strategies, 146–147
suitability, 150
supportive research, 149
termination, 147
therapist active, 140–141
time limited, 140
treatment, 146–147

J

Jackson, D. D., 9

K

Khorakiwala, D., 91
Klerman, G., 137
Knekt, P., 65
Kobos, J. C., 53
Kowalski, K., 34
Kral, R., 34

L

LaCourt, M., 34
Lambert, M., 12
language in psychological suffering, 92
Leichsenring, F., 65
Levenson, H., 3, 54
Lillis, J.
    Acceptance and Commitment Therapy, 89
Linehan, M. M., 105–106, 112, 115
Lipchik, E., 34
long-term therapist, 19
Luborsky, L., 55

M

Maintenance Therapies in Recurrent Depression (MTRD), 138
Malan, D., 27, 54
Mandes, C., 9
Mann, J., 54
markers and interventions in EFT, 128–129
Maultsby, M. C., Jr., 76
medical model of ITP, 139
Mental Research Institute (MRI), 8, 9–11
Meyer, A., 138
Miller, G., 34, 164
Miller, S. D., 34
mindfulness
    acceptance and commitment therapy (ACT), 98
    dialectical behavioral therapy (DBT), 109, 116
mind-set in SST, 156, 159
miracle question, 42–43, 45
Molnar, A., 34

N

National Institute of Mental Health (NIMH), 149
National Institutes of Health (NIH), 149
nontraditional perspective, 34–35
Norcross, J. C., 28
Nunnally, E., 34
nurturance in dialectical behavioral therapy, 109

O

Oatley, K., 71
outcome focused brief theory, 23–24
outcome studies, 11–12

P

Pardes, H., 12
Pascual-Leone, A., 64
Paul, K. E., 165
Paykel, E., 137
Peller, J. E., 41
perspectives
    acceptance and commitment therapy (ACT), 91–92
    brief cognitive behavior therapy, 72
    dialectical behavioral therapy (DBT), 106–107
    emotion-focused therapy (EFT), 122–123
    interpersonal psychotherapy (ITP), 138
    single-session therapy (SST), 156
phases of SST
    beginning, 162
    decision, 161
    ending, 164
    follow-through/follow-up, 164
    middle, 162–164
    preparation, 161–162
Piaget, J., 76

Pincus, H. A., 12
pretreatment in DBT, 115–116
principles guiding practice
    acceptance and commitment therapy (ACT), 92–93
    brief cognitive behavior therapy, 72–77
    dialectical behavioral therapy (DBT), 107–111
    emotion-focused therapy (EFT), 123–124
    interpersonal psychotherapy (ITP), 139–141
    single-session therapy (SST), 156–159
    solution-focused brief therapy, 35–37
    time-limited dynamic psychotherapy (TLDP), 56–59
principles in action
    acceptance and commitment therapy (ACT), 93–100
    brief cognitive behavior therapy, 77–84
    dialectical behavioral therapy (DBT), 112–117
    emotion-focused therapy (EFT), 125–132
    interpersonal psychotherapy (ITP), 141–150
    single-session therapy (SST), 159–166
    solution-focused brief therapy, 37–48
    time-limited dynamic psychotherapy (TLDP), 59–65
problem deconstruction discourse, 37
problem-free talk, 38–39
Prochaska, J. O., 28
Psychoanalytic Therapy: Principles and Applications (Alexander and French), 54
psychological flexibility, 89, 91–93, 101

R

Rank, O., 6, 53
rational emotive therapy (RET), 71
relationship questions, 48
research. *See* supportive research

S

scaling questions, 44–45
Schacht, T. E., 55
self as context in ACT, 96–97
self-development in EFT, 126
sessions in ITP, 144–146
Short-Term Cognitive Therapy Rating Scales (SRS), 85
short-term therapist, 19
Sifneos, P. E., 54
single-session therapy (SST), 154–166
    assumptions, 156–159
    case study, 163
    clinical guidelines, 164–165
    collaborative, 158–161
    constructive, 158
    do's and don'ts in, 165–166
    help at the point of need, 157–158
    history and contributors, 155
    maintaining focus, 161
    mind-set, 156, 159
    perspectives, 156
    phases of, 161–164
    power of the one, 156
    principles guiding practice, 156–159
    principles in action, 159–166
    quick fix nor superficial, 157
    strength-based, 158
    suitability, 166
    supportive research, 166
    working alliance, 159–161
solution-focused brief therapy, 33–49
    assumptions, 35–37
    case study, 38, 47
    collaboration, 40–42
    complainants, 40–41
    coping questions, 46
    customer, 41–42
    fast-forward questions, 43–44
    finding exceptions, 46–47
    finding solutions, 45–48
    goal setting, 42–44
    history and contributors, 33–34
    identifying resources, 46
    miracle question, 42–43, 45
    nontraditional perspective, 34–35
    principles guiding practice, 35–37
    principles in action, 37–48
    problem deconstruction discourse, 37
    problem-free talk, 38–39
    relationship questions, 48
    scaling, 44–45
    scaling questions, 44–45
    suitability, 48–49
    supportive research, 48
    task development, 48
    visitors, 40
strategies
    interpersonal psychotherapy (ITP), 146–147
    time-limited dynamic psychotherapy (TLDP), 65
strength-based single-session therapy, 158
Strupp, H. H., 55
Stulz, N., 12

suitability
    acceptance and commitment therapy (ACT), 101
    brief cognitive behavior therapy, 85
    brief theory, 27–28
    dialectical behavioral therapy (DBT), 117
    emotion-focused therapy (EFT), 132
    interpersonal psychotherapy (ITP), 149
    single-session therapy (SST), 166
    solution-focused brief therapy, 48–49
    time-limited dynamic psychotherapy (TLDP), 65–66
Sullivan, H. S., 138
supportive research
    acceptance and commitment therapy (ACT), 101
    brief cognitive behavior therapy, 84–85
    dialectical behavioral therapy (DBT), 117
    emotion-focused therapy (EFT), 132
    interpersonal psychotherapy (ITP), 149
    single-session therapy (SST), 166
    solution-focused brief therapy, 48
    time-limited dynamic psychotherapy (TLDP), 65

T

Talmon, M., 166
    Capturing the Moment: Single Session Therapy and Walk-In Services, 155
targets of therapy in DBT, 112–114
task completion and focus in EFT, 126
task development, 48
termination of treatment in ITP, 147, 149
Teten, A. L., 83–84
therapeutic alliance, 25, 27, 40, 65, 85, 159
therapeutic relationship
    acceptance and commitment therapy (ACT), 93
    emotion-focused therapy (EFT), 124–125
therapeutic tasks in EFT, 126–129
therapeutic work in EFT, 126
therapists
    interpersonal psychotherapy (ITP), 140–141
    proactive agent of change, 23
therapy outside the office walls, 26
time limited
    brief cognitive behavior therapy, 83–84
    interpersonal psychotherapy (ITP), 140
time-limited dynamic psychotherapy (TLDP), 52–66
    as focused, 58
    as process oriented, 58
    assessment, 60
    assumptions, 56–59
    attachment and relationships, 56
    case conceptualization, 59
    case study, 61
    change outside of therapy, 59
    circular causality, 56–57
    client's struggle, 57–58
    conceptualization, 60
    cyclical maladaptive pattern, 62
    experience to understanding, 63–64
    experience, understanding, change, 64
    experiential–affective theory, 56
    experiential learning, 62–63
    goals, 58, 60
    here-and-now attachment, 55
    history and contributors, 53–54
    intrapsychic to interpersonal, 55
    maladaptive patterns schematized, 56
    principles guiding practice, 56–59
    principles in action, 59–65
    shift in perspective, 55–56
    strategies, 65
    suitability, 65–66
    supportive research, 65
    therapist as active, 58
    treatment planning, 60
Toner, P., 12
transformation in EFT, 131–132
treatment
    emotion-focused therapy (EFT), 130–132
    interpersonal psychotherapy (ITP), 146–147
    time-limited dynamic psychotherapy (TLDP), 60
Treatment of Depression Collaborative Research Program, 149

V

validation in DBT, 108
values in ACT, 98
van Ommeren, M., 165
visitors, 40

W

Walter, J. L., 34, 41
Watzlawick, P., 9
    Change: Principles of Problem Formation and Problem Resolution, 10
Weakland, J., 9
    Brief Therapy: Focused Problem Resolution, 10
Weiner-Davis, M., 34
Weissman, M., 137

Wilks, C.R., 106
Wilson, K. G., 91
Wolpe, J., 85
    on brief cognitive behavior therapy, 70
workability in ACT, 93
working alliance
    emotion-focused therapy (EFT), 125
    single-session therapy (SST), 159–161

Y

Young, J., 155

Z

Zettle, R. D., 91

About the Author

Richard D. Parsons, Ph.D. is Professor Emeritus from the Counselor Education Department at West Chester University. He has over 40 years of university teaching experience in counselor preparation programs. Prior to his university teaching, Dr. Parsons spent nine years as a school counselor in an inner city high school. He has had a private clinical practice for over 40 years and serves as a consultant to educational institutions and mental health service organizations throughout the tri-state area of Pennsylvania, New Jersey, and Delaware. Dr. Parsons is the recipient of many awards and honors, including the Pennsylvania Counselor of Year award.

Dr. Parsons has authored or co-authored over 100 professional articles, books, and book chapters. His most recent books include: *Facilitating Growth Through Lifespan Development*; *Understanding and Facilitating Group Process*; *Connecting with the Expert Within*; and *Cognitive Therapy: Principles and Practice*, all published with Cognella. Dr. Parsons also serves as the creator and editor of two series of books, a series of 24 books targeting counselor educators, *Counseling and Professional Identity* (SAGE Publications) and a 10-book series, *The Cognella Series on Student Success* (Cognella Academic Publishing).